TOWARD A

NORTH

AMERICAN

COMMUNITY

Lessons from the Old World

for the New

TOWARD A

NORTH

AMERICAN

COMMUNITY

Lessons from the Old World

for the New

ROBERT A. PASTOR

Institute for International Economics
Washington, DC
August 2001

Robert A. Pastor is the Goodrich C. White Professor of International Relations at Emory University. He was a fellow at the Carter Center (1985-98) and founding director of its Latin American and Caribbean Programs and Democracy and China Projects. He served as director of Latin American and Caribbean affairs on the National Security Council (1977-81) and has been a foreign affairs consultant to the government, business, and nongovernmental organizations. He is the author or editor of 14 books, including *Exiting the Whirlpool: U.S. Foreign Policy Toward Latin America and the Caribbean* (2001), *A Century's Journey: How the Great Powers Shape the World* (1999), and *Congress and the Politics of U.S. Foreign Economic Policy* (1980).

INSTITUTE FOR INTERNATIONAL ECONOMICS
1750 Massachusetts Avenue, NW
Washington, DC 20036-1903
(202) 328-9000 FAX: (202) 328-5432
http://www.iie.com

C. Fred Bergsten, *Director*
Brigitte Coulton, *Director of Publications and Web Development*
Brett Kitchen, *Director of Marketing*

Typesetting and printing: Automatic Graphic Systems, Inc.
Cover photo: Reuters/Jim Bourg

Printed in the United States of America
03 02 01   5 4 3 2 1

Library of Congress Cataloging-in-Publication Data

Pastor, Robert A.
    Toward a North American community : lessons from the old world for the new / Robert Pastor.
        p. cm.
    Includes bibliographical references and index.
    ISBN 0-88132-328-4
    1. Free trade—North America. 2. Canada. Treaties, etc. 1992 Oct. 7. 3. North America—Economic integration. I. Title.

HF1746.P375   2001
337.1'7—dc21   2001044357

Contents

Tables

Figures

Preface

Economic integration among the world's major economies, especially in Europe and North America, has been a central component of the research program of the Institute for International Economics throughout its existence. This new study compares the two experiences, drawing lessons from the European record for North America. It makes a strong case for converting the North American Free Trade Agreement (NAFTA) into a community similar to, but also quite distinct from, the European Union over the next decade or so.

This book is also unique in its basic approach to NAFTA itself. Criticism of NAFTA is widespread in the United States and even the proponents of trade liberalization seldom defend it, let alone hold it up as a model, despite its dramatic successes since inauguration in 1994. Author Robert A. Pastor, to the contrary, stands the usual criticism on its head, arguing that the main problem of NAFTA is what it *failed* to do. He suggests that it did not go nearly far enough in promoting "deep integration" among its three member countries, and that they should now move to do so in order to achieve the agreement's unrealized potential.

Pastor's book is extremely timely in light of the arrival of Vicente Fox as President of Mexico in late 2000 and George W. Bush as President of the United States in early 2001. Early in their respective terms, President Fox presented a series of bold proposals that move in the direction of a North American Community, as proposed in this study, and President Bush indicated a responsiveness to seriously consider such ideas. Hence a vision that might have been deemed unrealistic only a year ago has clearly entered the realm of the possible and deserves serious consideration by policy communities and the public in all three countries of North America.

Pastor has unique qualifications to present such a vision. He has had both practical governmental experience, as director of Latin American Affairs on the National Security Council, and extensive research background as the author of 14 books, including three on US–Mexico relations and another on US trade policy. One of those books was coauthored with the brilliant current Foreign Minister of Mexico, Jorge G. Castañeda. Pastor had been personally invited by Fox to organize the international observation of the Mexican election on July 2, 2000, and the two of them had several opportunities to discuss the issues in the book. President Fox's admiration for the proposals and the book is inscribed on the back cover. We hope that the volume will help elevate the debate on both North American relations and US trade policy, and that is why we decided to release it at the time of President Fox's state visit to Washington in September 2001.

The Institute for International Economics is a private nonprofit institution for the study and discussion of international economic policy. Its purpose is to analyze important issues in that area and develop and communicate practical new approaches for dealing with them. The Institute is completely nonpartisan.

The Institute is funded largely by philanthropic foundations. Major institutional grants are now being received from the William M. Keck, Jr. Foundation and the Starr Foundation. A number of other foundations and private corporations contribute to the highly diversified financial resources of the Institute. About 31 percent of the Institute's resources in our latest fiscal year were provided by contributors outside the United States, including about 18 percent from Japan. Special funding for this project was provided by the Rockefeller Brothers Fund.

The Board of Directors bears overall responsibility for the Institute and gives general guidance and approval to its research program—including the identification of topics that are likely to become important over the medium run (one to three years), and which should be addressed by the Institute. The Director, working closely with the staff and outside Advisory Committee, is responsible for the development of particular projects and makes the final decision to publish an individual study.

The Institute hopes that its studies and other activities will contribute to building a stronger foundation for international economic policy around the world. We invite readers of these publications to let us know how they think we can best accomplish this objective.

C. Fred Bergsten
Director
August 2001

Point of Departure and Acknowledgments

In elementary school, I learned that I was a US citizen, but it did not occur to me until about two decades ago that I was also a resident of North America. At the time, I was the director of Latin American affairs on the National Security Council, and I was coordinating an interagency review of US relations with Mexico. I traveled there for consultations and met informally with a close Mexican friend and fellow graduate of the Kennedy School of Government at Harvard University. He was then a middle-level official in Mexico's Budget Department. I asked what he thought about the idea of expanding the US-Canadian Automotive Agreement—a free trade sectoral agreement dating back to 1965—to include Mexico and make it "North American" or, alternatively, to adapt the model for the United States and Mexico. He told me that he had already analyzed the agreement and concluded that it did not serve either US or Canadian interests and therefore did not see any reason to apply it to Mexico.

My friend's name was Carlos Salinas de Gortari. I disagreed with his analysis and continued to press him on the issue of free trade on subsequent visits. He consistently opposed the idea until the spring of 1990 when, as president, he made an even more sweeping proposal than I had contemplated.

His initiative led to the North American Free Trade Agreement (NAFTA), which came into effect on 1 January 1994. "North America" became more than a term of geography; it defined a new entity and offered the citizens of its three countries the possibility of a new and unique relationship. NAFTA proved to be a watershed event not just for Mexico but also for all of North America and the world. It was the first significant free trade area involving industrialized countries and a developing one, and it spurred virtually the entire hemisphere to try to extend the model to a Free Trade Area of the Americas (FTAA).

NAFTA's purpose was to reduce and eliminate barriers to trade and investment. But it lacks institutions to coordinate policy among the three governments or even to take into account the different levels of development. Having lived in Mexico in the mid-1980s and written a book, *Limits to Friendship* (Alfred Knopf, 1988), with an eloquent Mexican nationalist, Jorge G. Castañeda, who became Mexico's foreign minister in December 2000, I was very sensitive to the differences between our two countries and to their divergent perspectives on history. In a second book, *Integration with Mexico: Options for U.S. Policy* (Century Foundation, 1993), which I wrote during the NAFTA negotiations to try to frame the issues for the subsequent debate in Congress, I examined some ideas on ways to improve NAFTA. I also questioned the point of departure of the NAFTA negotiators. They were asking how to dismantle barriers; I thought it would be wiser to ask how we could facilitate integration between three such different countries and economies. In a third book, *The Controversial Pivot: The U.S. Congress and North America* (Brookings Institution, 1998), which I coedited with Rafael Fernandez de Castro, we tried to explain why the promise of NAFTA was unfulfilled, why a new partnership had failed to replace the dysfunctional paternalism of the past. The reasons, we concluded, were the lack of a compelling vision and a structure that would bring the vision alive and the unhelpful role played by the US Congress. The purpose of this book is to offer a vision together with a comprehensive proposal that would permit the three governments of North America to lift their relationship to a new level.

To research this book, I spent the past two years studying the European Union's (EU) experience integrating poorer countries. In the spring and summer of 1999, I was invited to participate in a faculty seminar on the EU directed by Professor Tom Remington of Emory University's Claus M. Halle Institute for Global Learning. I visited Europe twice for extensive interviews and was convinced there was much to be learned of relevance to NAFTA. Dr. C. Fred Bergsten, the director of the Institute for International Economics, agreed and provided both a forum and support for trips to Ottawa and Mexico City to interview officials and other leaders.

In Brussels and throughout Europe, I learned about the EU's experience in reducing disparities between rich and poor countries, but few took NAFTA seriously. Rather, Europeans seemed to be more interested in learning about the federal experiment of the United States. Canada also did not take NAFTA very seriously. From Ottawa's perspective, the United States loomed so large that North American issues were viewed solely in bilateral terms. In the United States, a heated contest for the presidency evoked strong statements by both Al Gore and George W.

Bush in favor of strengthening US-Mexican relations, but NAFTA was hardly mentioned, and comments on Mexico seemed aimed more at an emerging ethnic voting bloc than to the country to the south. Canada was also absent from the US debate, and NAFTA was not heard during the contest for the Canadian Parliament, which culminated with elections on 27 November 2000. Only in Mexico did a leader have a vision of a deeper, more modern North American relationship. I met with that leader, Vicente Fox Quesada, both during the campaign and after his election, and I was convinced he wanted to redefine the agenda for the three countries. This book is intended to develop that agenda.

My learning experience in the course of researching and writing this book reflects as long a journey as I have traveled in writing any previous book. I am indebted to the hundreds of policymakers, scholars, business-men, and other leaders who I interviewed in Europe, Canada, the United States, and Mexico. Former US Ambassador to Canada Gordon Giffin, an old friend, was especially generous of his time in helping me arrange interviews with senior politicians and officials in all the major political parties and groups in Canada, and I have also profited from many conversations on the subject with Mexico's Foreign Minister Jorge G. Castañeda.

I have also had the benefit of presenting some of the ideas in this book at the following institutions: Ghent Management School in Belgium on 17 May 1999; the Institute for International Economics on 30 March 2000, and on 11 April 2001; Canada's Ministry of Trade and Foreign Affairs on 9 May 2000; the Norman Patterson School of International Affairs at Carleton University in Ottawa, Ontario, on 11 May 2000; the Asia Pacific Economic Cooperation meeting in Manila on 24 July 2000; and the University of Alberta on 24-25 May 2001.

Let me thank the following people for generously giving me their time, ideas, and in most of the cases, their detailed comments on previous drafts: C. Fred Bergsten, Claude Barfield, Jorge G. Castañeda, Steve Charnovitz, Michael Chriszt, John Coatsworth, I. M. Destler, Desmond Dinan, Richard Feinberg, Isaiah Frank, Ted Gerber, Daniel Gros, Michael Hart, Dorothy Heisenberg, Randall Henning, Alexander Hicks, Gary Hufbauer, Michael Kergin, Catherine Mann, Maureen Molot, Jack Mutti, Scott Otteman, Hugo Paemen, Tom Remington, Riordan Roett, Mario Lopez Roldan, Jeffrey Schott, John Todd Stewart, Edwin Truman, Phillip Warf, and Paul Wonnacott.

I would especially like to thank Dan Ciuriak and Sidney Weintraub for exceptionally detailed and constructive suggestions on the entire manu-script. Miguel Basañez was generous in sharing data from the new World Values Survey, which I used in chapter 7. Charles Hankla and Benjamin Goodrich were extremely able and helpful research assistants and I am especially grateful for their help in constructing the tables. I accept responsibility for any errors that may remain.

Robert A. Pastor
August 2001

Redesigning NAFTA for the 21st Century

For the first time in history, all three countries of North America—Canada, Mexico, and the United States—held democratic national elections in the same year, 2000. Perhaps this was an omen that their political trajectories had begun to converge after two centuries in which their differences seemed far more important. The leading candidates for the highest office in each land debated issues intensely, but in all three countries, the agendas were almost exclusively domestic. The North American Free Trade Agreement (NAFTA), which had been so controversial a decade before, was barely mentioned, if at all, in any country. NAFTA's advocates did not take credit for it, although trade, investment, and social and economic integration had accelerated. Nor did the opponents of NAFTA bemoan its negative effects—the peso crisis in Mexico; the bailout organized and substantially funded by the United States; or the weak Canadian dollar. NAFTA, as politicians in all three countries informed me, was "not an issue anymore."[1]

It should have been. And it should be. NAFTA has been a scapegoat for disgruntled or uncompetitive groups in each country, but it has been a success for what it was designed to do. By reducing and eventually eliminating trade barriers among the three countries, NAFTA has gener-

---

1. I conducted interviews in Ottawa with leaders of the major parties in May 2000 and in Mexico in June and July 2000.

ated spectacular growth in trade and investment while improving national productivity and competitiveness. And the soaring traffic has not been just in goods. In the last year of the 20th century, people legally crossed the US-Canadian border 200 million times and the US-Mexican one 300 million times.[2] This amounts to nearly 1.4 million crossings a day. The integration that preceded NAFTA and was accelerated by it created striking opportunities for North America—but also dangerous vulnerabilities. The purpose of this book is to offer ideas on how the three governments can take advantage of the opportunities and take steps to reduce the vulnerabilities due to integration.

What's wrong with NAFTA is not what it did, but what it omitted. The agreement did not envisage any unified approach to extract NAFTA's promise, nor did it contemplate any common response to new threats. NAFTA simply assumed that the peoples of North America would benefit from the magic of a free marketplace, and that the three governments would resolve old or new problems. But in the absence of a compelling vision to define a modern regional entity, and lacking institutions to translate that vision into policies, the old patterns of behavior among the three governments remained. This meant that the US penchant for unilateralism and the Canadian and Mexican preference for bilateralism have trumped NAFTA's promise of a novel trilateral partnership.

Evaluations of NAFTA—both positive and negative—have tended to focus on the balance of trade and capital flows and the creation and loss of jobs. These are important issues, but they are hardly sufficient to take the pulse of such a complex, dynamic phenomenon. These fail, for example, to take into account the reorganization of large corporations with plants in all three countries, or the way in which environmental groups have reached across borders to press for higher standards, or the new alliances between labor unions in the United States and the Mexican government to assure the rights of migrants.

Few analysts of NAFTA have sought to learn from the experience of the longest-running, most successful regional trading scheme, the European Union (EU). Few leaders have proffered a vision of a future relationship among the North American countries. The exception is the new president of Mexico, Vicente Fox Quesada. His inauguration on 1 December 2000 represented a historic change for Mexico—the first peaceful, democratic transfer of power in the country's history. Fox has studied the European Union's experience in integrating poorer countries on its periphery, and he boldly proposed replacing the Free Trade Area with a common market. George

---

2. For the most recent data on the two-way traffic across the US-Canadian border, see Department of Foreign Affairs and International Trade of Canada, *Canada-US Partnership: Building a Border for the 21st Century* (Ottawa, December 2000, 2); and for the US-Mexican border, see "Welcome to America: The Border is Vanishing Before Our Eyes," *Time: Special Issue*, 11 June 2001, 38.

W. Bush, the new president of the United States, and Jean Chrétien, the reelected prime minister of Canada, both acknowledged the importance of the three-sided relationship and affirmed their interest in improving it. But neither defined the path to amelioration, nor did they signal any interest in establishing a common market.

Fox was persistent, however. He invited Bush to his ranch in Guanajuato on 16 February 2001, and persuaded the new US president to endorse a joint communiqué entitled the Guanajuato Proposal, a fulsome statement of common goals and principles. "Among our highest priorities," the two presidents promised, "is unfettering the economic potential of every citizen, so each may contribute fully to narrowing the economic gaps between and within our societies." Fox and Bush went further, pledging to consult with the Canadian prime minister, and then "we will strive to consolidate a North American economic community whose benefits reach the lesser-developed areas of the region and extend to the most vulnerable social groups in our countries."[3] Fox proposed that labor be permitted to move freely in North America, though he recognized that this might not be possible for 20 years or more, given the wide divergence in incomes. He suggested a compensation fund to assist the development of the poor regions of Mexico. He and his foreign minister, Jorge G. Castañeda, modeled their proposals on Europe's experience. Bush and Chrétien promised to study these ideas.

This book aims to take the skeleton of Fox's idea and graft a body onto it. I will analyze NAFTA's successes and shortcomings, seek to draw some lessons from the European Union, and propose ways for NAFTA to incorporate and adapt those lessons.

The Crisis of 1994 and NAFTA's Flaw

On 1 December 1994, at the end of the first year of NAFTA, a new Mexican administration under President Ernesto Zedillo took office. Three weeks later, after allowing a 15 percent depreciation, his government let the Mexican peso float, and it sank like a stone, losing about 40 percent of its value. The first reaction by Robert Rubin, the director of the National Economic Council in the US administration of Bill Clinton—who had just been named Secretary of Treasury—was "to let the market sort it out."[4]

---

3. "Toward a Partnership for Prosperity: The Guanajuato Proposal, Joint Communiqué," 16 February 2001, www.presidencia.gob.mx.

4. Cited in David Sanger, "The Education of Robert Rubin," *New York Times*, 5 February 1995, III, 1, 3. For a fuller description of what occurred, see Robert A. Pastor, "The United States and the Americas: Unfilled Promise at the Century's Turn," in *Eagle Rules? Foreign Policy and American Primacy in the Twenty-First Century*, ed. Robert J. Lieber (Upper Saddle River, NJ: Prentice Hall, 2002).

Soon after that, both governments began a long stumble that lasted more than a month before they could assemble a rescue package of $53 billion that would include $20 billion from the US Exchange Stabilization Fund. By the time the two governments reached an agreement, the initial damage had been compounded. Mexico's economy was in a shambles; its hopes of using NAFTA as a highway to the industrial world were dashed; 1 million jobs had been lost; and most of its major banks had failed.

Moreover, NAFTA was so discredited that President Clinton, who had heralded it as a model for the hemisphere just weeks before the crash, barely uttered the phrase again in that or in his next term. The issue and the agreement seemed to disappear from the policy debate, not just in the United States but in all three countries. And the ripple effects of the peso crash extended far beyond North America. One week before, 9-11 December 1994, 34 democratically elected presidents in the Americas met at a summit in Miami and promised to negotiate by 2005 a Free Trade Area of the Americas (FTAA). The decade ended with that promise unfulfilled. Indeed, President Clinton could not even extract the authority from the US Congress to negotiate any trade agreements.

This pivotal peso crisis had multiple causes. Mexico had suffered severe political setbacks during 1994, including the assassinations of the presidential candidate and secretary general of the governing Institutional Revolutionary Party (PRI). These events struck fear in the public and in the financial markets. Foreign capital began to flee. To reattract foreign investment, the Mexican government lifted interest rates and denominated its short-term bonds in dollars. By the end of the year, foreign investors had stopped buying the bonds and had begun to redeem them, causing a crisis of solvency that led to a wholesale exit of capital, much of it by Mexicans, and the resulting devaluation.

In retrospect, some analysts believed the crisis was due to the lack of transparency in Mexico's financial system. No doubt Mexico's weaknesses played a role in the crash, but one also needs to look more closely at the flow of international capital. In 1993, large amounts of money moved to emerging markets like Mexico's, but the next year, when the economies of the industrial countries recovered, the capital returned.

Some economists rang alarm bells in the fall of 1994 that Mexico's finances were overextended and its currency was overvalued, but the awkward truth is that policymakers in the three countries did not anticipate or plan for a financial crisis in the weakest member. NAFTA did not contemplate regular, high-level consultations, let alone any coordination among the three central banks or three treasury departments. The three leaders did not consult with each other. When Zedillo and his designee for finance minister traveled to Washington to meet with Clinton and his aides in November 1994, they were ready to request help from the United States, but they found Clinton utterly preoccupied by his party's loss of

Congress in elections that month. Clinton's advisors had been in contact with their counterparts, but neither side proposed ways to preempt the catastrophe that some saw coming.[5]

The peso crisis has been analyzed in great detail elsewhere.[6] It was due to an unfortunate collision between a political crisis and an overvalued peso. The premise of this book is that *the peso crisis was also a metaphor for both the success and the inadequacy of NAFTA*. The success was reflected in the expansion of trade and capital flows; the inadequacy was manifest in the lack of institutional capacity among the three governments to monitor, anticipate, plan for, or even respond to such a serious problem. NAFTA, in brief, was defined too narrowly, and the three governments paid a price for that myopia, albeit a price that varied among the three countries. Even worse, the three governments have not learned the lesson of 1994; they still apparently fail to understand the many dimensions of the phenomenon of North American integration.

The inescapable conclusion is that similar collective problems will emerge in the future, although in different guises, and that there is no institutional capacity to address them. New leaders, lacking a historical memory, may well repeat the old mistakes. After decades of trying to resist the multiple pressures toward integration with the United States, the governments of Canada and Mexico recognized that their efforts were worse than fruitless; they had become counterproductive. They reversed course and negotiated an agreement that accelerated a process of social and economic integration among natural but very unequal trading partners. The agreement eliminates trade and investment barriers, but it assumes that the social, economic, and political consequences of dismantling those walls will be trivial. NAFTA's charter (with the partial exception of the side agreements on labor and the environment) overlooked the concept of "externalities"—that markets generate unintended but costly social, environmental, and political consequences.

The "dark side" of integration also was ignored. As barriers to legitimate trade declined, the opportunities for illegitimate trade naturally increased. Governments cannot erase impediments to trade and travel between them without also facilitating drug trafficking, illegal migration, money laundering, and illicit arms sales. Indeed, this is both the supreme paradox and the most intractable problem associated with free trade areas: how can nation-states facilitate integration without widening opportunities for crime? Or conversely, how can governments retard or stop such crimes without unduly restricting legal trade?

---

5. This is based on interviews with senior Mexican and US government officials.

6. The most complete, balanced, and astute analysis can be found in Sidney Weintraub, *Financial Decision-Making in Mexico: To Bet a Nation* (Pittsburgh: University of Pittsburgh Press, 2000).

NAFTA's authors had incorporated a provision to allow each country to leave NAFTA if it failed, but there were no provisions to handle the "success" of freeing capital movements by institutionalizing consultation and, to the extent possible, coordination among the central banks. The three governments dealt routinely and usually bilaterally with such issues as drugs, immigration, debts, trucking, and taxes, but there were few if any mechanisms to relate these issues to each other or to NAFTA. As a result, one country's drug policies sometimes make it more difficult to address shared concerns on immigration, and policies on Mexico's repayment of its debt have the unintended effect of encouraging immigration. Because NAFTA is bereft of institutions, the three countries rarely see— let alone address—the connections between the problems or how implementing different policies may lead to their acting at cross-purposes.

An extraordinarily complex process of integration is under way, but the three countries still tend to focus on one problem or one commodity, two countries at a time. The issues are drugs and immigration; the commodities are softwood lumber, sugar, fruit, and vegetables. We continue to bilateralize and compartmentalize, though these problems only fester when we do so. We have not allowed our imaginations to recognize and seize the opportunities presented by the emergence of a formidable new region.

More than 400 million people live in the three countries of North America, which cover 21.3 million square kilometers of territory (see table 1.1). Their combined gross product in 1999 was nearly $10 trillion. In territory, population, and product, NAFTA is larger than the 15-nation European Union. There is a convergence among the countries on the rate of population growth, because Mexico's annual growth rate has declined sharply since the mid-1970s—from 3.4 to 1.9 in 1999. This growth rate still exceeds that of its northern neighbors, but Canada and the United States are virtually the only two industrial countries with net population growth—largely because of immigration—and of course, Mexico's population growth is diminished by emigration. The population profiles, however, are complementary, with Mexico's average population being much younger than its two northern neighbors. The life expectancy of Mexicans is also increasing faster than that of Americans and Canadians, but it is still 5-7 years behind. The level of education of its students remains quite low by Canadian and US standards.

Of the many bonds of economic integration among the three countries, trade is growing fastest, and NAFTA has accelerated a trend that began in the mid-1980s (see table 1.2).[7] In the past two decades, Mexico's total

7. A measure of the growing integration is the increase in trade among the three regional partners as a percentage of their total trade. Mutti looks at US-Mexican trade and calculates "trade intensity indices" (e.g., US exports to Mexico as a percentage of its total exports) and, although he finds that the intensity index for US imports from Mexico increased by about 40 percent between 1993 and 1999, it declined slightly for exports. He concludes that integration began in the 1980s and that its full effects have not yet occurred. See John Mutti, *NAFTA: The Economic Consequences for Mexico and the United States* (Washington: Economic Strategy Institute, 2001), 27-30.

Table 1.1 Indicators for the three countries of North America, 1990-99

Indicator	United States 1990	United States 1999	Canada 1990	Canada 1999	Mexico 1990	Mexico 1999	NAFTA 1990	NAFTA 1999	United States (as percent of NAFTA) 1990	United States (as percent of NAFTA) 1999
GDP (millions of dollars)	5,554,100	8,708,870	572,673	612,049	262,710	474,951	6,389,483	9,795,870	86.9	88.9
Per capita GDP (current)	22,216	30,992	21,610	19,744	3,048	4,896	17,616	23,951		
Area (thousands of square kilometers)	9,364		9,971		1,958		21,293			
Population (millions)	250	281[c]	26.5	31	86.2	97	362.7	409	69	69
Average annual growth rate 1990-99 (percent)	1.2	1.2	1.2		1.9					
Life expectancy at birth[a]	76	77	77	79	70	72				
Percent of GNP spent on education[b]	6.7	5.4	6.9	6.9	4.7	4.9				
Secondary school net enrollment ratio (percent)	94	96	84	95	67	66				
Total exports of goods (millions of dollars)	393,587	693,000	127,688	238,450	40,711	136,660	561,986	1,068,110	70	65
Percent of exports of goods to North America	28.4	36.2	75.3	86.4	46.4	86.0	42.8	54.7		
Total imports of goods (millions of dollars)	495,252	1,059,200	115,242	215,560	41,592	142,063	652,086	1,416,823	76	75
Percent of imports of goods from North America	24.5	29.5	66.6	70.0	50.4	62.0	33.5	41.3		

a. Data are from 1990 and 1998. The 1998 figure was computed by averaging the life expectancies for males and females.
b. Data are from 1980 and 1997.
c. Population is for 2000.

Sources: World Bank, World Development Report (1992 and 2001) for GDP, per capita GDP, area, life expectancy, percentage of GNP spent on education, and secondary school net enrollment ratio. Trade data are from International Monetary Fund, Direction of Trade Statistics Yearbook (1990); World Trade Organization, International Trade Statistics, 2000, http://www.wto.org/english/res_e/statis_e/stat_toc_e.htm; Bureau of Transportation Statistics, North American Transportation in Figures, 2000, http://www.bts.gov/itt/natf.html; International Monetary Fund, Direction of Trade Statistics Yearbook, 1990; and Inter-American Development Bank, ESDB Query Facility, 2000, http://database.iadb.org/esdbweb/scripts/esdbweb.exe.

trade increased seven times; Canada's and the United States', more than three times. More significantly, all three countries' trade with each other increased at a far more rapid rate than world trade (see table 1.3). Canada and Mexico rely on the United States to purchase more than 80 percent of their exports, and the United States now sells more than a third of all its exports to its two neighbors. A thick web of commerce, finance, and interdependence has been spun across the continent of North America. But the challenge of integrating three such disparate economies is clearly beyond the capacity of NAFTA, as it is currently constituted.

Lessons from the Old World

Even as Canadians and Mexicans struggled to shore up their distinct currency crises, Europe was trying to combine 12 or more currencies into 1—a feat of heroic proportions in a world in which islands of 10,000 people demanded sovereignty. Across the ocean sat the longest-lasting, most successful experiment in integration among sovereign states—the European Union[8]—and yet only a few considered drawing any lessons from its experience.[9] This is partly because the origin, purpose, and composition of the European Union were quite different from those of NAFTA. The European Union was born of two cataclysmic wars and a fervent desire for peace; its purpose and model was to build a community; and its members were more equal in size and power than was true of NAFTA. In addition, many Americans were skeptical as to whether the experiment with a unified currency would succeed, and they also viewed the thick EU "social safety net" as a cause of Europe's higher unemployment and therefore as hardly a model worth replicating.

There are two other reasons why the EU "model" was viewed as having limited relevance. First, the income disparity between Mexico and its two

---

8. Europe's Common Market began as the European Coal and Steel Community in 1951 and was transformed by the Treaty of Rome into the European Economic Community (EEC) in 1957. Later, it became the European Community (EC) and subsequently, after the Treaty of Maastricht in 1991, the European Union (EU). I will use "EC," "EU," or the Union to refer to the European entity.

9. A few did ask the questions, but the answers were very preliminary. See, e.g., Albert Fishlow, Sherman Robinson, and Raul Hinojosa-Ojeda, "Proposal for a North American Regional Development Bank," paper prepared for a conference sponsored by the Federal Reserve Bank of Dallas (14 June 1991); Donald J. Puchala, "The European Communities and the North American Free Trade Area," paper prepared for a conference on NAFTA at the Carter Center of Emory University (12 February 1992); and Robert A. Pastor, *Integration with Mexico: Options for US Policy* (New York: Twentieth Century Fund, 1993), chap. 5.

Table 1.2 North American trade with the world, 1980-99
(in millions of current dollars)

Country	1980	1990	1999
Exports			
Canada	67,730	127,688	238,450
Mexico	18,031	40,711	136,660
United States	220,781	393,587	693,000
Total	306,542	561,986	1,068,110
Imports			
Canada	61,004	115,242	215,560
Mexico	21,087	41,592	142,063
United States	256,959	495,252	1,059,200
Total	339,050	652,086	1,416,823
Total trade (exports and imports)			
Canada	128,734	242,930	454,010
Mexico	39,118	82,303	278,723
United States	477,740	888,839	1,752,200
Total	645,592	1,214,072	2,484,933

Sources: World Trade Organization, International Trade Statistics, 2000, http://www.wto.org/english/res_e/statis_e/stat_toc_e.htm; US Bureau of Transportation Statistics, North American Transportation in Figures, 2000, http://www.bts.gov/itt/natf.html; International Monetary Fund, Direction of Trade Statistics Yearbook, 1990; and Inter-American Development Bank, ESDB Query Facility, 2000, http://database.iadb.org/esdbweb/scripts/esdbweb.exe.

wealthy northern neighbors is much wider than that between poor and rich European countries, and therefore the prospect of reducing it seemed remote. Second, NAFTA is just a free trade area, whereas the European Union passed that threshold decades ago, on its way to becoming a customs union (with a common external tariff), a common market (with free movement of labor and capital), and finally an economic and monetary union.

Nonetheless, having identified the differences, one could still profit from analyzing the EU experience. The European Union reduced the volatility that disproportionately harmed its weak economies. And, during 40 years of trial and error, the Union significantly narrowed the disparities in income between its rich and poor members. The question, therefore, is not whether the Union developed the ideal model, but whether there are elements of its experience that NAFTA could learn from, adapt, and adopt. We will examine Europe's policies to see which ones worked best to narrow the gap between rich and poor countries and which policies were least effective.

The virtual disappearance of the issue of NAFTA from the politics of the three countries suggests that NAFTA may have descended to the peculiar resting place that controversial issues, like the Panama Canal

Table 1.3 Trade within North America and intraregional trade as percent of total world trade, 1980-99

	Exports						Imports					
	1980		1990		1999		1980		1990		1999	
Country	Dollars	Percent	Dollars	Percent	Dollars	Percent	Dollars	Percent	Dollars	Percent	Dollars	Percent
Canadian trade with												
Mexico	547	0.8	562	0.4	1,100	0.5	153	0.3	1,497	1.3	6,420	3.0
United States	53,614	79.2	95,611	74.9	205,020	86.0	46,208	75.7	75,286	65.3	144,430	67.0
Total	54,161	80.0	96,173	75.3	206,120	86.4	46,361	76.0	76,783	66.6	150,850	70.0
Mexican trade with												
Canada	153	0.8	458	1.1	6,420	4.7	547	2.6	458	1.1	1,100	0.8
United States	13,149	72.9	18,418	45.2	111,100	81.3	19,773	93.8	20,491	49.3	87,000	61.2
Total	13,302	73.8	18,876	46.4	117,520	86.0	20,320	96.4	20,949	50.4	88,100	62.0
United States trade with												
Canada	46,208	20.9	83,674	21.3	163,900	23.7	53,614	20.9	91,380	18.5	201,400	19.0
Mexico	19,773	9.0	28,279	7.2	87,000	12.6	13,149	5.1	30,157	6.1	111,100	10.5
Total	65,981	29.9	111,953	28.4	250,900	36.2	66,763	26.0	121,537	24.5	312,500	29.5
NAFTA total[a]	133,444		227,002		574,540		133,444		219,269		551,450	

a. Differences between intraregional imports and exports in 1990 and 1999 reflect differences in national trade accounts.

Sources: World Trade Organization, *International Trade Statistics, 2000*, http://www.wto.org/english/res_e/statis_e/stat_toc_e.htm; US Bureau of Transportation Statistics, *North American Transportation in Figures, 2000*, http://www.bts.gov/itt/natf.html; International Monetary Fund, *Direction of Trade Statistics Yearbook*, 1990; and Inter-American Development Bank, *ESDB Query Facility, 2000*, http://database.iadb.org/esdbweb/scripts/esdbweb.exe.

treaties, go after terrible predictions about their impact are proven wrong or forgotten. It simply left the public's radar screen.

Scholars, however, have continued to examine NAFTA, and several have looked at the European Union's experience for lessons. Let us review some of the literature. In *The New American Community*, Rosenberg views NAFTA as just one small step toward an entity that encompasses all the nations of the Americas and is almost indistinguishable from the European Union. His experience has been in Europe—not in the Americas—and thus it is not surprising that he borrows extensively from Europe's treaties and institutions and does little to adapt them. Indeed, his proposal verges on being almost a literal translation of the European Union into American, with an occasional modest change in language. For example, he suggests that an alternative name for a unifying Commission could be the "Executive Branch," but its role would be the same as that of the European Commission. It would initiate legislation, ensure the compliance of the three governments, administer common policies, and negotiate trade agreements with countries in other regions. The "Executive Branch" would be organized like the European Commission, with directorate-generals and cabinets. As in Europe, the Council of Ministers would be the principal decision-making body, deciding on legislation, coordinating members' economic policies, and so on.[10]

Several studies have focused on EU regional policies. Sweet offers a comprehensive description of the regional policies of Europe and also of the three governments of North America. He traces US regional policy back to the Franklin D. Roosevelt administration's New Deal, but describes its fuller development during John F. Kennedy's and Lyndon Johnson's administrations. Since then, and particularly since Ronald Reagan's administration, the federal government has given less attention to helping poor regions. Nonetheless, the US General Accounting Office still lists 340 federal economic development programs administered by 13 executive departments and agencies, with an annual core budget of about $6 billion.[11] He then describes Canada's policies toward its provinces, Mexico's policies toward its rural areas, and the European Union's regional and cohesion programs. He examines various European funds and evaluates their benefits and costs, concluding that the EU Structural Funds "led to a significant improvement in the economic performance of most recipients."[12]

---

10. Jerry M. Rosenberg, *The New American Community: A Response to the European and Asian Economic Challenge* (Westport, CT: Praeger, 1992), esp. chaps. 8 and 9.

11. Morris L. Sweet, *Regional Economic Development in the European Union and North America* (Westport, CT: Praeger, 1999), 257.

12. Sweet, *Regional Economic Development*, 130.

López Roldán, a Mexican scholar, recognized that the Mexican government's regional policy could not transfer the kinds of resources to poor regions as did its neighbors and the European Union. Of course, NAFTA did not envisage any policy for the poor regions of Mexico, but he recommends that the North American governments establish a system of structural funds to reduce disparities.[13]

Grinspun and Kreklewich view NAFTA as a product of a neoliberal economic philosophy and the hegemonic power of the United States and its corporations. The authors accept that the challenge is no longer whether to integrate with the world economy but rather how, and they propose that new institutions be established to strengthen popular participation and balance the unhealthy weight of multinational corporations. They point to the regime on intellectual property rights to show that large corporations have imposed a set of rules that serve their interests rather than the public's. The rules limit the free flow of information, technology, and trademarks to the detriment, in their view, of poor people and countries. The authors are not very specific as to how to achieve a new equilibrium—except to say that Europe's experience has been better balanced, partly because of its institutions and its social charter.[14]

MacMillan returns to the original question of relevance but reaches a very different conclusion. She sees the European Union and NAFTA as so different that one cannot extract meaningful lessons. The Union is more legalistic, with supranational institutions like the European Court of Justice that can insist on the supremacy of EU law over national law. Moreover, the Union has its own tax base, albeit a relatively small one, and common policies on agriculture, antitrust, and so on. NAFTA has none of these.[15]

Gianaris examines the evolution of the European Union and NAFTA and its policies on trade, industrialization, joint ventures, and fiscal and monetary affairs, but he stops short of drawing a comparison or asking whether lessons from one region's experience are useful for the other.[16] Similarly, the United Nations Economic Commission for Europe commis-

13. Mario López Roldán, "Tres Experiencias Europeas en Materia de Integración Económica Regional que Pueden Ser Utiles para Mexico en el Process de Integración de America del Norte," Madrid, photocopy (January 1996).

14. Ricardo Grinspun and Robert Kreklewich, "Institutions, Power Relations, and Unequal Integration in the Americas: NAFTA as Deficient Institutionality," in *Economic Integration in NAFTA and the EU*, ed. Kirsten Appendini and Sven Bislev (New York: St. Martin's Press, 1999).

15. Gretchen M. MacMillan, Managing Economic Convergence in the EU, in *Toward A North American Community: Canada, the US, and Mexico*, ed. Donald Barry (Boulder, CO: Westview Press, 1995).

16. Nicholas V. Gianaris, *The North American Free Trade Agreement and the European Union* (Westport, CT: Praeger, 1998).

sioned studies on the integration process within Europe and between the European Union and a number of Eastern European countries. A chapter was added on the US-Canadian Free Trade Agreement (FTA), but no explicit comparisons were made that might help the reader draw some lessons.[17]

In summary, the literature has grown on the subject of the European Union and how its programs might help North America. A more practical question is why Canadians and Mexicans have not insisted on drafting a social charter—or, until Fox, why they have not sought funds to reduce disparities. Canadians have given considerable thought to the concept of "social cohesion," and its implications for trying to build a community within Canada, but they have not applied this concept to Mexico or a North American Community.[18] One would think that, to compensate for their relative weakness, Canadians or Mexicans would seek ways to collaborate and pursue North American answers to collective problems. But that has not been the case. Why?

From the periphery of the continent, it is hard to see over the US elephant. Since the onset of NAFTA, Canada's and Mexico's trade with the United States has grown from about two-thirds to more than 80 percent of their total trade. Interviews with leaders in both countries whose political philosophies are spread across a wide spectrum led me to conclude that both countries are utterly absorbed with their own problems. To the extent that they look at the world, they invest most of their energy in their bilateral relationship with the United States.

Canadians and Mexicans initially approached each other, hoping for an informal alliance against the colossus, but they soon realized that this was not a productive approach. Each was averse to being used to serve the other's purposes, and the United States took offense at being the target of their collaboration. Each then retreated to the bilateralism of the past. Neither country has shown much interest in establishing trinational institutions, in part because they suspect that the United States is uninterested and that their proposals would not prosper. The United States, whether as a government or society, has not displayed an excess of imagination on North American issues, perhaps believing that its economic weight and the existing configuration of the relationship assures outcomes favorable to its interests.

All this could change if Fox persists with his agenda for a common market. The United States—with its large, growing Mexican American

---

17. United Nations Economic Commission for Europe, *Economic Integration in Europe and North America* (New York: United Nations, 1995).

18. See The Standing Senate Committee on Social Affairs, Science, and Technology, *Final Report on Social Cohesion* (Ottawa, June 1999); and Jane Jenson, *Mapping Social Cohesion: The State of Canadian Research*, Study F03 (Ottawa: Canadian Policy Research Network, 1998).

population—cannot afford to ignore his proposal, and might see an advantage in taking it seriously. If the United States begins negotiating a deeper relationship with Mexico, Canada cannot afford to sit on the sidelines. In brief, *Fox might introduce a new dynamic* into a static equation.

If and when the Bush administration persuades Congress to approve trade-promotion authority (previously described as "fast-track"), trade negotiations in the Americas will experience a jump-start. For the past several years, the principal trading initiative in the hemisphere has originated with the four countries of Mercosur. Chile and Bolivia associated with it. On 31 August and 1 September 2000, the Brazilian president invited all of his freely elected colleagues from South America to open discussions on a South American Free Trade Area (SAFTA). It was reported that Brazil hoped the talks would strengthen South America's bargaining power vis-à-vis the United States and NAFTA. On 1 December 2000, however, Chile turned away from Mercosur—in part because tariff rates were high—and initiated trade talks with the United States, despite the fact that the US president does not have authority to complete such an agreement. The Chilean decision is a reflection of the overweening power of the US market. The United States generates 76 percent and its two neighbors add 9 percent of the combined gross product of all the Americas.[19] When the Congress grants the president authority, the negotiations for the FTAA will become serious very quickly.

Organization of the Book

In chapter 2, to explain the limitations and the potential of NAFTA, I identify parameters for comparing NAFTA with the European Union and with two Asian entities, Asia-Pacific Economic Cooperation and the Association of South East Asian Nations—each of which is based on a model that addresses the global challenge of integration in ways unique to its region. One principal challenge of the 21st century is to find effective mechanisms for integrating developing countries into the global economy. Foreign aid is essential to lift countries from poverty, but the path toward sustainable economic growth requires trade, and one path toward that goal is to connect with a major trading scheme—the European Union or NAFTA. A recent World Bank report concluded that "selecting high-income countries as partners is often likely to be the best option for developing countries," but to ensure that such schemes respond to the needs of the poor countries "will require the creation of mechanisms to

---

19. See World Bank, *World Development Indicators 2000* (Washington: World Bank, 2000), table 7.1, 252-53.

ensure an equitable distribution of gain."[20] That is one more reason why NAFTA needs to be redesigned: to develop new policies to reduce income disparities.

Chapter 3 describes and evaluates the European Union's regional and cohesion policies. What led the Union to place such value on reducing disparities? Which programs were most effective, and why? What lessons can be drawn for a North American community? Chapter 4 examines NAFTA and its evolution, asking what problems have emerged and what opportunities have been missed.

The heart of the book resides in chapters 5 and 6, where I try to respond to NAFTA's limitations with in-depth proposals for a deeper relationship. Much of the analysis is based on lessons that I extract from the European Union and adapt to the special circumstances of North America. The goals of NAFTA need amending, and I describe the institutions that should be established and how their mandate would differ from those in the European Union. Then, I identify and suggest North American policies for infrastructure and transportation, trade, and macroeconomic policies and a common currency. Chapter 6 offers North American plans for customs and immigration, energy, regional development, and education. Of course, many other sectors are in need of comprehensive, continental consideration, but the ones in these chapters are illustrative of what could be done.

In chapter 7, I address the question of whether the entire exercise is quixotic. A trilateral approach has often foundered on the preference of Canada and Mexico for bilateralism and the United States' disposition to go it alone. I offer some ideas for how the governments can be reorganized to consider a trilateral approach. But are the governments ready to give up their sovereignty and develop common approaches? Are they prepared to establish new common institutions? To answer these questions, I explore historical and contemporary understandings of "sovereignty" and consult public opinion surveys. The rather surprising conclusion is that the people of North America are way ahead of their leaders. A majority of the public in all three countries is willing to support North American political union if they could be convinced that it would improve their lives and not threaten their cultural identity.

At the end of chapter 7, I develop three grand options for North America, and then explain why a fourth incremental, practical option should instead be chosen. That fourth option should aim to "deepen" the relationship among the three countries along the lines sketched in chapters 5 and 6.

Finally, chapter 8 looks beyond NAFTA to the Free Trade Area of the Americas, and beyond that to implications for the world's political

---

20. World Bank, *Trade Blocs: A Policy Research Report* (New York: Oxford University Press, 2000), x–xi.

economy. Should the United States deepen its relationship with its neighbors or widen it first to include the nations on its periphery? How should NAFTA relate to the FTAA and to the World Trade Organization (WTO)? Which path ought to have priority? I argue that we ought to pursue a deeper NAFTA, a wider FTAA, and global trade talks at the same time, because each is addressing a distinct set of issues. Moreover, the fact that the United States has three sets of options will generate competition and, it is to be hoped, more progress in all the talks.

Should NAFTA Be Deepened?
Is This the Moment?

Although there are groups within each NAFTA member state that would prefer to renounce or fundamentally alter the agreement, the three governments are all reasonably satisfied with it. And they have reason to be: Their trade and investment with each other have expanded far more rapidly than with the rest of the world, and many of their corporations have become continental and more competitive. And yet everyone knows the dangers of complacency. In a rapidly changing world, one cannot expect to maintain one's place, let alone grow, if one sits still. As Will Rogers once said: "Even if you're on the right road, if you sit down, you can get run over." *There are seven compelling reasons why the three governments of North America need to reevaluate NAFTA and seize this moment to explore aggressively new paths to deepen the relationship.*

First, NAFTA has not changed the pattern of the United States' relations with its two neighbors. This relationship is driven by deep-seated emotions and highly organized domestic interests, and most of the hard problems are addressed in forums that lack trinational rules. Some interests seek protection from competition—such as dairy and textiles in Canada; corn and services in Mexico; and lumber, sugar, and trucking in the United States. Other groups seek to deflect attention from local problems, such as when the United States seeks answers to its drug problems by condemning Mexico, or Mexico criticizes US immigration policies for its unemployment problem. Many of these problems are confronted again and again in ways that erode the relationship. In the end, the asymmetry of power makes solutions difficult, and often leaves a bitter taste. The only way to change these old habits is to submit them to a new structure—one based on rules rather than power or a sense of inferiority. The best time is at the beginning of national administrations, when there is a honeymoon period, and that opportunity is multiplied by three because the three leaders were recently inaugurated within months of each other.

Second, NAFTA has failed to deal with the contradictions inherent in the problem of integrating such diverse economies and societies. The most basic contradiction is that the elimination of barriers to trade in legal goods also makes it easier to smuggle illegal goods, and the steps normally taken by a government to prevent smuggling inevitably impede the exchange of legal goods. As the United States tries to stop drugs from coming across its borders, and as Mexico tries to stop illicit guns coming from the United States, legitimate businesses have to pay for the delays— often more than the amount of the tariff that was eliminated. There are ways to cope with these contradictions, but they require new formulas for cooperation.

Third, to sustain and to strengthen a cooperative spirit, the three governments should explore common approaches to other foreign policy issues. They might begin with developing a single approach to trade policy, as it relates to global trade talks and third countries. Cuba might provide a second opportunity. Since Fidel Castro came to power in 1959, the three governments have adopted very different approaches to Cuba. None have been successful, except in irritating the others. It might not be possible for the three to bridge the differences, but their relationship would benefit and their policies would be more effective if they succeeded.

Fourth, the three governments need to discuss controversial issues like a common currency. As the three economies become more highly integrated, major shifts in foreign exchange rates have a huge impact on trade and on domestic businesses. Insofar as exchange rates are fundamentally undervalued, they could lead to unwarranted industrial restructuring, or they could aggravate protectionism. US efforts to countervail Canadian wheat and lumber products are due in part to Canada's undervalued currency. A single currency would solve many of these problems, but it might create others. That is a plea to address the issue now rather than delay until a full-blown crisis strikes.

Fifth, the three countries are undergoing a profound process of social integration because of immigration. For Canada and the United States, immigration has become a growing source of population growth and employment. For Mexico, emigration and remittances have a pervasive psychological and financial effect. No issue looms as important for Mexico in 2001 as immigration. But the United States will need to take into account the distributive consequences and the social tensions inherent in immigration before responding to Fox's proposals for more visas. Even as US leaders express their condolences on the death of illegal migrants in the Arizona desert, an increasing number of Arizona ranchers take the law into their own hands. The many-sided issues of immigration can only yield a coherent response if the three governments first place them in a broader context.

Sixth, innumerable opportunities have not been addressed because we are looking at the relationship from the wrong direction. For example, although more than 75 percent of the goods exchanged by the three countries each year are carried by trucks, a trucker must cross 64 separate jurisdictions in North America, and the variation in safety standards and working conditions is so wide that it becomes impossible for the trucker to keep his costs low. NAFTA would benefit from a forum and an office whose responsibility would be to devise a North American plan for transportation and infrastructure, and for other issues as well.

Seventh, the most compelling practical reason to approach NAFTA with a different mindset is its original premise's lack of realism. The agreement was negotiated as if the three countries were of equal size and economic weight. That unrealistic assumption permitted a rule-based formula to eliminate trade and investment barriers, and in the long term, that is probably the best approach. In the short term, however, it ignored the uneven economic development, different vulnerabilities, and wide disparities in income and employment among the three countries.

These wide disparities ought to focus the minds of the countries' leaders, for several reasons. They are the principal motives for migration among the well-off ("brain drain") and the poor alike, thus contributing to a widening gap separating Mexico from its neighbors. No solution to the immigration problem is possible without a significant reduction in the gap between incomes in Mexico and in the United States. It is also difficult to conceive of a sense of community until there is a greater balance in the relationship between the one poor and two rich countries of North America. And without such a sense of community, it will be difficult to deal with problems, such as water shortages or transnational crime. The fact that integration is not reducing the gap is not an argument against integration; it merely suggests that additional steps are essential. The main argument for deepening NAFTA, however, is the simplest: *Problems can no longer be contained in any of the three countries, and new opportunities benefit all three.*

For all these reasons, the United States and its neighbors have an opportunity at this moment in history to create a *community of diversity* and to build a *model that gives a boost to the middle class of the developing world.* The United States does not need to reach across the world to seize that opportunity because it is right at its borders. Nor is the World Trade Organization (with its more than 142 member countries) likely to be the best forum. A trinational unit might be the optimal level at which to experiment with new approaches. The proposal by Fox offers an agenda, but new institutions are needed to organize the issues, provide concrete ideas, and stimulate leaders to make bold decisions.

2

One World or Three?

The point in history at which we stand is full of promise and of danger. The world will either move toward unity and widely shared prosperity or it will move apart into necessarily competing economic blocs. We have a chance, we citizens of the United States, to use our influence in favor of a more united and cooperating world. Whether we do so will determine, as far as it is in our power, the kind of lives our grandchildren can live.[1]

—President Franklin D. Roosevelt
12 February 1945

A cryptic irony haunts the corridors of international trade negotiations. Although governments have spent the last half-century crafting a global trading system, businesses have divided the system into three regions. The irony has a second layer: The country that has worked hardest to forge a single world trading system is the same one that is fashioning the most formidable challenge to it.

During the Second World War, some of the most heated disagreements between US President Franklin D. Roosevelt and British Prime Minister Winston Churchill concerned imperial trade preferences. Churchill was determined to maintain the British Empire, and Roosevelt was just as certain that imperialism should end, and world trade should be free of its influence. Roosevelt's vision prevailed, although not before he died. In 1947, the United States invited 22 countries to Geneva to discuss ways to reduce trade barriers and establish a rule-based global trading system. As part of a global compromise, France and the United Kingdom were

---

1. In a message containing the Bretton Woods proposals to the US Congress, cited in Sidney Ratner, *The Tariff in American History* (New York: Van Nostrand, 1972), 155.

permitted to retain exclusive trade arrangements with their colonies for a period, and after independence, the former colonies received trade preferences. But both France and the United Kingdom were compelled to accept global rules that allowed nondiscriminatory access to trade by all the world's businesses.[2]

The resulting General Agreement on Tariffs and Trade (GATT) established a framework that permitted tariffs to decline and world trade to grow by more than 15 times by the end of the century. Trade expanded at more than twice the rate of the world's production, doubling its interdependence. Despite its unparalleled success, however, GATT and the World Trade Organization that replaced it in 1995 did not produce one world; it produced at least three, and the United States, the champion of globalism, sat at the center of one of those—North America. How could it happen that three regional trading systems—East Asia, the European Union, and North America—emerged from a single set of global rules, and how important are these trading units? What are the common and distinctive characteristics of each regional trading scheme, and which elements are worth replicating? The economic-gravity model can explain why trade coalesced in proximate regions,[3] but what led the United States to deviate from the principle of a single, nondiscriminatory world system that it had so long defended?

These three regions now dominate the world economy, accounting for nearly 80 percent of the world's production and trade (figure 2.1). Although the countries in each region trade with those in other regions, trade within each region has increased more rapidly than trade among them. From 1980 to 1999, the exports of EU nations to each other increased from 53.2 percent of their trade with the world to 61.7 percent (table 2.1). For East Asia, intraregional exports as a percentage of total global exports expanded from 28.8 to 39 percent in the same period. (Part of the reason for the increase was the expansion of trade by China.) Exports from the three countries of North America amounted to less than a third of their total exports in 1980; by 1999, intraregional exports constituted 54.6 percent of their total exports. Intraregional imports as a percentage of total imports also increased in all three regions. Regionalism, in short, has been growing at a much faster pace in the past two decades than globalism, and the fact that these three regions are responsible for about 80 percent of all world trade confirms the new shape of the tripartite trading system.

---

2. See Richard N. Gardner, *Sterling-Dollar Diplomacy: Anglo-American Collaboration in the Reconstruction of Multilateral Trade* (Oxford: Clarendon Press, 1956); and Robert A. Pastor, *Congress and the Politics of U.S. Foreign Economic Policy* (Berkeley: University of California Press, 1980), chap. 3.

3. Jeffrey A. Frankel, *Regional Trading Blocs in the World Economic System* (Washington: Institute for International Economics, 1997).

Figure 2.1 The world's three main regions: Gross product and trade, 1998

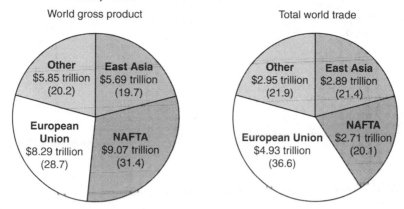

World gross product

Other $5.85 trillion (20.2)	East Asia $5.69 trillion (19.7)
European Union $8.29 trillion (28.7)	NAFTA $9.07 trillion (31.4)

Total world trade

Other $2.95 trillion (21.9)	East Asia $2.89 trillion (21.4)
European Union $4.93 trillion (36.6)	NAFTA $2.71 trillion (20.1)

NAFTA: North American Free Trade Agreement

Notes: Total trade is total of exports and imports of goods and services. *North America:* Canada, Mexico, and the United States. *European Union:* Austria, Belgium, Denmark, France, Germany, Greece, Ireland, Italy, Luxembourg, the Netherlands, Portugal, Spain, Sweden, and the United Kingdom. *East Asia:* Association of South East Asian Nations (ASEAN), China, Japan, and South Korea. Numbers in parentheses are percent of total.

Source: World Development Report 2000, World Bank, Washington.

These three regional trading areas are the largest by far, but they are not alone. A World Bank study found a "veritable explosion of regional integration agreements (RIAs) in the last fifteen years." The WTO requires that each member notify it when it reaches such an agreement. By 1999, the WTO recorded 194 such agreements; nearly half had been registered just since 1990.[4] Most of these agreements represent associations with the European Union—for example, with Eastern Europe, the Mediterranean, and Turkey—but there has also been a proliferation of RIAs in Latin America, the Middle East, Southeast Asia, and Sub-Saharan Africa. Most arrangements involve countries at comparable levels of development; the two major exceptions are NAFTA and the less formal Asia Pacific Economic Cooperation (APEC).

Still, the three most significant schemes for trade and production remain the European Union, NAFTA, and APEC. Part of the reason for the increased importance of EU intraregional trade is simply the expansion of its membership to 15 countries during the past 40 years. The growth of intraregional trade among the NAFTA countries is quite another thing. One might expect that Canada and Mexico would rely more on the US market because of NAFTA, but the United States is the major trading

---

4. World Bank, *Trade Blocs: A Policy Research Report* (New York: Oxford University Press, 2000), ix, 1.

Table 2.1 Intraregional trade for three world regions, 1980-99

Trade	1980	1990	1999
Intraregional exports as percent of total exports			
North America	32.60	42.80	54.60
European Union	53.21	60.58	61.69
East Asia	28.75	35.03	39.06[a]
Intraregional imports as percent of total imports			
North America	29.50	33.50	41.30
European Union	48.19	57.92	59.25
East Asia	23.42	35.39	48.95[a]

a. Figures drop Taiwan and add Brunei, China, Myanmar, and Vietnam.

Notes: North American figures include Canada, Mexico, and the United States. European Union figures for 1980 include Belgium, Denmark, France, Germany, Ireland, Italy, Luxembourg, the Netherlands, and the United Kingdom. The 1990 figures add Greece, and the 1999 figures add Austria, Finland, and Sweden. The Asian figures for 1980 and 1990 include Hong Kong, Indonesia, Japan, Malaysia, the Philippines, Singapore, South Korea, Taiwan, and Thailand.

Sources: Organization for Economic Cooperation and Development (OECD), Monthly Statistics on Foreign Trade, July 1992; OECD, Historical Statistics on Foreign Trade, 1965-1980, 1982; International Monetary Fund, Direction of Trade Statistics Yearbook, 1984, 1991, 1992, 1994, 1996, and Quarterly Report, June 2000.

nation in the world. It purchases and sells more goods and services in the world than any other country. Had the US market not been as open as it is, Asia would not have recovered so quickly after its financial crisis in 1997. Therefore, what is surprising is the growing importance of the North American market for US business. In 1990, Americans sold 28 percent of their goods to Canada and Mexico; by 1999, they were selling 36.5 percent there.

Does the emergence of three blocs represent a defeat for Roosevelt's vision of one world? No. The regionalism of the past 50 years is qualitatively different from the imperial blocs of the previous century. Imperial powers defined the terms of trade in their jurisdiction; competition was excluded or restricted to the empire's businesses. Today's regionalism is not a fortress; it acts within a global framework of rules. Regions are not permitted under those rules to exclude the goods from particular countries; indeed, the external tariff should be no different from the one defined by the WTO. The barriers to trade and investment around these new regional units are theoretically no higher than the barriers around any of the nation-states that adhere to WTO rules.

Within these new regional areas, nation-states try to eliminate or harmonize other barriers. Tariffs and nontariff barriers, which had been the principal focus in the old trade agreements, are only one part of more comprehensive schemes today. The European Union, NAFTA, and many of the new trade agreements cover services, intellectual property rights, government procurement, and a host of sectors that had not been included in previous agreements. As such, these regional schemes can be viewed as "laboratories" for experimenting with new ways to rationalize production and improve the quality of life.

Why have these new regional schemes emerged? There are numerous theories, and many are not incompatible. Some regional agreements were established for security reasons—to build new webs of cooperation to preclude a recurrence of wars. Economic motives obviously play a large role. Seeking to improve the living standards of their people, governments seek RIAs to enlarge their markets, diminish transaction costs, increase competition, reduce the prices of consumer goods, encourage foreign investment, and lock in macroeconomic policy reforms. One scholar found that countries seek to join RIAs when they judge that the economies are doing better within the schemes than outside them.[5]

Finally, geography has asserted itself, encouraging businesses to trade and invest more in countries that are closer to home. Most people have attributed the growing interdependence in the world to sharply declining costs of transportation and communications. Such transaction costs have declined markedly over time, but they continue to vary inversely with distance, making neighbors "natural trading partners."[6] It was imperialism—not free trade—that created "unnatural" trading patterns. The United Kingdom, for example, was the principal trading partner of Australia, Canada, and India. With the end of imperialism, and the emergence of a single set of global trading rules, geography and economics replaced politics as the principal factor explaining trading patterns. In brief and with a trace of irony, the global trading system made it possible for countries to trade more with their neighbors, and this trend encouraged governments to fashion stable, predictable regional integration areas.

From Global Rules to Regional Trade

Given US determination to strengthen the global trading system, how can one explain the change in US policy toward accepting and participating in regional groups? After the Second World War, the first new and significant deviation from a global trading system occurred when France, Germany, and four other countries established the European Coal and Steel Community in 1951. The preamble to its constituting treaty emphasized security motives: "Considering that world peace may be safeguarded only by creating efforts equal to the dangers which menace it . . . [the six countries

---

5. For this theory and a description of the others, see Walter Mattli, *The Logic of Regional Integration: Europe and Beyond* (Cambridge: Cambridge University Press, 1999).

6. Frankel, *Regional Trading Blocs in the World Economic System.*

are] resolved to substitute for historic rivalries a fusion of their essential interests . . ."[7] US policymakers judged that peace in Europe was worth an economic detour from a global trading system, and the Soviet threat was a second reason why the US government would consistently support European unity.

Europe also had a second reason to seek unity. A report written by Paul-Henri Spaak in 1956 urged the establishment of a Common Market to reverse the continent's decline: "Europe, which once had the monopoly of manufacturing industries . . . today sees its external positions weakened, its influence declining, and its capacity to progress lost in its divisions."[8] By the 1960s, Europe's economies had recovered and had begun to compete against the United States. The US government realized it was promoting the development of a formidable competitor, but it continued to believe that world peace and prosperity would be better served by a united Europe than a divided one.

At the same time, the United States was determined to try to maintain a uniform trading system and so, in the Kennedy Round of trade negotiations beginning in 1962, US negotiators pressed the Europeans to accept a level playing field. The United States also resisted proposals to establish its own preferential trade agreements with Latin America or other areas in the 1960s. The United States did not deviate from this policy until 1982, when President Reagan proposed the Caribbean Basin Initiative, a one-way free trade agreement with the small economies in the Caribbean and Central America. Soon after, the United States signed a free trade agreement with Israel. Because both agreements were with small, strategically vulnerable countries, no serious objections were raised regarding the implications for the GATT.

The decision to negotiate a US-Canadian Free Trade Agreement, reflecting the largest bilateral trading relationship in the world and, subsequently, the North American Free Trade Agreement, were of a different magnitude, heralding the beginning of a significant regional entity. Indeed, the first reaction by senior officials in the White House Office of the Special Trade Representative (STR) was negative. Their first priority was an open world trading system, and they did not want to pursue an initiative that could jeopardize completion of the Uruguay Round of world trade talks, but President Bush realized the political significance of NAFTA and instructed his negotiators to proceed expeditiously.[9] He signed the agreement in December 1992.

---

7. Cited in Walter Mattli, *The Logic of Regional Integration: Europe and Beyond* (Cambridge: Cambridge University Press, 1999), 69.

8. Cited in Mattli, *Logic of Regional Integration*, 70.

9. Frederick W. Mayer, *Interpreting NAFTA: The Science and Art of Political Analysis* (New York: Columbia University Press, 1998), 41-43.

Two challenges faced by regional trading areas are how to deepen integration by harmonizing domestic policies and how to enlarge the regions by incorporating new members. In March 1998, the European Union launched its most complex negotiations: to integrate 12 Eastern and Southern European countries. It also signed an agreement with 12 Mediterranean countries to establish a free trade area by 2010. In December 1994, the United States and 33 other countries in the western hemisphere pledged to complete negotiations for a free trade area by 2005.

East Asia is one of the most dynamic trading areas, but it does not have a regional group comparable to the European Union or NAFTA. Instead, it has two different organizations. One, the Association of South East Asian Nations (ASEAN), was established in 1967 with 5 nations (Indonesia, Malaysia, Philippines, Singapore, and Thailand). It expanded gradually to 10 members, and in 1992 agreed to establish a free trade area during the next 15 years. The other organization, Asia Pacific Economic Cooperation, a group of 21 countries including China, Japan, and the United States, agreed to establish a free trade area on both sides of the Pacific by 2020. With the periods allotted for phasing in the tariff and nontariff schedules, both the Americas and Asia should theoretically complete their free trade areas at roughly the same time. The targets, however, are probably too optimistic.

Nonetheless, the declaration of goals by APEC, ASEAN, and the Summit of the Americas all rest on the premise that economic growth depends on trade. They also agree that deepening and enlarging their regions can improve their firms' competitiveness and their countries' growth prospects.

The enlargement of these regional trading areas is especially significant because it represents an avenue toward modernity for faster-growing developing countries. The international development banks have increasingly focused on lifting the poorest countries and people. But for the poor to retain hope, they will also need to see that developing countries that succeed can find room among the industrial democracies. Much of the success of the middle-class countries in East Asia, Latin America, and Southern Europe has been derived from trade. The ability of these countries to join the industrial world depends to a great extent on whether they are allowed to join the new regional clubs of industrial countries. That is still one more reason why the enlargement of the European Union and NAFTA has a wider significance for the world.

Reconfiguring the World: Three Regional Models

From the end of the Second World War until 1989, the Berlin Wall symbolized the pivotal division in the world between East and West, between communism and democracy. As that fracture described the world's preoccupation with security, a second division—between North and South—defined two worlds in terms of relative wealth and poverty. With the collapse of the Berlin Wall, scholars sought new ways to define the landscape. Some, like Ohmae, saw the crumbling of "the modern nation-state—that artifact of the 18th and 19th centuries" to be replaced by "a borderless economy, a truly global marketplace."[10] Garten saw a coming clash between three new "empires"—the North American Empire, the German Empire, and the Japanese Empire—competing with each other, primarily on an economic chessboard.[11] With distance and academic detachment, Tonelson viewed the Cold War as "only a pause" in a 20th-century struggle between the same three powers.[12]

There are two problems with these perspectives. First, they fail to distinguish between two arenas of competition—the security and the economic. Each has different rules. A trade dispute is more likely to be resolved by a court or by negotiations than a conflict over territory or sovereignty. Second, these perspectives overlook the extent to which all three powers have a stake in the same international system. In the security arena, the three powers all are members of the United Nations; Japan and the United States are joined by a security treaty, and Germany and the United States, by the North Atlantic Treaty Organization (NATO). All three countries also play pivotal roles in the International Monetary Fund, the World Bank, and the WTO—the three pillars of the international economic system.

The security arena involves zero-sum conflicts over territory, sovereignty, status, and influence, but the rules changed after the Second World War as the ends and means of world politics were transformed.[13] Although it was not obvious at the time, the establishment of the United Nations in 1945 tolled the end of imperialism, a system by which great, and not so great, powers could acquire and govern sovereign states by force. That goal—to acquire territory and countries—had defined much of world history.

Perhaps the only change more fundamental than the global shift from imperialism to self-determination was the means by which nation-states pursued their ends. Up until the advent of nuclear weapons, states tried to amass as much firepower as they could, believing that the threat and

10. Kenichi Ohmae, *The End of the Nation State: The Rise of Regional Economies* (New York: Free Press, 1995), 7-8.

11. Jeffrey E. Garten, *A Cold Peace* (New York: Times Books, 1992).

12. Alan Tonelson, "America, Germany, and Japan: The Tenacious Trio?" *Current History*, November 1995: 353-58.

13. For an elaboration of these themes, see Robert A. Pastor, ed., *A Century's Journey: How the Great Powers Shape the World* (New York: Basic Books, 1999), esp. chaps. 1, 6, and 9.

use of these weapons would mean greater influence, territory, and wealth. Nuclear weapons, as the major powers learned, could not be used for any effective purpose other than to deter their use by one's rival. They also meant that the major powers had to be far more cautious about confronting each other than at any previous moment in world history.

The changes in the security arena and the end of the Cold War meant that the second arena—economic competition—would rise in importance. Economic contests tend to be positive-sum games in which nation-states define the rules of the market, and the market sets the prices for goods. During the Cold War, ideologies of economic development were surrogate weapons of a larger struggle. The end of the Cold War resulted in the compression and reconfiguration of the stark struggle between communism and capitalism. Whereas the old spectrum of economic ideas had been wedged between two concepts that seem extreme today—state control of the economy and an entirely free market—today's spectrum represents different shades of a mixed economy. Indeed, the three regional groups offer distinct variations on a neoliberal theme.

The attractiveness of each regional model depends, theoretically, on the values that each person or country holds most dear. Actually, the pragmatic strain of the modern world judges the attractiveness of the model by the relative success of each region's economy, and this has changed over time. In the 1980s, the success of the Japanese economy attracted considerable interest in their approach directed by the Ministry of International Trade and Industry to facilitate technological development. "Industrial policy," a variation on a Japanese theme, was the key to economic development—at least until the Japanese economic bubble burst. In the 1990s, the longest economic boom in US history made the US quasi-laissez-faire model seem to be the one worth imitating. Japan adapted the US model by discarding its guarantees of permanent work, and Japanese firms began firing workers. Canada, Europe, and Latin America also cut some holes in their security net, made their labor policies more "flexible," and even began to reduce taxes. If the US economy flags and the euro currency soars in the first decade of the 21st century, people may turn to Europe's model.

Each region has a personality that is a composite of various factors that are reflected in its regional trade agreement—in the agreement's origin and timing, its objectives and policies on internal disparities, the composition of its membership, its security foundation, the nature of its governing authority, and the philosophy that defines its distinctive vision.

The European Union is the most integrated of the regional trading regimes, partly because it is the only common market that permits the free movement of goods, services, capital, and labor among its 15 members. It was born from two devastating wars and a compelling dread (see table 2.2).

Table 2.2 Parameters of three regional trade areas

Parameters	European Union	NAFTA	East Asia
Origin	Fear of war	Secure market	Reaction to others
Objectives	Unity, solidarity; common market	Lower trade and capital barriers; competitiveness	Cooperation; WTO; prevent other blocs
Policy on disparities	Reduce	Ignore	Oppose idea
Composition	Members (even)	Unbalanced	Unbalanced
Security base	NATO	Rio Pact/US-Canada	Rivalry: China, Japan, United States
Authority/ institutions	Supranational; national governments	National governments; dispute-settlement mechanisms	National governments
Philosophy	Social market economy	Regulated free market; litigious dispute-settlement procedures	FDI networks; export platform

FDI = foreign direct investment
NAFTA = North American Free Trade Agreement.
NATO = North Atlantic Treaty Organization.
WTO = World Trade Organization.

The preamble to the treaty for the European Coal and Steel Community, established in 1951 as the first "practical" step toward a united Europe, began by recognizing "that world peace can be safeguarded only by creative efforts," and the countries resolved that "age-old rivalries" need to be replaced by a merging of interests that would form "the basis for a broader and deeper community among peoples long divided by bloody conflicts." Six years later, in the Treaty of Rome establishing the European Economic Community, six European nations (Belgium, France, Germany, Italy, Luxembourg, and the Netherlands) were "determined to lay the foundations of an ever closer union among the peoples of Europe."[14]

As its membership expanded in distinct stages from 6 to 15, the EC broadened and deepened its mandate. In February 1986, the 12 members of the European Community signed the Single European Act (SEA), which declared their intent of speaking "with one voice" and acting "with consistency and solidarity in order more effectively to protect its common

14. "Preamble to the Treaty of Rome," in *The European Union: Readings on the Theory and Practice of European Integration*, ed. Brent F. Nelsen and Alexander C-G. Stubb, 2d ed. (Boulder, CO: Lynne Rienner Publishers, 1998), 13-15.

interests." On 7 February 1992, at Maastricht, the leaders of the 12 countries signed the Treaty of European Union and dedicated themselves to defining a common citizenship, forging a united foreign and security policy, and establishing a single currency (the euro).[15]

Since its beginning, the European Community has established as one of its key objectives the need to "reduce the differences between the various regions and the backwardness of the less favored regions." With the first EC enlargement in 1973 to include Denmark, Ireland, and the United Kingdom, the British pressed for a more concerted approach to help poor regions, and George Thomson, a British EU commissioner, was given the responsibility of overseeing EC regional policy. The subsequent enlargement to include Greece (1981) and Portugal and Spain (1986) led to a significant restructuring and infusion of aid into these countries and Ireland. The European Union's model has been described as a "social market economy," combining a system of markets with "a commitment to the values of internal solidarity and mutual support." This requires a sharing of responsibilities between member states and the Union and, in the words of an EU report, a "recognition that wide disparities are intolerable in a community, if the term has any meaning at all."[16] To join the Union, prospective members have to meet precise standards for both economic and social policies and democracy and civil liberties.

The European Union has an elaborate supranational organization that is unique among all the regional integration agreements. At the top is the European Commission, an executive branch, composed of commissioners appointed by each member government, and charged with harmonizing policies among the countries. The Commission is increasingly accountable to a European Parliament elected by the people of Europe rather than the nation-states, but the Council of Ministers is responsible for approving legislation. The European Court has played a critical role in ensuring that EU directives are implemented in each state, and citizens can challenge their states if they feel their rights have not been respected.

. The North American Free Trade Agreement was born of different soil, and until Fox it aspired to be nothing more than the basis for a region in which goods, services, and capital would be traded freely, but labor's movements would be restricted. Until Fox raised the idea of a common market, no other leader in the three countries had even broached a preliminary step—a customs union with a common external tariff. NAFTA is also silent on an issue—internal disparities—with which the European

---

15. *The European Union: Readings*, 45-47, 69-70. The Treaty on European Union was approved at the Maastricht meeting of the European Council on 9-10 December 1991, and signed in Maastricht on 7 February 1992. The treaty came into force in late 1993 after 12 countries ratified it.

16. European Commission, *First Report on Economic and Social Cohesion, 1996* (Luxembourg: Office for Official Publications of the European Commission, 1996), 13.

Union is preoccupied, although income and employment gaps are far wider in North America than in Europe.

The origin of NAFTA was the growing fear in Canada and Mexico that a resurgence of US protectionism could devastate their economies. The only way to make the US market secure and stable was to negotiate a free trade area. Having long sought free trade, the United States could not reject the idea when its neighbors finally proposed it. Although the debate in the United States churned up fears of jobs lost to its low-wage neighbor Mexico, the agreement was approved.

The goals of NAFTA, as specified in the preamble to the agreement, speak of strengthening "the special bonds of friendship and cooperation among their nations"—not their peoples; of expanding and securing markets; of establishing rules consistent with the GATT; and of preserving each nation's "flexibility to safeguard the public welfare."[17] The two-volume treaty aims to reduce trade and investment barriers and to establish a framework for resolving disputes, but not to create a community of people of North America or to promote the well-being of all the people. The provision mentioning accession by other countries is brief and vague, allowing a country to accede to the agreement "subject to such terms and conditions" as the parties may decide in the future (Article 2204). It also allows each country to withdraw—just by giving 6 months notice (Article 2205).

After his inauguration in January 1993, President Clinton insisted on adding two side agreements on labor and the environment, and on establishing commissions to encourage each government to fulfill its promises in each area. These side agreements are fully consistent with the goals of the treaty—to expand trade, respect the sovereignty of each nation, and avoid sharing responsibilities or establishing any supranational authority. The philosophy is to liberalize the continental market, regulate sectors nationally but not in a manner that could be a disadvantage for the business of the other countries, and let each state cope with any transnational problems. NAFTA includes a state-of-the-art dispute-settlement mechanism with clear deadlines, but the courts are ad hoc and therefore cannot develop a historical memory. The style of NAFTA's governance is laissez-faire, reactive, and legalistic: Problems are defined by plaintiffs and settled by litigation. There is no mechanism for defining problems in a proactive way or addressing them from a continental perspective.

Asia has not resolved the first question as to which organization represents its interests. The only truly Asian regional organization is ASEAN, a group of 10 disparate countries in Southeast Asia whose per capita income ranges from the market economies of Malaysia ($4,530) and Thai-

---

17. *The North American Free Trade Agreement between The Government of the United States, The Government of Canada, and the Government of the United Mexican States* (Washington: US Government Printing Office, 1992), iii.

land ($2,740) to the communist government of Vietnam ($335). The widening of ASEAN to include Burma, Cambodia, and Laos, and the financial and political crises in Indonesia and the Philippines, have impeded progress toward the goal it declared in 1993 of establishing an ASEAN Free Trade Area within a decade.

The organization that has appeared to take the most initiative in the region is Asia-Pacific Economic Cooperation, though it has been dismissed as "four adjectives in search of a noun." APEC was founded in 1989 with 12 members. By 1997, the group had expanded to 21 nation-states, including Canada, China, Japan, Russia, Mexico, and the United States. Its membership accounts for about half of global output and 42 percent of world trade, but that is because it includes most of the major economic powers outside Europe.[18]

APEC sits at the other end of the spectrum from the European Union. If the Union has built too many institutions and NAFTA too few, then APEC has not seriously contemplated any institutions that could implement its goals—at least until now. The philosophy of the Asian member states seems to approach mercantilism, although members of the group swear their allegiance to the WTO. The Japanese market is of growing importance to the rest of Asia, but the US market remains the region's preeminent one, and in many ways, the region can still be viewed as an export platform for selling goods to the United States. Using their multinational corporations and trading companies, the Japanese have taken the lead in establishing industrial networks that have integrated many Asian economies into a larger regional unit.[19] An indication that East Asia is more a platform for exporting than an integrated region is that its intraregional exports are the smallest proportion of its total exports—39 percent—of all the three regions (see table 2.1).

Feinberg describes APEC and the Free Trade Area of the Americas as "non-identical twins." Both regional summits made their decisions to establish a free trade area in 1994, with the intention of completing and implementing the entire process by 2020. Neither has a centralized bureaucracy, though both have small, constrained secretariats. The FTAA negotiating style—modeled on NAFTA and the WTO—involves bargaining and reciprocity, whereas APEC encourages voluntary measures and individual action plans. Both seek trade liberalization across a wider agenda than just tariffs and nontariff barriers, but the FTAA has more political coherence because all the countries are democratic and members of the Organization of American States.[20]

18. For data and background information on APEC, see http://www.apecsec.org.

19. See Peter J. Katzenstein and Takashi Shiraishi, eds., *Network Power: Japan and Asia* (Ithaca, NY: Cornell University Press, 1997), and especially the chapter by Richard F. Doner, Japan in East Asia: Institutions and Regional Leadership.

20. Richard Feinberg, "Comparing Regional Integration in Non-Identical Twins: APEC and the FTAA," *Integration and Trade* 4, no. 10: 3-30.

In contrasting the three regional models—from the most integrated and institutionalized in Europe to the least in Asia—one factor that is present in the European Union and NAFTA and absent in East Asia is a militarily secure foundation. NATO guarantees Europe's security and encourages Europeans to find a common identity. Moreover, although the United States is the strongest power in NATO, many of the other governments have sufficient strength to assure that it remains an alliance of partners. North America is also built on a foundation where none of the three countries fears war with its neighbors. For a century or longer, the borders between the United States and its neighbors have not been defended by troops or bases. Unlike in Europe, however, North America has a single dominant power, the United States. And although Canada and Mexico do not fear military aggression, they live in constant anxiety that some unilateral US decision could adversely affect their economies. Still, no one doubts there is a secure foundation under both the European Union and NAFTA. That does not apply to East Asia.

In East Asia, a complex three-sided rivalry between China, Japan, and the United States precludes the kind of cooperation that seems almost a prerequisite to a free trade agreement. The absence of a "security community" in Asia, in Karl Deutsch's phrase, may explain the relative incoherence of the Asian regional trading group.[21] Without a consensus on security, the member states are unlikely to have the kind of confidence in each other that is needed to build a framework of cooperation. Each has to be very careful and tentative in diminishing its capacity to deal with future threats. Other explanations for the relative weakness of the Asian trade regime as compared with NAFTA and the European Union focus on the dearth of institutions and the diversity of norms and goals among its many members.[22]

Asian governments lack a coherent regional vision, and indeed, APEC is a Pacific Rim entity that includes all three NAFTA members. APEC's principal mission has seemed defensive from both sides of the Pacific. Japan and Asia wanted the United States in APEC to prevent its market from closing, and the United States wanted to prevent the emergence of an Asian group that excluded it. That might have shaped the origin of APEC; but today, some suggest that a unified Asia is beginning to emerge, and APEC or perhaps "ASEAN plus 3" (China, Japan, and South Korea) might be the vehicle.

---

21. For an examination of Deutsch's concept and application to various regions, see Emanuel Adler and Michael Barnett, eds., *Security Communities* (Cambridge: Cambridge University Press, 1998).

22. For a systematic comparison of APEC and other regional groups in Asia and North America, see Vinod K. Aggarwal, Comparing Regional Cooperation Efforts in the Asia-Pacific and North America, in *Pacific Cooperation*, ed. A. Mack and J. Ravenhill (Sydney: Allin and Unwin, 1994), 40-65.

Bergsten reports a "new Asian challenge," a series of ideas that Asian leaders are considering, including an Asian currency and monetary fund, annual summit meetings, and an East Asian or a Northeast Asian free trade area.[23] He notes in another article that Japan has begun free trade talks with a number of countries, and ASEAN plus 3 has held annual summits for 3 years in a row to sketch a new vision of economic cooperation.[24] If this occurs, then East Asia could become the "third pole" or region. But in the meantime, it has not reached a comparable level to that of the European Union or NAFTA in regional coherence, rules, and institutions.

The European Union and NAFTA:
A More Focused Comparison

To understand the relevance of the European Union's experience for NAFTA, we need to focus more intensely on the differences and similarities between the two entities. From 1960 to 1999, EU gross product expanded from less than $200 billion to $8.3 trillion as the member states expanded from 7 to 15 (see table 2.3). In comparison, the gross product of the three countries of North America grew from $565 billion to $9.8 trillion. But the aggregate size of the two region's economies masks the unevenness of its membership. In 1960, the US gross domestic product was 2.5 times larger than that of all 7 EC countries. At the end of the 20th century, the US GDP exceeded that of all 15 EU countries by $500 billion, and Canada and Mexico added another trillion dollars. A similar distribution is evident in comparing population (see table 2.4). The United States had 10 million more people than the EC 7 in 1960, and all of NAFTA exceeded the EU 15 by 34 million people in 1999.

An examination of the tables on GDP and GDP per capita (table 2.5), however, illuminates a key difference between the two regions (i.e., the relative balance among the EU countries and the asymmetry within North America). In both GDP and population, the European Union is characterized by four strong nation-states—France, Germany, Italy, and the United Kingdom—numerous middle powers, and some very small nation-states. The most powerful state—Germany—has about a fourth of the EU gross product and 7 percent of the world's product. The center and power of

---

23. C. Fred Bergsten, "The New Asian Challenge," Working Paper 00-4. Institute for International Economics, Washington, photocopy (March 2000); and C. Fred Bergsten, ed., *Whither APEC? The Progress To Date and Agenda for the Future* (Washington: Institute for International Economics, 1997).

24. C. Fred Bergsten, "Towards a Tripartite World: East Asian Regionalism," *The Economist*, 15 July 2000, 23-26.

Table 2.3 Gross domestic product of Europe and North America, 1960-99 (in millions of current dollars)

Group or country	1960	1970	1980	1990	1999	1999 as percent of world GDP
EC/EU total	196,509	482,433	2,844,712	5,574,100	8,277,649	27
Germany[a]	72,765	188,612	819,206	1,522,710	2,081,200	7
France	61,318	141,525	666,090	1,002,400	1,410,260	
United Kingdom	71,864	120,670	534,240	921,120	1,373,610	
Italy	39,550	93,258	446,432	954,680	1,149,960	
Spain	11,220	37,026	209,346	481,260	562,245	
Netherlands	11,297	31,577	170,044	241,050	384,766	
Belgium	11,016	26,520	120,760	181,800	245,706	
Sweden	13,195	32,872	120,872	151,740	226,388	
Austria	6,363	13,524	83,184	140,880	208,949	
Denmark	6,500	15,795	64,730	88,050	174,363	
Finland	4,572	11,255	53,665	84,650	126,130	
Greece	4,080	10,206	50,410	99,600	123,934	
Portugal	2,934	6,399	29,420	116,160	107,716	
Ireland	2,642	3,975	17,712	46,560	84,861	
Luxembourg	563	941	5,498	8,340	17,561	
NAFTA total	565,410	1,096,359	3,260,853	5,934,746	9,795,870	32
United States	513,316	981,745	2,706,294	5,135,000	8,708,870	29
Canada	40,626	81,564	267,550	503,820	612,049	
Mexico	12,744	33,050	196,042	295,926	474,951	
World	1,346,474	2,917,900	10,704,486	21,354,000	30,212,000	

EC = European Community.
EU = European Union.
NAFTA = North American Free Trade Agreement.
a. Data include statistics on the former West Germany only, except for 1999.

Sources: World Bank, World Development Indicators CD-ROM, 1999; United Nations, Compendium of Social Statistics, 1980 and 1998; World Bank, World Development Indicators Database, http://www.worldbank.org/data/dataquery.html; and Heston and Summers, Penn World Tables, http://datacentre.chass.utoronto.ca:5680/pwt/pwt.html.

North America is the United States, with almost 90 percent of the region's gross product and 29 percent of the world's.

Beyond the sheer difference in weight among the three countries of North America, perhaps the more important disparity is the income differential between the two industrial countries of North America and Mexico (see table 2.5). The per capita GDP of the United States, Canada, and Mexico in 1960 was $2,836, $2,257, and $354, respectively. The average for all North America was $2,406, with the United States representing 118 percent of the average and Mexico 15 percent. Nearly four decades later, the differences between the three countries did not change very much. The US per capita GDP was 7.9 times higher than Mexico's in 1960 and 6.5 times higher in 1999. In comparison, the gaps within Europe were

Table 2.4 Population of Europe and North America, 1960-99
(in millions)

Group or country	1960	1970	1980	1990	1999	1999 as percent of world population
EC/EU total	171	189	260	328	375	6
Germany[a]	55	61	62	63	82	1
France	46	51	54	56	59	
United Kingdom	52	55	56	57	59	
Italy	50	54	56	58	58	
Spain	30	34	37	39	39	
Netherlands	11	13	14	15	16	
Belgium	9	10	10	10	10	
Sweden	7	8	8	9	9	
Austria	7	7	80	8	8	
Denmark	5	5	5	5	5	
Finland	4	5	5	5	5	
Greece	8	9	10	10	11	
Portugal	9	9	10	11	10	
Ireland	3	3	3	4	4	
Luxembourg	0.3	0.3	0.4	0.4	0.4	
NAFTA total	235	276	328	363	409	7
United States	181	205	227	250	281	5
Canada	18	21	25	27	31	
Mexico	36	50	67	86	97	
World	446	3,610	4,428	5,257	5,975	

EC = European Community.
EU = European Union.
NAFTA = North American Free Trade Agreement.
a. Data include statistics on the former West Germany only, except for 1999.

Sources: World Bank, *World Development Indicators CD-ROM*, 1999; United Nations, *Compendium of Social Statistics*, 1980 and 1998; and World Bank, *World Development Indicators Database*, http://www.worldbank.org/data/dataquery.html.

much more modest. In 1999, the per capita GDP of Germany was 2.4 times that of Portugal, the EU's poorest country.

There also are differences in the way Europeans and Americans view income disparities and the possible instruments for alleviating them that might shed some light on the political philosophies of the two entities. Only 29 percent of Americans believe that "it is the responsibility of government to reduce the differences in income between people," whereas 61 percent of (western) Germans, 64 percent of the British, and 81 percent of Italians believe their governments have such a responsibility.[25] One

25. These opinions were given in a survey cited by Derek Bok, *State of the Nation* (Cambridge, MA: Harvard University Press, 1998), 157.

Table 2.5 GDP per capita for Europe and North America, 1960-99
(in current dollars)

Group or country	1960	1970	1980	1990	1999
EC/EU total	1,149	2,553	10,941	16,994	22,049
Germany[a]	1,323	3,092	13,213	24,170	25,372
France	1,333	2,775	12,335	17,900	23,869
United Kingdom	1,382	2,194	9,540	16,160	23,238
Italy	791	1,727	7,972	16,460	19,948
Spain	374	1,089	5,658	12,340	14,266
Netherlands	1,027	2,429	12,146	16,070	24,349
Belgium	1,224	2,652	12,076	18,180	24,034
Sweden	1,885	4,109	15,109	16,860	25,559
Austria	909	1,932	1,040	17,610	25,841
Denmark	1,300	3,159	12,946	17,610	32,794
Finland	1,143	2,251	10,733	16,930	24,411
Greece	510	1,134	5,041	9,960	11,763
Portugal	326	711	2,942	10,560	10,782
Ireland	881	1,325	5,904	11,640	22,768
Luxembourg	1,877	3,137	13,745	20,850	40,650
NAFTA total	2,406	3,972	9,942	16,349	24,434
United States	2,836	4,789	11,922	20,540	31,915
Canada	2,257	3,884	10,702	18,660	19,999
Mexico	354	661	2,926	3,441	4,875

EC = European Community.
EU = European Union.
NAFTA = North American Free Trade Agreement.
a. Data include statistics on the former West Germany only, except for 1999.

Sources: World Bank, World Development Indicators CD-ROM, 1999; United Nations, Compendium of Social Statistics, 1980 and 1998; World Bank, World Development Indicators Database, http://www.worldbank.org/data/dataquery.html; and Heston and Summers, Penn World Tables, http://datacentre.chass.utoronto.ca:5680/pwt.

might conclude that this variation explains why the European Union has a "regional policy" for narrowing disparities, and NAFTA does not, except that other data blur this fine point. For example, 94 percent of Americans believe that "our society should do what is necessary to make sure that everyone has an equal opportunity to succeed."[26] And the US government does invest in a wide range of programs to give children an equal start and also to compensate for unemployment, old age, and ill health. The United States spends much more than Europe on health and education per capita. But the United States spends more privately; and the European Union, publicly. In addition, the United States has an efficient mechanism through the Federal Reserve system and via the progressive income tax and earned-income tax credit to mitigate inequalities between regions

26. *Ibid.*

and economic classes.[27] Through the tax system, the wealthiest 8 percent of the US population (earning above $100,000) paid nearly two-thirds of all taxes, and the poorest 60 percent paid about 12 percent of total taxes.[28] (The wealthiest will benefit from President Bush's tax cut, approved by Congress in May 2001, but the ratio of tax payments should not change that dramatically.)

In Canada, two provinces—Ontario and Quebec—account for about two-thirds of the country's GDP—and provincial per capita incomes vary considerably. Like the United States, Canada has multiple policies to reduce the disparities between individuals and provinces. Canada's Department of Regional Industrial Expansion (DRIE) invests in depressed regions and encourages businesses to do the same. Its average annual expenditure of $235 million between 1968 and 1973 doubled during the next 8 years. These funds, however, were roughly 3-6 percent of total fiscal transfers during the same periods. Recognizing the diminished effect of DRIE, Parliament abolished the agency in the late 1980s and replaced it with smaller regional offices. By 1993, due to the growing effects of free trade with the United States, Canada decided to promote more even development among the provinces by compelling them to reduce the barriers that impeded trade and the flows of capital and labor among them.[29]

Without government transfers, the people in Newfoundland earn about two-thirds of the per capita income of those living in Ontario. After the government's corrective measures are incorporated into the data, provincial per capita incomes vary by 14-16 percent of the national average. In 1995, in the Atlantic provinces, for example, government programs succeeded in raising the average provincial per capita income from 71 to 77 percent of that in Ontario.[30]

The differences among the states of Mexico are far wider, and the capacity of the government to reduce those disparities is less. In 1995, about half of domestic production (48.6 percent) was concentrated in Mexico City and the states of Jalisco, Mexico, and Nuevo Leon, and 25

---

27. For a summary and analysis of the redistribution of fiscal transfers each year, see http://www.nemw.org/fedspend99.pdf.htm. For a good summary of the distinctiveness of the states and regions in the United States, see "America's States and Regions: How Similar? Where Different? Sectionalism at Century's End," *The Public Perspective: A Roper Center Review of Public Opinion and Polling* 9, no. 4 (June/July 1998).

28. Data provided by the US Treasury Department and US Congress, House Ways and Means Committee, published in the *New York Times*, 26 July 1999, A11.

29. Michael Howlett, Alex Netherton, and M. Ramesh, *The Political Economy of North America: An Introduction*, 2d ed. (New York: Oxford University Press, 1999), 309-11.

30. *Ibid.*, 106-08.

Table 2.6 Ratio of three richest to three poorest states or provinces in North America, 1997

Canada	United States	Mexico
2.1	1.9	4.1

Sources: For Canada, Statistics Canada, http://www. statcan.ca/english/pgdb/economy/economic/econ50.htm. For Mexico, Instituto Nacional de Estadistica Geografia e Informatica, gross domestic product at constant prices, 2000, http://www.inegi.gob.mx/difusion/ingles/portadai.html. For the United States, Bureau of the Census, http:// www.census.gov/hhes/income/income99/99tabled.html.

of the 32 states accounted for less than 3 percent each of total production.[31] Per capita income in the southern states of Chiapas, Guerrero, and Oaxaca is 62 percent less than per capita income in the Northeast, and health and education statistics mirror that difference.[32] Because government expenditures as a percentage of the GDP of Mexico are about a third of that of the United States and Canada, the government's capacity to try to equalize inequalities is weak.

It is therefore not surprising that the gap between the three richest states or provinces and the three poorest states or provinces is roughly twice as large in Mexico as in its two northern neighbors.[33] (see table 2.6). This poses a serious problem for Mexico but also, as we shall see, for all of North America.

The Regional Advantage

The trend toward the development of three great world regions is not incompatible with a global trading regime. On the contrary, the challenges that preoccupy these regions—such as standards, domestic policies that unintentionally function as nontariff barriers, and agriculture programs— have also eluded international organizations. If effective solutions can be found at the regional level, they might be applied globally. In this sense,

---

31. Mauricio A. Gonzalez Gomez, "Crisis and Economic Change in Mexico," in *Mexico Under Zedillo*, ed. Susan Kaufman Purcell and Luis Rubio (Boulder, CO: Lynne Rienner Publishers, 1998), 55.

32. Elvia Gutierrez, "Disturbing Trend Haunts Economic Development: Regional Disparities Are Alarming," *El Financiero International Edition*, 31 May 1999, 15.

33. The ratios for Canada and Mexico reflect the gap in gross domestic product by provinces and states. For the United States, the ratio reflects the gap in incomes per household in each state.

the regional schemes can function in the way that states are supposed to act in a federal system, as opportunities to experiment with policies that, if successful, could become national laws.

Every step toward integration seems to encounter an almost insurmountable obstacle labeled "sovereignty." And yet in the experience of the European Union, such debates on sovereignty have impeded negotiations only for limited periods. Eventually, the member-states find ways to deal pragmatically with a problem, laying aside the ideological debate—or rather redefining it—so as to permit a new transnational approach.

North America also has experience with this pattern. After its revolution in the second decade of the 20th century, Mexico's quasi-religious devotion at the altar of "sovereignty" was a seemingly impossible barrier to discussing issues related to the promotion of foreign investment or free trade with the United States. But this began to change after the debt crisis of the mid-1980s. The government shifted the debate, gradually but definitively, and few protested when the Mexican president proposed a free trade agreement with the United States that involved dismantling all trade and investment barriers. While Mexican policy was spinning 180 degrees, the word "sovereignty" could barely be heard.

The three regions have very distinctive purposes and policies. Yet—just as governments can learn from others' experience—so can regions. No region has devoted as much time and resources or experimented with more responses to the problem of inequalities than the European Union. In the next chapter, we will explore its experience in depth—beginning with a description of its policies and how they evolved, and continuing with an assessment of their effectiveness. Our principal focus will be the economic dimension—disparities of income and employment—but we will also examine political and policy implications.

3

The European Union and Its "Cohesion" Policies: An Evaluation

The traumas of two devastating wars and the Great Depression moved Europe's leaders to undertake the most radical experiment in international relations since the Treaty of Westphalia ushered in a world of modern nation-states. Europe's purpose was nothing less than forging a new cooperative framework to transcend the nation-state. Nations would not disappear, but barriers between them would be dismantled, and new supranational institutions would be established. Over time, member-states would devolve responsibilities to these institutions for the common good of Europe.

Among the many goals that the European Community defined at its creation was the reduction of disparities among its members. Because no one knew how to achieve that goal, and because other objectives—notably, eliminating barriers to trade—assumed a higher priority, little attention was given to this issue in the beginning, other than establishing two institutions—the European Social Fund (ESF) and the European Investment Bank (EIB)—to promote economic development and also try to reduce inequalities.

A decade later, as the European Union accepted new members, Jacques Delors, the president of the European Commission, began to reshape its institutions and provide significant additional funds to reduce disparities. By the time the Union faced the post-Cold War challenge of incorporating Eastern Europe, the modest effort to reduce disparities had grown so large that EU officials proudly compared it in scope and magnitude to the Marshall Plan—only on a permanent rather than an emergency basis.

In this chapter, we will examine the European Union's institutions and review the evolution of its "regional" or "cohesion" policies so that we might assess its effectiveness and draw lessons that might be of use in North America.

Europe's Designs

The Treaty of Rome, signed by six European governments on 25 March 1957, established the European Economic Community to "lay the foundations of an ever closer union among the peoples of Europe." The goals were explicit:

- "to ensure the economic and social progress of their countries by common action to eliminate the barriers which divide Europe;

- "to strengthen the unity of their economies and to ensure their harmonious development . . . ; [and]

- "to pool their resources to preserve and strengthen peace and liberty . . ."[1]

Although the aims were lofty, Europe embarked on a practical, step-by-step journey, mainly because European leaders were divided on the ultimate goal—whether their Community should be a family of nations, a confederation of states, or a unified European government. For that reason, the member-states have had great difficulty relinquishing their veto powers and accepting a decision-making process that would permit more rapid consolidation of the unit. Although the European budget has grown, and European institutions extended their domain, the EU budget only amounted to 1.27 percent of EU GDP by 1996, as compared with the central-government expenditures of its members, which ranged from 28.4 percent of GDP (in Greece) to 44.6 percent (France) in 1998.[2]

Nonetheless, at critical moments in the European Union's evolution, when paralysis bred crises, the governments did overcome their parochial interests and made the difficult decisions that permitted the experiment to advance.[3] The leaders narrowed the scope of the "unanimity rule," by

---

1. Preambles to the Treaties Establishing the European Communities, in *The European Union: Readings on the Theory and Practice of European Integration*, ed. Brent F. Nelsen and Alexander C-G. Stubb (Boulder, CO: Lynne Rienner Publishers, 1998).

2. For the European Union, see http://www.europa.eu.int/comm/budget/en/financementbudget/index.htm. For the range of European government expenditures, see World Bank, *World Development Report 2000/2001* (New York: Oxford University Press, 2001), table 14, 300-01. Also see European Commission, *First Report on Economic and Social Cohesion, 1996* (Luxembourg: Office for Official Publications of the European Commission, 1996), 6.

3. For the development of this thesis, see Andrew Moravcsik, *The Choice for Europe: Social Purpose and State Power from Messina to Maastricht* (Ithaca, NY: Cornell University Press, 1998).

which all decisions required a consensus. More decisions were made in more areas based on majority voting, and they pressed forward to a Single European Market. On 7 February 1992, the 12 European governments signed the Treaty on European Union in Maastricht, the Netherlands, to establish an economic and monetary Union with a common citizenship and a common foreign and security policy. By then, the European Court held sway throughout the region, and people could seek redress from their governments by appealing to the Court. The European Parliament, directly elected since 1979, attracted politicians of greater stature, who insisted on greater accountability by the Commission.

Some politicians, like Margaret Thatcher, complained that "the Brussels bureaucracy" was making decisions for the member-states and reintroducing the kinds of economic controls that she had removed in the United Kingdom. Complaints about the EU bureaucracy were chronic, and some were justified. The bureaucracy, after all, did not get smaller, and although some agencies outlived their usefulness, they did not disappear. This is, of course, the iron rule of bureaucracy, and it is especially applicable to international organizations.

Nevertheless, the EU Commission was manned by some of the most sophisticated civil servants in the world. They were sensitive to Thatcher's concerns and enlisted national and subnational officials for various projects.[4] To address concerns of a "democratic deficit" (the lack of accountability by international civil servants), the Union adopted the principle of "subsidiarity," whereby decisions would be made as close to the people as possible. Perhaps the EU Commission's most useful contribution was its most modest—the compilation of data and analyses on all European sectors and issues. The data permitted the national leaders to visualize Europe-wide and cross-border problems from a continental rather than just a national perspective.

From Goals to Programs

The Treaty of Rome included references to two instruments that would define Europe's initial approach to the problem of reducing disparities within the Community. The European Investment Bank would make loans in lagging regions, and the European Social Fund would provide money for vocational training and for facilitating movement by workers into other areas or jobs. The European Agricultural Fund (different from the Common Agriculture Policy, or CAP) began providing grants to farmers in 1968 to help them to modernize their equipment and operations, and

---

4. For Thatcher's view of Europe as a "family of nations" and Jacques Delors' contrasting view of "a necessary union," see Nelsen and Stubb, eds., *European Union: Readings*, 49-68; and for a condensed version of the Maastricht Treaty, 69-70.

in subsequent years to develop rural areas. Until 1973, most of the resources were funneled into Southern Italy.

The first institution that focused exclusively on the problem of regional disparities was the European Regional Development Fund, which was established in 1975 after the Union was enlarged to include Denmark, Ireland, and the United Kingdom. The ERDF's purpose was "to help to redress the main regional imbalances in the Community."[5] Roughly 85 percent of ERDF-funded projects in the 1970s and 1980s were used for infrastructure, and 91 percent of its funds went to the poorest regions in five countries—France, Germany, Italy, Greece, and the United Kingdom. Member governments cofinanced the projects. The budget increased eight-fold in the first 10 years of the program (1975-84), but that only amounted to an eighth of what was spent for the Common Agricultural Policy.

The enlargements of the 1980s (Greece, Spain, and Portugal) coincided with the leadership of Jacques Delors, the president of the European Commission, who used the moment to transform the mandate, the programs, and the amount of funds devoted to the task. The Single European Act of 1986, which he shepherded to eliminate roughly 300 intra-Union barriers by 1992, included a new concept and a more precise set of goals under the title of "Economic and Social Cohesion" (Article 130A-E):

> In order to promote its overall harmonious development, the Community shall develop and pursue its actions leading to the strengthening of its economic and social cohesion. In particular, the Community shall aim aid at reducing disparities between the levels of development of the various regions and the backwardness of the least favored regions, including rural areas.[6]

The premise of the European Community was that its people shared fundamental interests, and therefore progress should be measured in terms of *lifting the entire community* in a fair and equitable manner. "Imbalances," the EC report on cohesion writes, "do not just imply a poorer quality of life for the most disadvantaged regions . . . [but also] an under-utilisation of human potential and a failure to take advantage of economic opportunities which could benefit the Union as a whole."[7] The operational definition of "economic cohesion" was convergence of basic incomes, rates of employment, and competitiveness. "Social cohesion" could be measured in universal systems of social protection and mutual support. This would mean a reduction of the incidence of poverty and improvements in productivity and the quality of life. Under the "Delors I" 5-year plan (1989-93), adopted by the Community in 1988, the budget for

---

5. Reiner Martin, *Regional Policy in the European Union: Economic Foundations and Reality* (Brussels: Centre for European Policy Studies, 1998), 81-83.

6. European Commission, *First Report on Economic and Social Cohesion*, 1996, 13.

7. *Ibid.*, 13.

Structural Funds for the poorer countries would gradually double in real terms, to 60 billion ECUs. By the end of the plan, the regional funds would amount to almost 30 percent of the total budget and about 0.3 percent of EC GDP.

The end of the Cold War and the negotiations for the Maastricht Treaty led to Delors II (a 6-year plan, 1994-99), which boosted funding for cohesion by 50 percent, up to 0.46 percent of the EU GDP. The Maastricht Treaty also created two more cohesion instruments: the Cohesion Fund for the four poorest countries—Greece, Ireland, Portugal, and Spain—and the European Investment Fund for poor regions. The Cohesion Fund would also be used to help poor countries stabilize their economies so that they might be able to qualify for economic and monetary union. In addition, a new Committee of the Regions (Article 198-C) was established to permit Europe's regions to have direct representation in Brussels.

The proliferation of funds necessitated reorganization, and the Union divided them into two groups. The largest share was devoted to Structural Funds, which included the ERDF (50 percent of total Structural Funds), the European Social Fund (30 percent), Agriculture (17 percent), and Fisheries (3 percent). The Structural Funds were grants and amounted to 170 billion ECUs during the 1994-99 period, or about a third of total Community spending. The Union also allotted 15.5 billion euros for the Cohesion Fund's four poor countries for grants for projects during a 7-year period, rising from an annual level of 795 million euros in 1993 to 2.8 billion euros in 1999. This, however, represented only about 10 percent of the money allocated to the Structural Funds. The total budget for 2000-06 amounts to 195 billion euros (at 1999 prices). This represents 1.27 percent of the EU GDP in 1999 (table 3.1).[8]

The Structural Funds aim at six different targets or areas: (1) regions where development is lagging (70 percent of total Structural Funds); (2) regions suffering from industrial decline (11 percent); (3) long-term and youth employment (5 percent); (4) training for workers (5 percent); (5) adjustment in agricultural (rural) and fisheries sectors (9 percent); and (6) adjustment for sparsely populated areas (0.5 percent).[9]

The process of deciding on the distribution of the funds is, needless to say, complicated and shaped by a multitiered political process.[10] The objectives are sufficiently diverse that most member-states are eligible for some aid. Indeed, the Structural Funds are distributed to more than half

---

8. For the data, see http://www. europa.eu.int/comm/regional_policy/activity/funds/funds_en.htm.

9. *Ibid.*, 9.

10. For a description of the Structural Funds and the political process by which the funds are allocated, see Andrew Evans, *The EU Structural Funds* (New York: Oxford University Press, 1999).

Table 3.1 EU Structural and Cohesion Funds, 1992-2006

Funds	Percent of total fund	Date established	Objective	Funds 1992-93 (billions of EUR)	Funds 1994-99[a,b] (billions of EUR)	Funds 2000-06[b,c] (billions of EUR)	Total, 1992-2006
Structural Funds	100	1995[d]		26.7	170.0	195.0	391.7
European Regional Development Fund	50	1975	Economic development	11.1	85.0	97.5	193.6
European Social Fund	30	1957	Training, wage subsidies	9.7	51.0	58.5	119.2
European Agricultural Guidance and Guarantee Fund	17	1957	Agriculture	5.9	28.9	33.2	68.0
Financial Instrument for Fisheries	3	1993	Fisheries		5.1	5.9	11.0
Cohesion Funds	100	1993	Poor-country development	n.a.	15.5	18.0	33.5
European Investment Bank[e]	100	1958	Economic development	17.7[f]	133.1	n.a.	

n.a. = not available

a. For the Cohesion Funds, figures are for 1993-99.
b. Amounts for each subfund are estimates based on the percentage of the total Structural Fund budget they usually receive.
c. Predicted.
d. The four funds listed below were consolidated under Structural Funds in 1995.
e. Figures are for loans.
f. Number is for 1993 only.

Sources: European Union, http://www.europa.eu.int/comm/regional_policy.htm; Hix, *The Political System of the European Union* (New York: St. Martin's Press, 1999); and European Investment Bank Web site, http://www.eib.org/loans.htm.

Table 3.2 Distribution of Structural and Cohesion Funds, 1989-2006

Group or country	Total funds (annual average) (millions of ECUs)		Funds as a percent of GDP[a]
Cohesion countries			
Spain	111,564.0	(6,198.5)	1.1
Portugal	46,283.4	(2,571.3)	2.5
Ireland	16,000.8	(895.1)	1.6
Greece	50,922.0	(2,829.3)	3.1
Other EU countries			
Austria	3,096.0	(258.1)	0.11
Belgium	4,753.8	(264.1)	0.10
Denmark	1,818.0	(101.0)	0.06
Finland	3,459.6	(288.3)	0.26
France	36,275.0	(2,015.3)	0.13
Germany	58,181.0	(3,232.3)	0.14
Italy	61,905.6	(3,439.2)	0.30
Luxembourg	255.0	(14.2)	0.08
Netherlands	6,035.4	(335.3)	0.09
Sweden	3,153.6	(262.8)	0.12
United Kingdom	33,827.4	(1,879.3)	0.16

ECU = European currency unit.

a. GDP for 1996.

Sources: European Commission, *First Report on Economic and Social Cohesion* (Brussels, 1996); European Union, http://www.europa.eu.int/comm/regional_policy/; and Simon Hix, *The Political System of the European Union* (NY: St. Martin's Press, 1999).

the regions in the Union because every state has poor regions. This means that the biggest donors are among the largest recipients. Other than Spain, the two countries that have or are programmed to receive the most Structural Funds since 1989 are Italy and Germany, receiving 61.9 billion euros and 58.2 billion euros, respectively. France also received 36.3 billion euros in Structural Funds; and the United Kingdom, 33.8 billion (table 3.2).

The Cohesion Fund, which delivers the grants directly to central governments, was the product of a bargain struck at Maastricht by the Spanish prime minister. In exchange for receiving what would grow to become the most funds transferred to a single country—111.6 billion euros from 1989—Spain agreed to sign the treaty. The Cohesion Funds are spent on the environment, infrastructure, and research and development in the four countries whose per capita GDP is less than 90 percent of the EU average (Greece, Ireland, Portugal, and Spain). The decision on the amount allotted to each state is made by all the states. The EC Commission then decides on the specific projects in collaboration with the subnational governments.[11]

---

11. For a political analysis of the decision making that led to the various Structural and Cohesion Funds and how they are allocated, see Gary Marks, "Exploring and Explaining Variation in EU Cohesion Policy," in *Cohesion Policy and European Integration: Building Multilevel Governance,* ed. Liesbet Hooghe (Oxford: Oxford University Press, 1996).

The European Investment Bank has made loans for regional development to all member-states, and the amounts are significant. In 1999, the EIB approved loans of 33.4 billion euros,[12] but these loans are not considered part of the Structural or Cohesion Funds. The Union claims that the total amount allocated for Structural and Cohesion Funds amounted cumulatively to 6.5 percent of annual EU GDP during the decade 1989-99. In comparison, Marshall Plan aid during the period 1948-51 amounted cumulatively to 4 percent of annual US GDP.[13] But the comparison is misleading, both on statistical and substantive grounds. The EU aid was a 10-year total, and the Marshall Plan was for 4 years, but the denominator in both cases is the GDP in just the first year of the program. Also, the Union transferred the funds to itself, often to the same countries.

Nonetheless, in an age when foreign aid has been declining precipitously, the EU transfers represent a significant effort. In just the period from 1992 through 2006, the Union has or will transfer roughly 425.2 billion euros (table 3.1). What motivated the Union? First, equity and solidarity are goals that are mandated in the EU treaties. Second, if regions endured a shock or even a slow decline, the rest of Europe felt the negative consequences and therefore had an incentive to buffer the downturns in the poor countries. Fiscal transfers spread the burden of adjustment and assisted the adversely affected countries. Third, growth in the poor countries often readily translated into fast-growing markets for the goods of the rich countries. And fourth, the transfers shored up political support in the poor areas where the Union is unpopular or the government is weak.[14] With each enlargement, the strong EU countries felt it necessary to offer increasing funds to the poor applicants. Some view the side payments as necessary for the strong countries to secure the wider market.[15]

The dynamic of the bargain is pertinent to the contemporary challenge that the European Union faces in its negotiations with 12 Central and Eastern European governments (CEEs), which are poorer than any of the member-states. If the criteria for the CAP and Structural and Cohesion funds were to remain unchanged after these countries join, the Union would have to double or triple the funds. "No previous enlargement is comparable," Michel Barnier, the EU commissioner for regional affairs, told the European Parliament in February 2001. "This time the Union's

---

12. For data and background on the European Investment Bank, see http://eib.eu.int/.

13. European Commission, *First Report on Economic and Social Cohesion, 1996*, 9.

14. Clifford J. Carrubba, "Net Financial Transfers in the European Union: Who Gets What and Why?" *Journal of Politics* 59, no. 2 (May 1997): 469-96.

15. This contrasts with the case of Mexico and most of Latin America, which evidently believe that they gain more from entry into a free trade area with the United States than Washington does.

surface area and population will grow by a third, but its gross domestic product by just 5 percent."[16] The income gap between the Union's poorest and richest regions would double. The Union therefore faces some hard choices. At a meeting of heads of state and government in Berlin in March 1999, its leaders discussed these issues in the framework of the Agenda 2000 package that would define its policies in the period 2000-06. The leaders agreed to an appropriation of 213 billion euros for regional policy (divided between 195 billion euros for Structural Funds and 18 billion euros for the Cohesion Fund). They also tightened the objectives and revised the criteria for allocations under Objective 1 (lagging regions), which receives 70 percent of the Structural Funds so that only regions whose per capita GDP was less than 75 percent of the EU average would receive funds.[17]

This decision, however, reflected, more or less, the status quo. The leaders had dodged the most difficult questions. The first issue was what to do about the CAP, which accounts for half of the EU budget. If the CEEs join, the Union would either have to elevate taxes or shut down the program. The CAP not only posed a problem for the budget but also for multilateral trade negotiations. A second issue was what to do about regional policy. Given the economic growth in the four poor countries, some in the European Commission had proposed that much of the regional funds should be set aside for the new applicants, but the Spanish prime minister protested vehemently. He was beginning an election campaign, and he could not afford to extract less from the Union than had his predecessor.[18]

Without a decision to reduce the Cohesion Fund, the French were not willing to contemplate a reduction in the CAP, particularly because the British insisted on keeping a rebate on their transfers. The German chancellor, who was hosting the event, also felt vulnerable politically because of a series of missteps after taking office, and he could not afford to have a summit meeting break up in disarray. It was far better for everyone to emerge reasonably satisfied than to have any member-states rail at the outcome. This, of course, was a recipe for inaction, and that was the result. Instead of making the hard but necessary decisions to reduce the CAP and begin to transfer the Structural and Cohesion funds into a much larger fund to facilitate the transition of new members, the EU leaders postponed the decisions. They did, however, allocate roughly 2.5 percent

---

16. Peter Norman, "Enlarged EU May Need to Boost Aid," *Financial Times*, 1 February 2001, 14.

17. European Union, "Reform of Structural Policy: Results of the Berlin Summit," *Newsletter* 62, March 1999.

18. This case is assembled from many interviews that the author had in March, June, and July 1999 in Brussels, Paris, Madrid, Cologne, and Frankfurt.

of the Structural Funds for "cross-border cooperation," which would be infrastructure projects between the Union and the CEEs.

A historically long, 5-day summit meeting in Nice in December 2000 affirmed the European Union's determination to complete a significant enlargement by 2004. They agreed to extend majority voting to 29 new policy areas, but each major power insisted on retaining a veto in critical areas.[19] No progress was made to break up the logjam on cohesion policy in Nice,[20] nor at a subsequent meeting in Brussels in May 2001.[21]

Evaluating EU Regional Policy

Economists agree that countries benefit from trade, but they divide on whether trade narrows or widens the gap between winners and losers—between countries and among groups within countries. To simplify, "convergence theories" (based on the Heckscher-Ohlin-Samuelson model) predict a convergence of factor incomes because capital will invest and deploy technology where it can gain greater returns. Conversely, "divergence theories" suggest that trade will widen existing disparities as firms locate in the same area to minimize the costs of their inputs. Moreover, rich countries devote more resources to developing their human capital (education, training) and investing in physical capital; thus, they can grow faster than those with fewer resources. This trend widens the gap for still another reason: Factors, especially labor, are not as mobile and prices are not as flexible as the convergence theories assume. The EU experience offers a good opportunity to test the two theories.

A World Bank analysis looked at income differences since the Benelux Union (Belgium, the Netherlands, and Luxembourg) was established in 1947 and concluded that the data "clearly shows an almost continuous convergence . . . Income differences narrowed by about two-thirds over the period [1947-81], due mainly to the more rapid growth of the lower income countries."[22] The European Commission focused its analysis on the four poor "Cohesion" countries, but in its first *Cohesion Report* in 1996,

---

19. Suzanne Daley, "European Union Reform: After 5 Days, A Yawn," *New York Times*, 12 December 2000, A8.

20. In his summary presentation to the European Parliament on the Summit Meeting, Romano Prodi, president of the European Commission, expressed disappointment that "little or no progress was made on cohesion, tax, regulation, and social legislation, all sensitive areas in which the Conference came up against the intransigence of some Member States." His speech can be found at http://www.europa.eu/int/rapid/start/cgi/gu.

21. "What's Ours Is Ours," *The Economist*, 24 May 2001.

22. World Bank, *Trade Blocs: A Policy Research Report* (New York: Oxford University Press, 2000), 51-52; see also fig. 3.8.

it found the evidence mixed as to whether the disparities in income and employment between the rich and poor member-states had narrowed. In its *Sixth Report* issued in February 1999, however, the Commission declared: "The evidence is now unambiguous: the GDP, or output, per head of poorer regions is converging toward the EU average." During the period 1986-99, per capita GDP in the four Cohesion countries *rose* from 65 to 78 percent of the EU average. As for the regions, per capita GDP in the 10 poorest regions *increased* from 41 to 50 percent of the EU average; and in the 25 poorest regions, from 52 to 59 percent.[23] The countries moved to close the gap considerably faster than the regions, but the narrowing of the differences within the regions was hardly trivial.

Although the disparities in income declined, the unemployment picture did not improve. Europe's economy recovered in 1994, but unemployment remained at 10 percent overall for the Union in 1998, and long-term unemployment—those out of work for a year or more—stood at almost half (49 percent) of the unemployed. In the 25 regions with the highest unemployment rates, the long-term unemployed accounted for 60 percent of the total unemployed.[24] Growth is unlikely to solve this problem, but the good news is that the poor regions experienced a relatively greater improvement in productivity, as indicated by the reduction of the gap in income.

Another way of looking at the unemployment problem is to realize that the poor regions, particularly those in the poorest states, had historically high levels of underemployment and flimsy safety nets—if they had any at all. As these poor states were integrated into the European Union, new investments tended to be more capital and technology intensive, meaning that jobs were created. But they were fewer and better jobs than what the regions had before. At the same time, the countries approved social legislation to assist the jobless.

In the summer of 1999, I sought answers to the puzzle of why unemployment increased in the face of accelerated development in Andalusia, one of Spain's poorest provinces with the highest unemployment. With considerable EU funding, Andalusia has built one of the most modern highways in Europe, a state-of-the-art telecommunications system, new colleges and universities, and fast-growing industries based on tourism. In the past, Andalusians traveled to northern Europe for jobs, but today, they will not even look for work in central Spain. Why not? The answer is that the area's development and Spain's democratic progress have created options for workers to find occasional, "informal" work and collect unemploy-

---

23. European Commission, *Regional Policy and Cohesion: Sixth Periodic Report on the Social and Economic Situation and Development of the Regions of the European Union* (Luxembourg: Office for Official Publications of the European Commission, 1999), i, 9.

24. *Ibid.*, i.

ment compensation. In a study of unemployment in Europe, Tsoukalis found that the high rates tended to reflect "seasonal labor patterns" usually associated with tourism or economies with high service components. He argues that productivity, which was improving in many of the poor countries, was a better indicator of convergence than unemployment.[25] So the unemployment figures might be inflated; instead of reflecting a widening gap in the quality of life, they might actually disguise a narrowing one.[26]

There is additional evidence that the figures on unemployment may mask more positive trends. Illegal migration into the EU countries (according to the European Commission) has been soaring—from about 40,000 in 1993 to an estimated 500,000 in 2000. Increasing numbers of undocumented migrants have come from Morocco to Spain and Portugal.[27] If unemployment were as severe as the figures suggest, these new migrants would have had difficulty finding work, and the unemployed would have migrated to rich areas of Europe. In fact, migration from one country to another within the European Union has declined. Only about 2 percent of EU citizens seek work in Europe outside their own countries. In comparison, Americans move from state to state more than five times as often as EU citizens change countries.[28]

Although all four Cohesion countries (Greece, Ireland, Portugal, and Spain) have made substantial economic progress since entering the Union, an analysis of the differences in their rates of growth might be a useful vehicle for assessing the effectiveness of EU regional policies (table 3.3). Ireland has been the most successful. Although burdened with a weak infrastructure and educational system, it took quick advantage of the Union and achieved the highest growth rate of any member-state in the first programming period (1989-93), averaging 5 percent annually, as compared with an EC average of 1.7 percent. In the second period (1994-99), it had 7t percent annual growth. Its inflation, balance of payments, and ratio of budget deficit to GDP also were better than the community average.[29] The result was a breathtaking advance: Ireland's per capita

25. Loukas Tsoukalis, *The New European Economy Revisited* (New York: Oxford University Press, 1997), 174.

26. Eduardo Moyano Estrada y Manuel Perez Yruela, eds., *Informe Social de Andalucia (1978-98)* (Cordoba: Instituto de Estudios Sociales Avanzados de Andalucia, 1999), esp. VI, Mercado de Trabajo y Estructura Ocupacional, 361-424.

27. Roger Cohen, "Illegal Migration Increases Sharply in European Union," *New York Times*, 25 December 2000, 1.

28. Suzanne Daley, "Despite European Unity Efforts, There's No Country Like Home," *New York Times*, 12 May 2001.

29. European Commission, *The Impact of Structural Policies on Economic and Social Cohesion in the Union, 1989-99* (Luxembourg: Office for Official Publications of the European Communities, 1997), 71.

Table 3.3 Growth of GDP in the Cohesion countries, 1986-99

Measure	Year(s)	Greece	Spain	Ireland	Portugal	EU 4[a]	EU 11[b]	EU 15[c]
Annual average	1986-96	1.6	2.8	6.2	3.5	2.9	2.0	2.1
percent change	1986-91	2.2	4.3	5.3	5.1	4.1	2.8	3.0
in GDP	1991-96	1.0	1.3	7.1	1.8	1.7	1.5	1.5
	1996-99	3.8	3.6	9.2	3.8	4.1	2.6	2.8
Annual average	1986-96	0.5	0.3	0.3	−0.1	0.3	0.4	0.4
percent change	1986-91	0.5	0.2	−0.1	−0.3	0.2	0.4	0.4
in population	1991-96	0.4	0.4	0.6	0.1	0.4	0.4	0.4
	1996-99	0.5	0.1	0.9	0.1	0.2	0.3	0.3
GDP per head	1986	59.2	69.8	60.8	55.1	65.2	107.7	100.0
(PPS)	1987	57.4	71.5	62.5	56.7	66.3	107.4	100.0
EU 15 = 100	1988	58.3	72.5	63.8	59.2	67.6	107.1	100.0
	1989	59.1	73.1	66.3	59.4	68.3	106.9	100.0
	1990	57.4	74.1	71.1	58.5	68.8	106.8	100.0
	1991	60.1	78.7	74.7	63.8	73.1	105.5	100.0
	1992	61.9	77.0	78.4	64.8	72.7	105.6	100.0
	1993	64.2	78.1	82.5	67.7	74.5	105.2	100.0
	1994	65.2	78.1	90.7	69.5	75.3	105.0	100.0
	1995	66.4	78.6	96.8	70.1	76.3	104.8	100.0
	1996	67.5	78.7	96.5	70.5	76.6	104.8	100.0
	1997[d]	69.2	77.8	96.4	70.7	76.3	104.8	100.0
	1998[d]	68.6	78.6	102.1	71.1	77.1	104.7	100.0
	1999[d]	69.3	79.6	105.1	71.8	78.2	104.5	100.0

PPS = purchasing power standards, a formula for reducing the distorted effect of exchange rates in order to compare the relative income of people in different countries.

a. EU-4 is Greece, Spain, Ireland, and Portugal.
b. EU-11 is the other 11 richer nations of the EU.
c. EU-15 is the 15 nations of the EU.
d. Numbers for 1997-99 are projections.

Source: Eurostat, calculations DGXVI; European Commission, *Sixth Periodic Report*, February 1999.

GDP rose from only 61 percent of the EU average in 1986 to 105.1 percent in 1999.[30]

The growth, however, was not evenly distributed within Ireland. Most of it was concentrated in the eastern part of the country, particularly in the service sector around Dublin. But there were other benefits to EU membership. Because agriculture remained an important part of the relatively undeveloped Irish economy, EU price supports helped Irish farmers modernize. With advice from EU financial advisors, the Irish government cut spending, privatized its state companies, and reduced interest rates,

---

30. European Commission, *Sixth Periodic Report*, 9.

and this stimulated both domestic and foreign investment, which helped lift the entire economy and made "the Irish success story" a model for others.

Ireland also received significant resources from the Union. For the decade beginning in 1989, it received 10.2 billion euros from both Structural and Cohesion funds, and the government matched that amount with counterpart investments. (Another 6 billion euros are programmed for the next 6 years.)[31] In addition, it received $10.4 billion in private investment linked to the projects funded by the Union—for a total of 31 billion euros. The Union transferred resources that were equivalent to 2.8 percent of Ireland's GDP. National counterpart funding raised the total investment to 5 percent of GDP.[32] This undoubtedly provided a significant boost to Ireland's development. Of the 10.2 billion euros in grants, about 35 percent went to education and training, 25 percent to infrastructure (roads, rails, and ports), and the rest to small and medium-sized enterprises and environmental projects.

EU technical advisers also helped Irish government officials fashion an outward-oriented development strategy, and they also encouraged the Irish central government to give greater attention to the views of officials at lower levels than they had ever done before. Indeed, the EU modus operandi served to mobilize local community groups to get involved in defining and implementing projects, and to encourage the central government to consult these groups regularly.[33]

The Economic and Social Research Institute in Dublin did an intensive analysis and evaluation of EU programs in Ireland and concluded that "no single factor can explain the economic turnaround." But it did identify three mutually reinforcing variables: the gradual accumulation of human capital, fiscal control and the maintenance of wage competitiveness, and a sharp increase in EU Structural Funds. These funds began to arrive in 1989, just when there was a substantial backlog of projects and urgent infrastructural needs. "Without the support of the structural funds," the report concludes, "congestion in public infrastructure and constraints in third level education would have limited the recovery."[34] Using several different models, the institute concluded that the combined effect in the period 1995-99 was to raise the level of GNP by 3-4 percent above what it would have been without EU funding.[35]

---

31. See table 3.2.

32. European Commission, *The Impact of Structural Policies*, 73-75.

33. Brigid Laffan, "Ireland: A Region Without Regions—The Odd Man Out?" in *Cohesion Policy and European Integration: Building Multi-Level Governance* (Oxford: Oxford University Press, 1996), 320-41.

34. Patrick Honohan, ed., *EU Structural Funds in Ireland: A Mid-Term Evaluation of the CSF, 1994-99* (Dublin: Economic and Social Research Institute, 1997), xv-xxi.

35. *Ibid.*, xviii.

Ireland's trajectory was astonishing, but the three other poor countries—Greece, Portugal, and Spain—also made progress. All three Southern European governments slowly opened their economies and began to
emerge from their authoritarian, protectionist shells in the early 1960s.
As tariffs declined, foreign investment arrived, and the result was that
the three countries witnessed important economic growth and an increase
in real wages during the decade 1963-73: 6.4 percent in Spain, 6.8 percent
in Portugal, and 7 percent in Greece. The labor force began to move out
of agriculture and into the industrial and service sectors. Between 1974
and 1976, the dictatorships ended, and the European Community, which
insisted they become democratic before becoming members, began to
discuss the terms of their entry.[36]

Despite its growth during the previous decade, Spain's infrastructure
and educational base were significantly below the EC average. Its per
capita GDP rose from 70 percent of the EC average in 1986 to nearly 80
percent in 1999. Like Ireland's, Spain's growth was uneven—with the
most prosperous areas in Madrid and Catalonia reaching the EC average
by 1996.[37] The scale of EU transfers to Spain tripled between the two
periods (1989-93 and 1994-99), and it is programmed to continue a high
level of aid until 2006. By that time, Spain would have received 111.6
billion euros—about the same as the other three Cohesion countries combined, and double the next highest recipient. Adding both the national-
counterpart funding and the private-sector financing for the EU projects,
the total amount of EU resources mobilized constituted about 1.5 percent
of Spain's average annual GDP in 1989, and 3.4 percent for the years
1994-99.[38] The investments were concentrated in infrastructure, primarily
roads, but attention and resources were also devoted to telecommunications. Within 5 years of its entry into the European Union, foreign businesses tripled their direct investment in Spain, giving rise to suggestions
that it was "turning into the continent's Sun Belt."[39]

During the past decade, Portugal has grown faster than Spain and the
European Union as a whole—but of course it started from a lower base.
Its GDP per capita increased from 55 percent of the EC average in 1986
to 72 percent in 1999. With a weaker economy, Portugal was affected much
more severely by the recession in the early 1990s, and its development has
been more unbalanced. Most of the country has remained poor, but the

---

36. See Otto Holman, *Integrating Southern Europe: EC Expansion and the Transnationalization
of Spain* (New York: Routledge, 1996).

37. European Commission, *Sixth Periodic Report*, 10.

38. European Commission, *The Impact of Structural Policies*, 45.

39. Stephen Greenhouse, "With Spain in Common Market, New Prosperity and Employment," *New York Times*, 15 January 1989, 1, 9; and Alan Riding, "Spain Aims for a Competitive
Edge in a Unified Europe," *New York Times*, 14 June 1992, F11.

average income of its two urbanized regions—Lisbon and Norte—now approaches the EU average.[40] EU aid of 46.3 billion euros from 1989 to 2006 will amount to about 4 percent of Portugal's GDP at the 1994 level, or 7.2 percent when central-government and private-sector funding are included. As in Spain, the EU emphasis on infrastructure was key to its development. During the past decade, the EU has financed and constructed or improved nearly 4,000 kilometers of roads, or almost half of all the roads in Portugal. It has also constructed or improved 640 kilometers of railroad and modernized almost the country's entire telephone network.[41] Also, as with Ireland and Spain, foreign investment transferred new technology and created higher-paying jobs.[42]

Greece, the poorest EU member-state, initially made the least progress after its entry into the Union because it had chronic fiscal and current account deficits for a decade. In 1994, its budget deficit as a percentage of GDP was 12.1 percent, but it sharply reduced the deficit since then, and its economy began to grow. Its per capita GDP rose from 60 percent of the EU average in 1986 to 69 percent in 1999. As its trade barriers declined and its macroeconomic policies improved, the income gap between Athens and the rest of the country began to widen, much as it did in the other Cohesion countries.[43]

Notwithstanding the Greek government's flawed economic policies, the European Union nearly doubled its aid in the second period, so that from 1989 to 2006, the Union will transfer 51 billion euros to Greece. Together with national and private funds, the total amount represented 4.5 percent of the average annual GDP in the 1989-93 period and 7.2 percent for 1994-99—quite a substantial amount. Repeated and credible reports of corruption have impeded Greek development, but the Union has helped the government address the problem to expedite critical projects on infrastructure (roads and subways) and telecommunications.

The magnitude of the transfers to all four Cohesion countries is significant, but to what extent do these funds contribute to growth and to the reduction of income disparities? To answer that question, one needs to estimate what would have happened in the absence of the assistance and compare that to what occurred after the aid was invested. Aid affects an economy in four ways. First, it increases the income that a country can spend on goods and services. Second, through improvements in infrastructure and education, it increases a country's productive potential. Third, it encourages a country to reset its priorities toward essential long-

40. European Commission, *Sixth Periodic Report*, 10.

41. European Commission, *The Impact of Structural Policies*, 111-21.

42. Peter Gumbel, "Portugal: A Recovery That East Europe Can Emulate," *Wall Street Journal*, 1 May 1992, A11.

43. European Commission, *Sixth Periodic Report*, 10-11.

term investment. And fourth, it has a multiplier effect, coaxing additional funds from private investors.

Four different models—using different assumptions and emphases—have been used to try to assess the specific aid effects. Some, like the Beutel Model, focus on the demand side. Others, like the Pereira Model, examine the supply side. Still others, like the Hermin and the Quest II models, incorporate both demand and supply. All of them suggest that EU funds were responsible for some of the growth, though they differ on the proportion.[44]

The difference between the uncommon success of Ireland and the initial stagnation of Greece underscores the importance of each country's policies—particularly macroeconomic policies, exchange rates, foreign investment policies, and the rule of law in constraining corruption. EU funds helped successful governments accelerate their growth. The European Union also helped reinforce the more responsible policymakers in weak governments.

A comprehensive, incisive study of the effect of regional and cohesion policies was done by Leonardi, who defines "cohesion" precisely and measures it among member-states and regions during the period 1970-91. Among the EU member-states, he finds, as others did, significant convergence. Using regression analyses, he tests various explanatory variables, including distance from the core countries, foreign investment, level of industrialization, unemployment, and EC funding. He finds that the best predictor of convergence is distance from the core countries, and the best explanatory variable is EC spending. Structural and cohesion aid, he concludes, "made a substantial contribution to economic investment and overall GDP in the three nations. [It] acted as a significant stimulus to the national economies, explaining in part the surge of these countries toward convergence."[45]

As to why Greece did not do as well as the other three Cohesion countries, Leonardi sees several factors. Greece joined the European Union at a time of a Europe-wide recession; and its weak infrastructure and notoriously corrupt administration led foreign investors to want to "remain aloof."[46] He also finds the gap between industrial and developing regions to have narrowed, and he explains it by "significant upward movement of the bottom regions."[47]

---

44. These models are summarized or developed in European Commission, *Sixth Periodic Report*, 80-82; and Martin, *Regional Policy in the European Union*, 100-03.

45. Robert Leonardi, *Convergence, Cohesion, and Integration in the European Union* (New York: St. Martin's Press, 1995), 133, 170-76. See chapter 3 for his methodology. In the period he studied, 1970-91, Greece was the only one of the four cohesion countries that did not make progress.

46. *Ibid.*, 134-36.

47. *Ibid.*, 116. Leonardi looks closely at the southern Italian case and believes that the lack of convergence is due to excessive government involvement and a lack of a market economy (chap. 5).

Leonardi did not assess whether Structural Funds or the Single Market were more important in explaining the convergence of the poor nation-states. The Organization for Economic Cooperation and Development (OECD) did such a study in 1994, and it concluded that it was "difficult to find strong evidence the single market program has yet had sizeable effects on aggregate output." The study estimated that the Single Market had improved GDP by perhaps 1.5 percent.[48] That is not exactly a trivial contribution to GDP, but it also does not compare with the kind of contribution that Leonardi attributes to the Structural Funds. The OECD study, however, suffered from the same problem as the others, including Leonardi: how to answer the counterfactual—what would have happened in the absence of the Single Market?

Of the Structural Funds, which policies and projects were most effective? Martin, in a report for the Centre for European Policy Studies, concluded that investments in two areas were most effective: infrastructure and human capital.[49] The European Union has emphasized these two areas, but it has also scattered considerable funds into projects in other areas, such as environmental protection, regulatory policies, new initiatives to provide low-interest loans to small and medium-sized businesses, and technical assistance.

The gap between rich and poor EU member-states narrowed faster than the gap between regions. A recent study by Boldrin and Canova failed to stress the distinction between these two gaps—among states and among regions—and as a result, *The Economist*, drawing from their report, concluded mistakenly that EU aid has not served a useful developmental purpose.[50] Boldrin and Canova's analysis focuses on the 211 "regions" within the European Union between 1982 and 1996. The most significant regional and cohesion aid was only transferred at the end of that period. Although they claim to disagree with the EU's analysis, in fact, their study confirms the EU reports' main conclusions—first, that the evidence was ambiguous by 1996; second, that there was less convergence among regions; and third, that there was convergence in incomes among the rich and poor states. By 1999, the Union found clear evidence of convergence. Boldrin and Canova also argue that one of the possible reasons for the lack of convergence among regions is that EU subsidies to the poor regions may have served to impede migration from them to rich regions. This, I suggest above, may be true, but it substantiates the argument that EU

48. Cited by Tsoukalis, *New European Economy Revisited*, 75-76.

49. Martin, *Regional Policy in the European Union*, 66-72.

50. Michele Boldrin and Fabio Canova, "Inequality and Convergence in Europe's Regions: Reconsidering European Regional Policies," *Economic Policy* (April 2001), 207-53; and "What's Ours Is Ours," *The Economist*, 24 May 2001.

funds have lifted the poor regions to the level where people no longer exercise the option to emigrate.

The failure to reduce significantly the gap among the 211 regions in the European Union is troubling, particularly because transfers within member-states exceed the funds that are made available by the Union. The major cause of those disparities is evident from a map of Europe. The rich regions are all congregated around the largest cities, and the poor regions are rural. Of course, the urban areas conceal within their midst even wider disparities between rich and poor than can be found between the cities and the farms, and those differences resist convergence despite high levels of resource transfers for welfare, unemployment compensation, and transportation and education subsidies. (And sometimes the measurement of the gap does not include these transfers.) Although farmers' incomes cannot match those of most urban workers—and that explains why you cannot keep them down on the farm—the cost of living in rural areas is lower, and much rural income might be underreported because of barter and other "informal" business activity.

Boldrin and Canova offer still more reasons why the data on regional disparities might be mistaken. First, the regions are very heterogeneous in size and population, but most are too small to be considered independent economic areas. Second, there is often very little relation between the activities occurring in the region and the official data. For example, research and development (R&D) expenditures are usually associated with urban areas because that is where corporate headquarters are located, although R&D usually is not done at corporate headquarters. Also, a city has higher per capita income, but that may be overstated because much of its labor comes from outlying regions with lower income. So, in brief, the gap that separates the income of urban from rural residents might appear wider than it really is. This conclusion is different from—if not the opposite of—the view that there has been no reduction in the wide disparities among regions.

Lessons from EU Experience

Recognizing the distinct points of departure of the European Union and NAFTA, let us extract 10 lessons from EU experience that may be of use in contemplating the future of North America.

1. **A declaration of goals.** From the beginning, Europe's leaders defined their mission in terms of community and solidarity. Their goal was that that the people of Europe would cooperate in new ways to bring peace and well-being to all. Those leaders who were most committed to this goal used the ideal of community to press for its attainment.

The first lesson, then, is that a clear statement of goals is necessary but not sufficient to construct a community of nations.

2. **Limiting institutions.** The European Union established too many supranational institutions; NAFTA made the opposite mistake of establishing almost none that are serious. The Union established six different funds for "regional policies," though many are duplicative or unnecessary. Inertia and vested interests make any changes in these institutions very difficult. The lesson is that policymakers should incorporate a "sunset" provision into every institution or funding mechanism, lest each assume a permanence that would diminish—not enhance—the region's capacity to reduce disparities.

3. **Convergence and conditionality.** The spectacular reduction in the income gap between the rich and poor countries of Europe in a relatively short period of time (since 1986) offers hope that regional trading schemes could be an effective vehicle to lift up middle-income countries. Among the many factors responsible for narrowing the gap were the establishment of the Single Market, foreign investment, and the massive EU aid programs. There is a consensus that these three factors contributed to the reduction of disparities, but there is some disagreement as to which is most important. An analysis of the different growth rates among the four Cohesion countries leads to the inescapable conclusion that national policy is a fourth critical determinant, and that conditionality multiplies the contribution of EU aid. If a recipient government, for example, runs up an excessive public deficit, the Union suspends its loans until the government corrects the deficit. The Union also insisted on democracy as a criterion for membership. The lesson is to use the first three factors—Single Market, foreign investment, and aid—to induce the recipient government to adopt the appropriate economic policies and political structures that will allow it to make best use of the resources.

4. **The best projects for regional assistance.** The European Union has funded almost every imaginable kind of project through multiple channels, but the consensus among analysts is that the funds were most effectively employed in projects aimed at infrastructure and higher-level education.

5. **Emigration.** One effect of convergence in incomes and social policies was to reduce the level of emigration from the poor countries and regions in the European Union. Although the gap within the Union was much narrower than within NAFTA, the lesson is indisputable: A reduction in disparities will also reduce the pressures to emigrate.

6. **Reducing volatility.** Although convergence did occur between rich and poor countries, the poor ones did not follow a straight path upward. Rather, what occurred is that the Cohesion countries outperformed the EU average in the boom years and did worse than the EU average during recessions.[51] The opportunities and the dangers of integration are much more serious for weak countries than for more advanced ones. Another study by Martin also found greater volatility among the weaker partners of an integration effort.[52] The lesson is that rich countries need to find ways to cushion the swings that poor economies suffer. Macroeconomic policy coordination and financial "buffer" or "swap" arrangements should be undertaken to protect poor countries from foreign exchange crises.

7. **Growing inequality within the "successful" poor countries.** In many cases, rapid integration tended to coincide with accelerating inequality among the regions of a poor country. More often, this is not because the poor became poorer but because the prosperous regions—the ones tied to the European Union by both exports and inward flows of investment—sped ahead. The poor regions grew more slowly, or their growth just halted. The lesson is that governments should monitor the progress of all regions of poor countries and institute mechanisms to assist those regions that are falling behind or not growing fast enough.

8. **Funds for the affluent and gaps among regions.** More than half of all EU Structural Funds go to poor regions in the rich countries, and several of the rich countries (notably Denmark and France) obtain large subsidies from the Common Agriculture Policy, which is half the EU budget. ("Regional policies" take 30-35 percent of the budget.)[53] One study questions whether there has been any reduction in the disparities among the regions, and therefore concludes that EU funds serve the goal of redistribution, not development.[54] Although this critique has flaws (analyzed above), it would be more efficient and desirable to concentrate the funds in the poor states. Having an EU project in each country gives the citizens of that country a sense of the continued presence and contribution of the Union, but the proportion of funds going to the rich countries should be sharply reduced. The lesson is to find inexpensive, symbolic ways to give the

51. European Commission, *Sixth Periodic Report*, 9.

52. Martin, *Regional Policy in the European Union*, 53-61.

53. See Tsoukalis, *New European Economy Revisited*, 202-22.

54. Boldrin and Canova, "Inequality and Convergence in Europe's Regions," 207-53.

donor countries a feeling that the fund is responsive to their concerns while concentrating the money where it is needed most.

9. **The benefits and pitfalls of politics and bureaucracy.** A large bureaucracy is needed to address the multilevel challenge of legislating, administering, judging, and enforcing EU rules and laws, of harmonizing all 15 member-state policies, and of negotiating the enlargement and relations with other governments. In response to criticism that the bureaucracy is too distant from the people, politicians in governments and the European Parliament have spawned an intrusive oversight process and have insisted on local involvement. This, in turn, has encouraged local groups to demand a larger slice of the pie— with consequences that are both positive (encouraging greater local involvement) and negative (inefficiency and diversion of funds for political purposes). The problem is to find the right balance; the lesson is to keep democracy at the core of deliberations as an organization deepens.

10. **The magnitude of the commitment.** The European Union appropriated truly significant funds to reduce disparities between rich and poor governments and regions, and these funds have made a difference in raising the incomes of the nation-states on Europe's periphery.

In sum, then, the countries of Europe recognized the importance of cooperation and solidarity because, unlike the countries of North America, they were desperate to avoid another European war and also because they understood that their ability to play an important global role required collaboration. The European Union committed significant resources to reduce disparities, but some of those funds were spent inefficiently. NAFTA has the benefit of learning from EU mistakes as well as successes.

4

North America's Journey

In 1990, when President Carlos Salinas of Mexico proposed a free trade agreement with the United States, the US gross domestic product was about 20 times larger than Mexico's and 10 times larger than Canada's. Asymmetry, whether in size of the economy or of the military, is the defining characteristic of the relationship of North America's three nation-states.

In contrast, the principal members of the European Union have economies that are closer in size. It is true that Germany's economy is 183 times larger than Luxembourg's, but the four largest economies—Germany, the United Kingdom, France, and Italy—all are much closer in population and per capita GDP than are the countries in North America. Between the richest and poorest EU member-states, the per capita GDP ratio has varied from 2.4:1 in 1960 to 3.3:1 in 1997—quite modest as compared with the 8:1 ratio between the United States and Mexico in 1960 and 1997, with some variations in between because of an overvalued exchange rate in Mexico (table 4.1).

Distances within North America

It is not just the asymmetry; history also counts. Europe's traumatic 20th-century history has been a unifying force since the Second World War. In contrast, North America has been divided by its history and, more precisely, by its memory of 19th-century conflicts.

Lacking a unifying or traumatizing motive, the governments of North America were reluctant to consider a framework that could advance inte-

Table 4.1 Ratio of GDP per capita between richest and poorest country in the European Union and NAFTA, 1960-97

Group	1960	1970	1980	1990	1997
European Community/ European Union[a] (1957)	2.37 (Luxembourg/ Italy)	1.82 (Luxembourg/ Italy)	2.33 (Luxembourg/ Ireland)	2.43 (Germany/ Greece)	3.31 (Denmark/ Portugal)
NAFTA (1994)	8.01 (United States/ Mexico)	7.25 (United States/ Mexico)	4.07 (United States/ Mexico)	5.97 (United States/ Mexico)	8.20 (United States/ Mexico)

NAFTA = North American Free Trade Agreement.

a. Considers only those nation-states that were members of the organization for each year.

Sources: World Bank, *World Development Indicators*, CD-ROM, 1999; United Nations, *Compendium of Social Statistics* (New York, 1980 and 1988).

gration. "Americans do not know, but Canadians cannot forget," writes Seymour Martin Lipset, "that two nations, not one, came out of the American Revolution." The United States of America emerged confident and proud of its revolution, and Canada defined itself to a considerable extent as "that part of British North America that did not support the [American] Revolution."[1] In 1812, the United States tried, but failed, to annex Canada, and the fear that the formidable Union army in 1865 might trek north to try once again to expel the British was the principal reason why Canadians sought independence, and why the British accepted it in 1867 in the form of a dominion within the British Empire. (Both judged correctly that the United States was less likely to make war against an independent Canada.)[2]

Canadians remained wary of a close relationship with the United States. In 1911, the Canadian prime minister lost an election for concluding a free trade agreement with the United States. Thirty-seven years later, Prime Minister William Lyon McKenzie King refused, at the last minute, to approve a free trade agreement with the United States, evidently fearing a similar political result.

Mexico's history has some similarities to Canada's, but its anxieties about the United States are more intense. Having lost its war and a third of its territory in the 19th century, and having suffered several military interventions in the early 20th century, Mexico's distrust of the United States was deeper than Canada's. Because it has been less stable, prosper-

1. Seymour Martin Lipset, *Continental Divide: The Values and Institutions of the United States and Canada* (New York: Routledge, 1991), 1, 42.

2. Michael Howlett, Alex Netherton, and M. Ramesh, *The Political Economy of Canada: An Introduction*, 2d ed. (New York: Oxford University Press, 1999), 163.

ous, and democratic, Mexico also bears a heavier sense of inferiority. For this reason, any proposal from the United States to reduce trade or investment barriers was usually met with a curt rejection—when officials deigned to respond.[3]

The rationale for a more distant relationship with the United States was most clearly articulated by a young intellectual in the 1980s. "In the case of two nations as disparate in size, power, and wealth as Mexico and the United States," wrote Jorge G. Castañeda, "the weight of economic superiority can be crushing and can lead to a permanent loss of significant attributes of sovereignty and cultural identity." Castañeda, who would become Mexico's foreign minister under the Fox administration, then felt that integration could lead to "political subservience in foreign policy and domestic affairs, as well as a progressive fading of the country's heretofore vigorous cultural personality." Mexico, he feared, could become "less Mexican," and therefore the best foreign policy was to keep Washington at arms' length.[4]

Given the history and the imbalance in power, perhaps the only way to have reached a North American Free Trade Agreement was for the United States' neighbors to lead. And, of course, that is what occurred in the mid-1980s—first in Canada, and then in Mexico. In the 1970s, the Liberal Party under Pierre Trudeau had given Canadian nationalism an edge that made many Canadians proud and others very uneasy. New laws promoted by Trudeau discouraged foreign investment and raised tensions with the United States, and when a deep recession struck Canada in 1982, businesses realized that the Canadian market was not large enough to permit them to grow. A Canadian observer wrote: "They [Canadian businessmen] wanted to become more export-oriented, but were reluctant to make the necessary investment in the face of continued trouble in the Canada-US relationship."[5] In 1984, a national election brought the Progressive Conservative Party under Brian Mulroney to power with a large majority. Although his party had also opposed free trade with the United States, Mulroney recognized a change in the public mood in favor of experimenting with more open trade with the United States. Reagan responded positively, and both governments negotiated a free trade agreement and signed it in 1988.[6] In the same year, Mulroney

---

3. In the 1970s, the US administration of Jimmy Carter proposed a number of possible agreements to minimize trade disputes, and Reagan, during his campaign and his administration, proposed a "North American Accord," a free trade agreement.

4. Robert A. Pastor and Jorge G. Castañeda, *Limits to Friendship: The United States and Mexico* (New York: Alfred A. Knopf, 1988), 241.

5. Michael Hart, *Fifty Years of Canadian Statecraft: Canada at the GATT, 1947-1997* (Ottawa, Canada: Centre for Trade Policy and Law, Carleton University, 1998), 168. Hart is a Canadian scholar and trade negotiator.

6. For two analyses of the issues and the agreement, see Paul Wonnacott, *The United States and Canada: The Quest for Free Trade* (Washington: Institute for International Economics, 1987); and Jeffrey J. Schott and Murray G. Smith, eds., *The Canada-United States Free Trade Agreement: The Global Impact* (Washington: Institute for International Economics, 1988).

called an election, and the free trade agreement was heatedly debated, with the Liberals expressing determined opposition. Mulroney won re-election, but by a narrower margin. There was uncertainty in Canada about the new trade agreement.

The reversal on free trade by Mexico and its president, Salinas, was even more startling than Mulroney's. Mexico had a history of defensive nationalism, particularly aimed at its northern neighbor, which was always more strident than Canada's. In the mid-1970s and the early 1980s, Mexico sharply restricted foreign investment and increased the state's role in the economy. When the debt crisis threatened to bankrupt the country in 1982, its leaders underwent a period of self-examination and emerged with the help of the International Monetary Fund and others to embark on a more export-oriented policy. This meant that the government sharply reduced tariffs and limitations on foreign investment; introduced fiscal discipline; and privatized state-owned corporations.

When Salinas took office in December 1988, he understood that the success of the Mexican economy depended on whether it could attract large sums of private investment. He went first to Western Europe, but found the governments focused on incorporating Eastern Europe after the end of the Cold War. Still interested in diversifying its relationships from excessive reliance on the United States, he went next to Japan. There, he was distressed to find the Japanese very cautious about challenging the United States in its neighborhood. He pondered his next step, realizing that the opening of Mexico's economy in the previous 5 years had left it vulnerable to arbitrary acts of protectionism by the United States, and that the Canadian Free Trade Agreement, which had just been concluded, had addressed that concern adequately. He therefore turned to Washington for a free trade agreement and for the key that would presumably unlock the door of foreign investment.[7] The United States had always been *the* problem and *an* opportunity for Mexico, but no one grasped the opportunity quite like Salinas did.

NAFTA: Description and Evaluation

NAFTA aimed to eliminate all trade and investment barriers and level the playing field in procurement, telecommunications, banking, services, and other sectors.[8] To secure the market, the three governments created a state-of-the-art dispute settlement mechanism. Instead of trying to estab-

---

7. This summary of Salinas' views on trade is derived from numerous interviews that the author had with Salinas from 1979 through 1994, particularly during the period 1989-92, when his views on NAFTA took shape.

8. For a description and preliminary analysis of NAFTA, see Robert A. Pastor, *Integration with Mexico: Options for U.S. Policy* (Washington: Twentieth Century Fund, 1993); and see Gary C. Hufbauer and Jeffrey J. Schott, *NAFTA: An Assessment*, rev. ed. (Washington: Institute for International Economics, 1993).

lish an institution to negotiate the reduction or harmonization of policies, as the European Union had done, NAFTA selected a few sectors and harmonized the policies in the agreement. The agreement was a minimal one that reflected the Canadian and Mexican fear of being dominated by the United States and the US antipathy toward bureaucracy and suprana-tional organizations. It was an "invisible hand," a classical liberal frame-work whose principal shared goal was to eliminate impediments to trade.

Except for a few objective analyses of NAFTA's effect on the three economies, most assessments of its progress resumed the debate that had been fought over the original agreement.[9] In a letter to Congress transmitting a mandatory 3-year assessment, President Clinton naturally defended the agreement: "NAFTA has already proved its worth to the United States during the three years it has been in effect." The Office of the US Trade Representative concluded in that report that NAFTA had had a "modest positive effect" on the US economy, and that it had helped Mexico to recover after the peso crisis much more quickly than it had after its 1982 debt crisis. Curiously, the report does not discuss NAFTA's effect on Canada, perhaps because that was less controversial in the United States. The report also describes some of the cases heard by the labor and environmental commissions and sees progress in both areas.[10]

On the other side, a coalition of opponents to NAFTA, including the Economic Policy Institute, the International Labor Rights Fund, Public Citizen, and the Sierra Club, produced a report entitled "The Failed Exper-iment: NAFTA at Three Years." The report concluded that US business had used NAFTA as a threat to reduce wages, that the United States had sustained major trade deficits with its neighbors, that NAFTA had contributed to Mexico's peso crisis and Canada's recession, and that NAFTA had been ineffectual on labor rights and silent as "an already heavily polluted border region [became] much dirtier and more danger-ous."[11] Another assessment 2 years later by Public Citizen concluded that conditions had deteriorated further.[12]

In an astute review of the debate on NAFTA, Weintraub shows how many of the arguments used by advocates and opponents circle around

---

9. For an excellent assessment of the original agreement, see Hufbauer and Schott, *NAFTA: An Assessment*; George Grayson, *The North American Free Trade Agreement: Regional Community and the New World Order* (Lanham, Md.: University Press of America, 1995); and William A. Orme, Jr., *Understanding NAFTA* (Austin: University of Texas Press, 1996).

10. Office of the US Special Trade Representative (USTR), *Study on the Operation and Effects of the North American Free Trade Agreement*, July 1997.

11. Economic Policy Institute et al., *The Failed Experiment: NAFTA at Three Years* (Washing-ton, 1997).

12. Public Citizen, Global Trade Watch, "NAFTA at Five: A Failure," December 1998, http://www.citizen.org/pctrade/nafta/reports/5years/htm.

similar criteria—related to the balance of payments or the gain and loss of jobs. He argues persuasively that these criteria are misleading and that a more useful assessment of NAFTA's progress would be based on its effect on total trade, productivity, intraindustry specialization, industrial competitiveness, environmental effects, and institution building.[13]

With regard to NAFTA's principal goals on trade and investment, the agreement has been a resounding success. In 1993, Mexican tariffs averaged about 10 percent, 2.5 times those of the United States. By 1999, Mexican tariffs had fallen to 2 percent, and import licensing and other nontariff barriers had been eliminated. Today, two-thirds of all US exports enter Mexico duty-free. Nearly all goods that were traded between Canada and the United States now enter duty-free. Agricultural products are the most sensitive, and thus free trade in this area has been delayed until 2008.

As barriers declined, trade and investment soared in all three directions during the 1990s. If we take its goal as aiming to reassure businesses in all three countries of a secure continental market, then we can use 1990, when negotiations began, as one benchmark. From that year to 1999, exports among the three North American countries climbed from $229.9 to $585.1 billion—an average annual rate of growth of 10.9 percent— double the rate of growth of the three countries' exports to the world.[14] Mexico's exports to the United States leaped from $18.4 billion in 1990 to $111 billion in 1999; and its imports from the United States, from $20 to $87 billion (see table 1.3).

Just from the moment NAFTA came into force in January 1994 until 1998, trade more than doubled among the three, and in 1997, Mexico leapt over Japan to become the second most important market for US goods and services—behind Canada. By then, the triangle was completed; Mexico and Canada had become each other's third largest trading partners, after the United States and the European Union.[15] The effect on Mexico is even more profound if one looks back to 1985 when it began reducing its trade barriers. That year, Mexico's total trade with the United States was $33 billion; 14 years later, it had expanded nearly sixfold, and in the process had transformed its economy. In 1981, oil accounted for 72 percent of Mexico's exports; by 1998, only 5.5 percent of Mexico's $117 billion worth of exports were oil, and 90 percent were manufactured goods.[16]

---

13. Sidney Weintraub, *NAFTA at Three: A Progress Report* (Washington: Center for Strategic and International Studies, 1997), chap. 2.

14. Inter-American Development Bank, *Integration and Trade in the Americas: Periodic Note* (December 2000), 115.

15. For Mexican-Canadian data, see Naomi Adelson, "About Face: The Move to Export-Led Growth," *El Financiero International Edition*, 14 June 1999, 3.

16. United Nations Economic Commission on Latin America and the Caribbean, *Economic Indicators*, table 18A, http://www.eclac.org/index1.html.

Even before Canada and the United States negotiated a free trade agreement, both countries were each other's most important trading partners. Still, from that sturdy base, from 1985 to 1998, total trade more than doubled—from $122 to $329 billion.[17] Of course, NAFTA is not alone responsible for this expansion, and it is difficult to estimate precisely how much the reduction in barriers due to NAFTA, as opposed to the Uruguay Round, accounts for the growth in trade. DRI/McGraw-Hill concluded that NAFTA had boosted trade between Mexico and the United States by $17 billion, which represented a $7 billion net US export increase from 1993 to 1996. Using a different model, the International Trade Commission concluded that there was "a strong statistical link between the increase in bilateral trade between the United States and Mexico and the implementation of NAFTA."[18]

Another study by a group of scholars from the University of California at Los Angeles (UCLA) showed that US imports from Mexico increased at an average rate of 6.4 percent in the 3 years before NAFTA and 20 percent in the years after it, but they also found that the imports of those commodities liberalized by NAFTA grew much less than those that were not affected by NAFTA liberalization. The expansion in Mexican exports was mostly in manufacturing and was due primarily to industrial integration by North American firms.

That same UCLA study examined the effects of NAFTA on jobs. Using a partial-equilibrium model that deliberately exaggerated an adverse effect on jobs by assuming that demand and productivity were fixed, the report indicated that as many as 300,000 jobs were lost during the period of 1990-97 due to import competition from Mexico and 458,000 due to imports from Canada. This is an average of 94,000 jobs lost *each year*. That figure, however, should be juxtaposed with the roughly 200,000 jobs that were being created *each month* during the 1990s. But those estimates of job loss were based on a model. The US Department of Labor actually certified that 46,826 workers lost their jobs due to Mexican imports from the date of NAFTA's approval in 1993 until July 1999, and about half as many (23,250) jobs were lost due to imports from Canada. The number of workers actually certified as unemployed because of NAFTA is less than 25 percent of the numbers estimated by the UCLA model. The point is that *the total number of jobs lost was trivial* in comparison with the more than 20 million jobs created from 1993 to 1999.[19]

---

17. For trade statistics, see http://www.ita.doc.gov; or http://www.wto.org/english/res_e/statis_e/stat_toc_e.htm.

18. For a summary of these and other studies, see USTR report, 4-28.

19. Raul Hinojosa et al., *The U.S. Employment Impacts of North American Integration After NAFTA: A Partial Equilibrium Approach* (Los Angeles: University of California at Los Angeles, 2000, http://naid.sppsr.ucla.edu). For the number of jobs, see *Economic Report of the President* (Washington: US Government Printing Office, 2000), 26.

Indeed, that simple comparison suggests that the entire debate about trade's effect on jobs may have been misleading. President Clinton had argued that NAFTA would create jobs; Ross Perot, that it would destroy jobs. Both were correct but missed the point. Trade, though a growing part of the US economy, was still relatively small, and thus the creation and destruction of jobs was more closely related to business cycles than exports and imports.

NAFTA's impact on Canada may have been as consequential as on Mexico. Although two-way trade between Canada and the United States had always been high, it had stagnated for the decade before the Free Trade Agreement; then it doubled. An econometric analysis of the data by Canada's Department of Foreign Affairs and International Trade concluded that two factors explained the growth: economic expansion in the United States and trade liberalization due to FTA and NAFTA.[20] This conclusion was supported in a study by Schwanen, who showed that the sectors liberalized by the FTA had grown fastest, and the composition of its exports shifted from raw materials to manufactured goods and automotive products. Most of the growth in trade has been intrafirm and intraindustry, just as has occurred in Mexico and the United States.[21]

On the issue of foreign direct investment (FDI), all three countries were ambivalent, although in different ways. About the only thing that Canada and Mexico feared more than having too much investment by the United States was that they would have too little foreign investment. Both were concerned that a free trade agreement would exacerbate their dependence on US multinationals. To the extent that the US public followed the debate on NAFTA, the one issue that seemed to preoccupy them the most was the one popularized by Perot—that US businesses would move to Mexico to take advantage of cheap labor. In fact, a number of unusual patterns can be detected that are quite different from these fears and predictions.

Salinas's fear that foreign investors would not come even if he built NAFTA proved unfounded. From 1990 to 1998, FDI in Mexico nearly tripled—from $29.9 to $83.3 billion. What was surprising was that the share of that investment owned by Americans declined from 64.2 to 61.8 percent. To what extent was this due to NAFTA? Graham and Wada argued that most of the decisions by US firms to locate in Mexico were made before NAFTA was even announced. They believe the triggering event for the first round of major investments was the decision in the mid-1980s to open Mexico's economy and in particular to reach agree-

---

20. Shenje Chen and Prakash Sharma, Department of Foreign Affairs and International Trade, "Accounting for Canadian Export Growth: 1983-1997," Trade and Economic Policy Paper 97-01, http://www.dfait-maeci.gc.ca.

21. Daniel Schwanen, *Trading Up: The Impact of Increased Continental Integration on Trade, Investment, and Jobs in Canada*, Commentary 37 (Toronto: C.D. Howe, 1992) and *A Growing Success: Canada's Performance under Free Trade*, Commentary 52 (Toronto: C.D. Howe, 1993).

Table 4.2 Flows of foreign direct investment to Mexico, 1990-98
(millions of dollars)

Year	1990	1991	1992	1993	1994	1995	1996	1997	1998
Flows to Mexico	2,634	4,762	4,393	4,389	10,973	9,526	7,619	12,830	10,238

Sources: Inter-American Development Bank and Institute for European-Latin American Relations (IRELA), *Foreign Direct Investment in Latin America: Perspectives of the Major Investors* (Madrid: IRELA, 1998), 36; United Nations Economic Commission on Latin America and the Caribbean, *Indicators* (Santiago, 2000), table C18.

ments with the United States on trade issues and on eliminating restrictions on foreign investment.[22] No doubt, this led to an important surge in foreign investment, but the decisions of the mid-1980s do not explain sufficiently two surges that occurred after 1990—first, in 1991 after trade talks began; and second, in 1994 after the agreement was approved (see table 4.2). From 1991 to 1993, average annual flows of foreign investment to Mexico increased by $4.5 billion, or 71 percent above that of 1990. During the period 1994-98, after implementing the agreement, the average annual level of FDI rose to $10.2 billion, or 127 percent above that of the previous period. The promise of NAFTA and then the reality affected those investment decisions at least as much, if not more, than the liberalization of the investment laws in the 1980s.

Canada's primal fear was that US corporations would purchase their national treasures, especially their oil.[23] The free trade agreement did stimulate major new investments, but the US share declined from 75 percent before the agreement to 68 percent in 1998.[24] The sharpest reduction was in the petroleum and mining sectors. Forty percent of US investments in Canada in 1966 were in those two sectors; by 1995, only 18 percent of US investments were in them. In contrast, during the past two decades, Canadian FDI in the United States has grown at an annual rate of 11 percent, which is more than twice the rate of growth of US investment in Canada.[25] By 1998, 53 percent of Canadian investment abroad, amounting to $126 billion, was located in the United States.[26]

---

22. Edward W. Graham and Erika Wada, "Domestic Reform, Trade and Investment Liberalization, Financial Crisis, and Foreign Direct Investment in Mexico," *The World Economy* 23, no. 6 (June 2000).

23. See, e.g., Kari Levitt, *Silent Surrender: The Multinational Corporation in Canada* (Toronto: Macmillan, 1970).

24. Department of Foreign Affairs and International Trade of Canada, *Opening Doors to the World: Canada's Market Access Priorities, 2000* (Ottawa, 2000); the data are also available at http://www.dfait-maeci.gc.ca or http://www.exportsource.gc.ca.

25. Gary C. Hufbauer and Jeffrey J. Schott, *North American Integration: 25 Years Backward and Forward*, Paper 3 (Ottawa: Industry Canada, 1998), 14-17.

26. Department of Foreign Affairs and International Trade of Canada, *Opening Doors to the World.*

The US-Canadian Free Trade Agreement, and subsequently NAFTA, triggered a veritable avalanche of foreign investment into and out of Canada. FDI in Canada averaged Cn$11.5 billion annually between 1993 and 1997, and then in 1998, the rate doubled to $22.9 billion—to a bring total FDI in Canada to Cn$217 billion in 1998, more than double the level before the free trade agreement went into effect a decade before. This investment transferred new technology and increased Canadian productivity. But the unusual dimension was that Canadian FDI abroad surpassed the incoming flow. By the end of 1998, total Canadian FDI abroad amounted to Cn$240 billion—more than three times the level before the FTA.[27] The connection between expanded trade and investment could not be demonstrated in a more compelling way.

One of the objectives in the preamble of NAFTA is to "enhance the competitiveness of their [Canadian, Mexican, US] firms in global markets." The automotive sector is the largest group of manufacturing industries in all three countries, and it constitutes roughly 40 percent of North American trade. Auto production is now continental. In 1962, with a highly regulated, protected auto sector, Mexico's automobile industry produced 67,000 cars. By 1997, after a series of decrees that liberalized trade in auto parts, Mexico produced 854,809 cars. It reserved 303,577 for the local market, and sold most of the rest to its two northern neighbors. By 1999, Ford was making its Escorts, General Motors its Silverados, and Chrysler its Ram Chargers in Mexico. Integration is a source of efficiency, but also of vulnerability. When autoworkers struck in Flint, Michigan, in 1998, General Motors plants in Silao, Saltillo, and Ciudad Juarez halted, and about 84,000 Mexican workers were idled.[28] Although Mexico's automaking capacity has been elevated, it still represents a relatively small proportion of total North American car production (8.2 million) and sales (9.3 million); the US proportion of the first was 73 percent, of the second, 89 percent.[29]

The auto industry is the most important and integrated in North America, but it is hardly unique in the way it has reorganized itself. In an analysis of surveys of the views of managers of US firms that have operations in Canada and Mexico, Blank and Haar concluded that NAFTA "intensified trends already underway toward the development of continental-wide strategies and the creation of North American production,

---

27. *Ibid.*

28. Brendan M. Case, "The United State of Mexico: Mexico Is Annexing Sectors of the U.S. Economy," *Latin Trade*, August 1999, 48-54.

29. For the data on production and sales and for analyses of the auto industry, see Sidney Weintraub and Christopher Sands, eds., *The North American Auto Industry under NAFTA* (Washington: Center for Strategic and International Studies, 1998), tables 1.2 and 1.3, 6-7; and Maureen Appel Molot, ed., *Driving Continentally: National Policies and the North American Auto Industry* (Ottawa: Carleton University Press, 1993).

marketing, and sourcing networks."[30] Many US multinationals have reorganized themselves as North American companies, with plants in all three countries that use the comparative advantage of each plant and that respond to a continental market rather than three separate national markets. The term "maquiladora," which was used to refer to assembly plants in Mexico, no longer captures the diversity and the advanced state of the new investments. Most of the new trade and nearly half of the total trade between Mexico and the United States is now intraindustry, which is just one more indication of the accelerating pace of integration in North America.[31]

The one foreign investment story that few anticipated was the growth of Mexican multinational corporations. In just one decade, beginning with fewer than 2,000 workers overseas in 1990, Mexican companies ventured into two dozen countries, employing about 70,000, with annual revenues of about $8 billion. CEMEX, the world's third largest cement company, and the Mexican food company Grupo Industrial Bimbo were the largest, but numerous Mexican auto parts companies were also exporting and investing in the United States and all over the world.[32] Corona replaced Heineken as the number one beer imported in the United States.[33]

Institutions and Flank Issues

The signatories of NAFTA deliberately wanted to avoid establishing any bureaucratic or supranational institutions. The core of the agreement was therefore self-executing or designed to be implemented by *each* government. Still, the dispute-settlement mechanism obviously needed some structure. The modus operandi was to create a "NAFTA Free Trade Commission," which was a "virtual" structure; that is, it was simply a phrase to describe periodic meetings among the trade ministers of the three countries, "with no permanent location or staff." Their meetings were intended to assess the implementation of the agreement, resolve any new disputes, and oversee the work of numerous committees established to

---

30. Stephen Blank and Jerry Haar, *Making NAFTA Work: U.S. Firms and the New North American Business Environment* (Miami: North South Center Press, 1998), 17, 23.

31. For the data on intraindustry trade, see "Mexican Economic Integration," *Banamex Review of the Economic Situation in Mexico* 76, no. 900 (December 2000), 500-06.

32. Joel Millman, "The World's New Tiger on the Export Scene Isn't Asian: It's Mexico: NAFTA Prodded Firms to Think Globally to Meet U.S. Challenge," *Wall Street Journal*, 9 May 2000, 1, 10.

33. Kenneth N. Gilpin, "In Mexico, Stocks Rise as Growth Slows," *New York Times*, 3 June 2001, 8.

address specific issues described in each chapter in the agreement.[34] Each government maintains a "NAFTA Secretariat," which technically assists the trade ministers, but in the case of the United States, the secretariat is a low-level staff person in the Department of Commerce. Weintraub described the Free Trade Commission as "completely a creature of the three trade ministries," with no independent authority. Indeed, he views this and the other structures established by NAFTA as "quite primitive."[35]

To settle trade disputes, the governments deliberately established a "mechanism" rather than a permanent court. The ad hoc procedure has the advantage of avoiding a permanent bureaucracy. But by hiring experts on a case-by-case basis rather than permitting judges to accumulate experience and expertise, each new set of "experts" may repeat mistakes, rediscover after a period of trial-and-error expeditious procedures, or simply find themselves outmaneuvered by corporate counsel with vastly more experience than themselves.

There are three distinct mechanisms for settling trade or investment disputes, and each country has used all of them to initiate complaints. Between 1994 and 2000, the largest number of cases (76) were handled under "Chapter 19," dealing with countervailing duties and antidumping. There were 16 "Chapter 11" cases dealing with investor disputes, and 4 cases of "Chapter 20" on other aspects of the agreement.[36]

From a Canadian perspective, Davey evaluated the process and the decisions and concluded: "The dispute settlement mechanisms of the [FTA/NAFTA] have worked reasonably well . . . the basic goal of trade dispute settlement . . . is to enforce the agreed-upon rules. By and large, these dispute-settlement mechanisms have done that."[37]

Among the concerns that have been raised about the dispute-settlement mechanisms, the most important relate to Chapter 11 on investment. Because one of the purposes of NAFTA was to encourage foreign investment, this provision was originally drafted to calm US investors' fears of expropriation by Mexico. No one had anticipated that it would be used in all three countries, in some cases to penalize the application of a more rigorous standard on chemical emissions than had existed when the corpo-

---

34. For a straightforward description and implicitly a defense of the dearth of staff and bureaucracy of the new institutions, see US General Accounting Office, *North American Free Trade Agreement: Structure and Status of Implementing Organizations*, GAO/GGD-95-10BR (Washington: US Government Printing Office, 1994).

35. Weintraub, *NAFTA at Three*, 69.

36. A full list of the cases was compiled by Antonio Ortiz Mena L.N., "Dispute Settlement Under NAFTA: The Challenges Ahead," appendix 1, Division de Estudios Internationales, Centro de Investigación y Docencia Económicas, Mexico City, photocopy (24 May 2001).

37. William Davey, *Pine and Swine: Canada-United States Trade Dispute Settlement—The FTA Experience and NAFTA Prospects* (Ottawa: Centre for Trade Policy and Law, 1996), 288-89.

ration first made the investment but that is what happened. The NAFTA side agreement on the environment encourages the upgrading of environmental standards, but Chapter 11 turned this provision on its head, by permitting companies to sue governments for any changes, including new environmental rules, that could diminish or harm their investment. These decisions were criticized not just because of the outcome but because the court proceedings were confidential.[38] Certainly, more transparency is essential, but the three governments should also take steps to narrow the scope of this provision.

The center of NAFTA is trade, investment, and global competitiveness, but on the flanks of the agreement are the issues of labor and the environment. These side agreements were grafted onto the core at the initiative of President Clinton, who was inaugurated after NAFTA was signed. The Canadian and Mexican governments did not share his concerns about the need to address labor or environmental issues, but both acquiesced because the United States did not press for any supranational authority to regulate common standards. Instead, the negotiations produced relatively innocuous commissions for cooperation among officials responsible for each area in the three governments. Both the Commission for Labor Cooperation (CLC) and the Commission for Environmental Cooperation (CEC) provide citizens, corporations, unions, and nongovernmental organizations (NGOs) with an avenue for presenting their complaints. In the case of the labor agreement, since 1994, the CLC received 23 complaints—14 directed against Mexico, 7 against the United States, and 2 against Canada.[39]

Both commissions have done some useful work, and nongovernmental organizations from Canada and the United States have helped their counterparts in Mexico to develop and pursue complaints. But both commissions reflect the caution of their governments. No one has criticized them for being too aggressive or trying to forge common responses on difficult questions such as pollution on the border or labor rights in the apparel industry.[40] The International Labor Rights Fund, an NGO advocate on labor rights, which has petitioned the CLC several times, viewed the labor agreement as "wholly inadequate to deal with the complex issues of cross-border labor regulation since it did nothing to correct the verified record

---

38. See Anthony DePalma, "NAFTA's Powerful Little Secret: Obscure Tribunals Settle Disputes, but Go Too Far, Critics Say," *New York Times*, 11 March 2001, III, 1, 13.

39. For the submissions, see http://www.dol.gov/dol/ilab/public/programs/nao; also see http://www.naalc.org.

40. See Jacqueline McFadyen, "NAFTA Supplemental Agreements: Four Year Review," Working Paper 98-4, Institute for International Economics, Washington, photocopy (1998); and Gary Hufbauer, Daniel C. Esty, Diana Orejas, Luis Rubio, and Jeffrey Schott. *NAFTA and the Environment: Seven Years Later*, Policy Analysis 61 (Washington: Institute for International Economics, 2000).

of nonenforcement of labor laws in Mexico, particularly in the maquiladora plants."[41]

The mandate of the commissions have transnational goals—for example, to improve working conditions, living standards, and labor principles in a cooperative way in all three countries. The commissions could do more if the three governments decide to expand the mandates and increase their autonomy and resources.

The two fears raised by environmentalists during the debate on NAFTA—that Mexico would become a "pollution haven" and that this would lower environmental standards in Canada and the United States— were not borne out by subsequent events. NAFTA did not worsen environmental conditions in the three countries, but it did not do as much as many had hoped to improve the intolerable conditions on the US-Mexican border. Two studies of the impact of the CEC concluded that it has "developed credibility in its nearly eight years as a North American policymaking body." Canadian and US environmentalists both in and outside government have worked closely with their Mexican counterparts to increase Mexico's capacity to monitor and enforce its environmental standards. Environmental officials in Mexico have noted that international support has helped them gain additional resources from their own governments. The CEC has also undertaken important projects on airborne pollutants and migratory species.[42]

During the debate on NAFTA in the US House of Representatives, President Clinton approved the proposal of Congressman Esteban Torres to establish a North American Development Bank (NADBank). The idea and the name had more weight than the mandate or the resources. It took considerable time before the NADBank became operational, but even then, its bilateral mandate limited its work to market-based loans for environmental projects on the border. On a parallel track, Mexico and the United States negotiated the establishment of a Border Environment Cooperation Commission (BECC) to assist border states and local communities to design and coordinate environmental infrastructure projects on the border area. The BECC, based in Ciudad Juarez, Chihuahua, involves local communities in the development of projects and then seeks financing from the private sector and NADBank, which is based in San Antonio, Texas. Mexico and the United States have each contributed $225 million

---

41. Cited in Latin American Working Group, Legislative Update, 6 February 1998, 5.

42. Gary C. Hufbauer, Daniel C. Esty, Diana Orejas, Luis Rubio, and Jeffrey J. Schott, *NAFTA and the Environment: Seven Years Later*, Policy Analysis 61. (Washington: Institute for International Economics, 2000); Jan Gilbreath, *The Environment and Trade: Predicting a Course for the Western Hemisphere Using the North American Experience*, joint publication of Mexico Project, Americas Program, Center for Strategic and International Studies, and Sustainable Americas Project, Yale Center for Law and Environmental Policy (Washington: Center for Strategic and International Studies, 2001), 46, 10.

of paid-in capital, which gives the bank a lending capacity of $2 billion. The combination of chronic poverty and rapid urbanization and industrialization on the border have created a multiplicity of health problems, involving water and waste treatment, solid and toxic wastes, and air pollution. The two institutions were very slow in getting organized, but by 2000, 29 projects had been started or completed.

There are varying interpretations of the effectiveness of these institutions. The Clinton administration in its 3-year evaluation in July 1997 defended the two institutions for improving the lives of border citizens, and the National Wildlife Foundation saw "promising potential" in the way the twin institutions were approaching the issues. Most everyone else has been critical. Public Citizen (an NGO) and the US General Accounting Office in 1996 found little evidence of improvement of the environment in the area. Researchers from UCLA and the National Council of La Raza also concluded that both organizations had done little.[43]

The most telling critique of these two border institutions was done by the staff of the NADBank at the request of its board in a draft paper that was posted on the World Wide Web. The report agreed that the health and sanitation of the border should remain the principal mission, but it acknowledged that "the Bank's lending capacity remains virtually untapped." Even in the 29 projects, the bank's loans were a minimal component. The report goes further: "The Bank's current lending capacity will *never* be fully utilized by water, wastewater, and solid waste projects" [*emphasis added*].[44]

The problem is twofold. First, the NADBank has a mandate to lend at market rates of interest for "sustainable" projects, but few communities in Mexico can afford to incur the kind of debt needed to fund these projects. They do not have the revenue to repay, and their residents could not afford higher utility prices. The interest rates are competitive but not affordable in Mexico, but the rates are not competitive in the United States because of the tax-exempt municipal finance market. Second, the bank

---

43. Public Citizen, *NAFTA's Broken Promises: The Border Betrayed* (Washington: Public Citizen Publications, 1996); US General Accounting Office, "Environmental Infrastructure Needs in the U.S.-Mexican Border Region Remain Unmet," Report to the Ranking Minority Member, Committee on Commerce, House of Representatives, GAO/RCED-96-179; USTR, Study on the Operation and Effect of NAFTA, July 1997; Angela Acosta et al, *A Latino Review of President Clinton's NAFTA Package: Part 2: The North American Development Bank, the Border Environment Cooperation Commission, and the U.S. Community Adjustment and Investment Program.* (San Antonio, TX: William C. Velasquez Institute, 1997); and Mark J. Spaulding and John J. Audley, *Promising Potential for the U.S.-Mexico Border and the Future: An Assessment of the BECC/NADBank Institutions* (Washington: National Wildlife Federation, 1997).

44. North American Development Bank, *Utilizing the Lending Capacity of the NADB*, draft, 20 June 2000, 4-5, see http://www.nadb.org/english/about_bank/overview/Overview _Text.htm.

has been reluctant to broaden its mandate and fund general infrastructure projects in the communities.

The NADBank's board of directors met on 16 November 2000 to consider the report. They decided that the bank should continue its focus on water pollution and wastewater treatment, but it also should consider financing other types of environmental infrastructure projects, including those outside the border region.[45] President Fox subsequently visited the bank and encouraged it to do more. These are important steps, but it is too soon to say whether the bank will be able to expand its capacity and improve significantly the quality of life on the border.

During the US debate on NAFTA, questions were raised about its impact on Mexico's political development. Some opposed NAFTA because they feared that the Institutional Revolutionary Party—which had governed the country since its revolution—would be so strengthened that it would postpone indefinitely any possibility of political liberalization. Others argued that rejecting NAFTA would encourage PRI hardliners to rebuild the walls—economically and politically—around Mexico, setting back the prospects for democracy. Mexico's subsequent political evolution proved a resounding rejection of the first argument. Through the course of the 1990s, as a result of new laws, Mexico's electoral institutions—primarily the Federal Election Institute and the Electoral Court—grew more independent, impartial, and professional. Gradually, public confidence in these institutions increased. In the 1997 national elections, the PRI lost its majority in Congress for the first time. And the first election for mayor of Mexico City was won by the leader of the leftist Democratic Revolutionary Party, Cuauhtémoc Cárdenas. This merely set the stage for the astonishing national contest on 2 July 2000. Vicente Fox Quesada, the presidential candidate of the Alliance for Change, whose core was the National Action Party (PAN), defeated the PRI candidate by a margin of 6 percent.[46] Few Mexicans would have predicted such a fundamental yet peaceful change.

How did it happen? The first breach in the armor of the hegemonic party-state occurred before the 1988 election with the defection of Cuauhtémoc Cárdenas, the former PRI governor of Michoacan and son of the revered president, Lázaro Cárdenas. Cárdenas' decision to contest the presidency opened the PRI's hitherto internal debate to the public and made criticism of the PRI and the government permissible. A second reason was the persistent demand for basic voting rights by the PAN and

---

45. See North American Development Bank, "Expansion of NADB Sectors of Activity, Board Resolution 2000-10," San Antonio, photocopy (16 November 2000).

46. See the following three articles on the Mexican election in *Journal of Democracy* 11, no. 4 (October 2000): Andreas Schedler, "The Democratic Revelation; Robert A. Pastor, Exiting the Labyrinth: Mexico's Path Toward Democratic Modernity;" and Sergio Aguayo Quesada, "The 'External Factor'."

Mexican NGOs.[47] Third, the opening of Mexico's economy put pressure on the government to open the political system. The international costs of domestic political repression or even manipulation increased, as portfolio investors seemed to be greatly influenced by rumors or signs of political instability. Mexico could not secure a stable flow of foreign investment or join the modern world with an authoritarian political system. In that larger sense, NAFTA, the culmination of Mexico's economic opening, had a decisive effect in encouraging the political liberalization of the country.

In assessing the overall impact of NAFTA, Mexico probably has been affected the most. Its economy suffered a severe recession in 1995 primarily because its government mismanaged its foreign exchange in the face of a number of political crises, but a contributing factor was its increased dependence on foreign capital. Mexico, however, recovered quickly from that setback, and through the remainder of the decade, it sustained annual growth rates averaging about 5 percent. Trade and investment, particularly with its two northern neighbors, increased, although much of the investment was concentrated on the border area, where it also exacerbated social and pollution problems.

Mexico's economic transformation began before NAFTA, but it was consolidated, and in some ways accelerated, by the trade agreement. The country's dependence on trade (exports plus imports as a percentage of GDP) tripled from 19.7 percent in 1983 to 58.7 percent in 1999. It changed from an oil-dependent economy to one based on manufactured exports. Labor moved out of the rural areas at an exceptionally fast pace. Indeed, in 1960, more than half of Mexico's labor force was in agriculture, accounting for only 16 percent of GDP. By 1999, 22 percent of the population was on Mexico's farms, but they only produced 5 percent of the country's output.[48] NAFTA delayed the reduction in agricultural barriers, and so very little, if any, of this migration can be attributed to the agreement. Nonetheless, in the long term, the movement of workers from rural areas to cities will have as big an effect on Mexico's capacity to adapt to industrial-world competition as any other part of the agreement.

Except for its farms in the north—mostly growing fruit and vegetables—which are geared to the US market, most of Mexico's farms are small, obsolete, or lack any credit. Under Salinas, the Constitution was changed to permit the sale of land in *ejidos* (Indian cooperatives), but the government had scarce funds for credit or assistance to the small farmers. Privatization of the sugar industry permitted new investment. Mexico

---

47. For an excellent description and analysis of this process, see Vikram K. Chand, *Mexico's Political Awakening* (Notre Dame, IN: University of Notre Dame Press, 2001).

48. For the data, see Michele Veeman, Terrence Veeman, and Ryan Hoskins, "NAFTA in the Next Ten Years: Issues and Challenges for Agricultural Trade and Policy," University of Alberta, Edmonton, photocopy (May 2001).

was a net importer of sugar at the time of NAFTA, but by 2000, it had a capacity to export considerably more than the quota the United States allowed—116,000 metric tons. That represented a fivefold increase in its quota at the time that NAFTA was approved, but the Mexicans had hoped for a 500,000-ton quota. While the United States protected its sugar industry, Mexico restricted imports of high-fructose corn syrup from the United States. Both governments took the other to a NAFTA panel.[49]

The impact on Canada was also quite pronounced. NAFTA deepened Canada's dependence on the US market, but it also helped diversify and internationalize its economy. With a history that has reflected considerable uncertainty as to whether it wanted to join its economy to the world's, Canada, since FTA and NAFTA, has made a clear commitment. Canada's trade as a percentage of GDP expanded from 52.4 percent in 1990 to 74.2 percent in 1999—making it the most trade-oriented country in the Group of Seven (or Eight).[50]

As for the United States, its total trade as a percentage of GDP increased by 25 percent during the 1990s—from 16 to 20 percent. Given the size of the US economy and the longest period of growth and job creation in its history, most analysts would say that NAFTA contributed to this success, but only marginally. Perhaps the greatest accomplishments of NAFTA were the least visible—the growing competitiveness and continentalization of industry, the social integration with its neighbors, the acceleration of economic integration, and the coalescence of the three countries more than at any moment in history.

The dispute settlement mechanism has managed trade-related problems satisfactorily, reducing the politicization of trade disputes. The other institutions—on labor, the environment, and border cooperation—have performed modestly, as the times demanded. From the perspective of the most populous, prosperous, and powerful of the three countries, NAFTA has already succeeded in establishing a framework that could lead to greater cooperation among the three North American countries and enhanced competitiveness in the world community.

What's Left? What's Wrong?

An evaluation of NAFTA should not be confined just to trade and investment criteria or the side agreements. One needs to view NAFTA as the

---

49. See US International Trade Commission, *The Year in Trade 2000: Operation of the Trade Agreements Program*, Publication 3428 (Washington, June 2001), 4-14-18 (also see http://www.usitc.gov); and Ginger Thompson, "Farm Unrest Roils Mexico, Challenging New President," *New York Times*, 22 July 2001, 1.

50. Department of Foreign Affairs and International Trade of Canada, *Opening Doors to the World: Canada's Market Access Priorities, 1999* (Ottawa, 1999), 1. See also table 1.1.

center of a unique social and economic integration process and of an effort to redefine the relationship between two industrial countries and a developing one. The most compelling form of integration not mentioned in NAFTA is that of people.

The flow of people, cultures, food, music, and sports across the two borders has surged even more than the trade in goods and services. In 1996, the first destination for most US tourists abroad was Mexico; 20 million Americans went. The second most popular destination for US tourists was Canada; 13 million traveled there. Third was the United Kingdom, with only 2.3 million US tourists. Of the millions of tourists who visit the United States each year, the vast majority (20 million) come from Canada. The next largest source is Mexico (7.5 million), and then Japan (3.7 million).[51]

The greatest impact, however, is not by the people who visit the other country for a few weeks, but by those who remain. Although Americans immigrate to Canada and Mexico, and Canadians immigrate to the United States and Mexico, the heaviest movement of people in North America has been from Mexico to the United States. Except during the violence of the revolution, the flow was hardly noticeable in the early part of the century. When Congress debated the first law to limit immigration to the United States, a majority voted to allow Mexicans to come without restriction. Congress thought Mexico deserved special treatment as a neighbor, but they also did not think many would come. "Remember," Senator Alva Adams said in 1924, "Mexico is not a populous country. It is not teeming with millions of people eager to leave ... There will be no great influx if the border is left open."[52] The Mexican population explosion after the Second World War combined with a liberalization of US immigration policy in 1965 to make Adams' words seem ironic, at best. Most Mexicans living in the United States have arrived in the past two decades. More than 3.5 million Mexicans have legally migrated to the United States since 1981, representing roughly a fourth of all US immigrants arriving during this period (table 4.3).

The increase in numbers of immigrants understates their social impact. Whereas the total population of the United States grew by 13.2 percent in the last decade of the 20th century, its Hispanic population increased 57.9 percent (from 22.4 to 35.3 million) and its Mexican population by 52.9 percent (from 13.5 to 20.6 million). The new immigrants have transformed Southern California, Texas, and parts of the Southwest, but the 2000 census suggests that the immigrants have spread much more widely than ever

---

51. Barbara Crosette, "Surprises in the Global Tourist Boom," *New York Times*, 12 April 1998, IV5; and Earl H. Fry, *Canada's Unity Crisis: Implications for U.S.-Canadian Economic Relations* (New York: Twentieth Century Fund Press, 1992), 78.

52. *Congressional Record*, Senate, 18 April 1924, 6625.

Table 4.3 Legal immigration to the United States, total and North American, 1901-98 (thousands of people)

Period	World	From Mexico (percent of world)	From Canada (percent of world)	From North America (percent of world)
1901-20	14,531.2	268.6 (1.8)	921.4 (6.3)	1,189.6 (8.2)
1921-40	4,635.6	481.6 (10.4)	1,033.0 (22.3)	1,514.6 (32.7)
1941-60	3,550.5	360.4 (10.2)	549.7 (15.5)	910.1 (25.6)
1961-70	3,321.7	453.9 (13.7)	413.3 (12.4)	867.2 (26.1)
1971-80	4,493.3	637.2 (14.2)	114.8 (2.6)	752.0 (16.7)
1981-90	7,338.1	1,653.3 (22.5)	119.2 (1.6)	1,772.5 (24.2)
1991-98	7,605.1	1,929.7 (25.4)	112.5 (1.5)	2,042.2 (26.9)

Sources: US Bureau of the Census, *Statistical Abstract of the United States*, 1999, 1986, 1968, 1948, www.ins.usdoj.gov/graphics.

before. Although half of all Hispanics live in California and Texas, during the past decade the Hispanic population of Oregon has doubled; of Minnesota, tripled; of Georgia, quadrupled; and of North Carolina, quintupled.[53]

In July 2001, the Mexican government published a report, "Mexico's Population in the New Century," which gives estimates of the Mexican-origin population in the United States that are comparable to the data in the US census report—about 21 million people, of which 8.5 million were born in Mexico, and about 3 million are undocumented. Like the US census as well, the Mexican report concludes that the Mexican-origin population was concentrated in just four states with half in California. But signs of dispersal to other states, particularly in the south, were evident and, more interesting, that they were also coming from a broader cross-section of Mexico. Indeed, the Mexican census, on which much of the report was based, found that residents from more than 96 percent of all Mexican municipalities have contact with relatives in the United States, many of whom send remittances. The Mexican report expressed concern that an increasing percentage of its best educated people—about 6 percent of those who received college or postgraduate degrees—have moved to the United States.[54]

Remittances have played a more and more important role in the relationship between Mexicans in the United States and their relatives. The Central Bank of Mexico has been refining its techniques for estimating

---

53. Betsy Guzman, US Bureau of the Census, US Department of Commerce, "The Hispanic Population: Census 2000 Brief," C2KBR/01-3, May 2001.

54. See Consejo Nacional de Poblacion, "Migracion Mexicana hacia los Estados Unidos," http://www.conapo.gob.mx/RELEVANTE/migracion.htm. For a summary of this study, see Susan Ferriss, "An Altered View of Mexican Immigrants," *Atlanta Journal-Constitution*, 12 July 2001.

the total amount of remittances since the 1980s. In 1996, it estimated that $4.2 billion was remitted.[55] Mexico's National Statistics Institute (INEGI) estimated that the total amount of remittances sent by immigrants since 1994 was $29.2 billion. However, more than 80 percent is used for consumption. The most recent Mexican government report estimates that Mexican workers send their families about $17 million a day, and in 2000, that amounted to $6.2 billion—in the past decade, $45 billion.[56]

When the US economy declines, some Americans react negatively to new immigrants. In 1994, Californians strongly approved Proposition 187 to deny illegal migrants schooling or social services. This was not an unreasonable proposition, because illegal migrants were not supposed to be in the United States. But to deprive children of health services or education because of their parents' transgression is both socially and morally mistaken. Moreover, the campaign to secure the approval of the proposition was widely perceived in the Hispanic community as racist. The violence by Arizona ranchers against undocumented workers is still one more symptom of the social tensions that accompany a large movement of people. These crimes provoke an understandable and harsh reaction in Mexico. The social integration of the two countries raises many difficult and awkward questions that need national understanding and leadership. A true NAFTA ought to provide an umbrella under which many of these issues should be addressed. At the moment, it does not.

Let me introduce six dimensions of NAFTA's inadequacy. Then, in the next two chapters, I will develop proposals to respond to them.

- *Hijacking NAFTA:* To sustain any complicated agreement requires that its partners accept their respective obligations, but NAFTA has not been strong enough to preclude special interests, acting through a government, from violating its provisions (e.g., trucking, sugar, magazines).

- *Beneath NAFTA:* Eliminating legal barriers to trade also facilitated the illegitimate side of integration (e.g., smuggling, drugs, money laundering, undocumented workers, and illicit arms). NAFTA did not address this contradiction.

- *Beyond NAFTA:* The premise of NAFTA is that its members would consult and develop a strong relationship that would permit them to forge common policies—on the environment and labor and perhaps

---

55. For an explanation of the problems in estimating the amount of remittances and a summary of existing estimates for Mexico and other countries in Latin America, see Deborah Waller Meyers, *Migrant Remittances to Latin America: Reviewing the Literature* (Washington: Inter-American Dialogue and Tomas Rivera Institute, 1998), 4-5.

56. "Remesas de Migrantes Equivalen a 83 percent de la Inversion de EU en México," *La Jornada*, 30 October 2000. For the more recent estimate, see Ferriss, "Altered View of Mexican Immigrants."

on foreign and trade policy. There has been little, if any, progress in this area.

- *Disintegrative pressures:* As we have seen in Europe, the process of integrating diverse economies also generates countervailing disintegrative pressure—accentuating economic volatility, deepening regional disparities, and widening income inequalities—which can erode support for integration. NAFTA has not begun to address these problems.

- *Coalescing pressures:* Integration affects the debate in neighboring countries on issues that are seemingly unrelated to trade, such as taxes, health care, and even gun control. Sometimes, the debate is framed so that the differences between countries are accentuated and the relationship suffers. The question is whether a framework for consultation could influence the debate so that the countries would want to borrow policy ideas from each other.

- *Missed opportunities:* The incentive system of NAFTA encourages governments to look after their own interests, and it lacks any institutions that could help the governments forge *North American policies* or define a common agenda.

Hijacking NAFTA

The purpose of NAFTA was to expand trade, and it certainly accomplished that, but the increased competition led powerful, but embattled, interest groups to try to escape the agreement's restraints. Each government faced these pressures. By and large, the dispute-settlement mechanisms served to deflect many of these groups into litigation, but a few cases endangered the agreement. The most significant involves transportation.

Trucks carry 75-80 percent of the trade among the three countries.[57] To accommodate the increase in traffic and to try to obviate bottlenecks at the border, NAFTA set a date—18 December 1995—when Mexican and US trucks would be allowed to deposit their cargo within 20 kilometers of the other side of the border. Then, on 1 January 2000, Mexican and US trucks were supposed to be able to travel in each other's country without impediment. The United States did not meet either deadline. The US Teamsters Union pressured the Clinton administration to deny access to Mexican trucks, and the Mexicans retaliated by denying access to US trucks.

The Teamsters were trying to avoid competition, though they claimed they were primarily concerned about lax Mexican safety standards. The US General Accounting Office found that fewer than half of the Mexican

---

57. US General Accounting Office, *Commercial Trucking: Safety and Infrastructure Under the North American Free Trade Agreement* (Washington: US Government Printing Office, 1996), 16.

trucks met US safety conditions, but the Mexican government agreed to meet US standards. With the onset of the 2000 election campaign, and the importance of securing political support from the Teamsters, the Clinton administration refused to implement the NAFTA agreement on trucking. In January 2000, the Mexican government requested an arbitration panel to finally rule on the issue, and on 29 November 2000, a five-person panel (two Mexicans, two Americans, and a Briton) ruled unanimously that the United States had violated the agreement.[58] The United States then appealed, but the appeal was rejected on 7 February 2001.

The Bush administration promised to comply with the ruling. The Federal Motor Safety Carrier Administration devised and announced a plan on 1 May 2001 whereby Mexican trucks have to apply for permission to drive on US roadways. If they are approved, they will not be inspected each time they cross the border, but they will still be subject to spot and roadside inspections and an 18-month audit. The Teamsters pledged to fight, and in June and July 2001, they succeeded in persuading a substantial majority of both Houses of Congress to pass a bill that would prohibit Mexican trucks from using US highways, except under highly discriminatory safety standards. The Bush administration had pledged that Mexican trucking would have unimpeded access to the United States by the end of 2001, but it was uncertain whether it would be able to fulfill that promise.[59]

Transportation problems extend beyond the problem of trucks crossing the border. US shipments are stopped at the US side of the border, where a Mexican forwarding company arranges the paperwork and fees. Then a Mexican "drayage" ("cost of carrying wagon") company secures the trailer and transfers it to its final destination. But the procedure can include as many as seven tractor and trailer transfers for a single shipment. The same applies to Mexican trucks going north.[60] Whatever savings might have accrued as a result of the diminution of trade barriers have been more than offset by the staggering inefficiency of the drayage system, which may remain even if the trucking problem is resolved.

Were the Teamsters the only interest group compelling a government to deny its obligations under NAFTA, one would be less concerned about the agreement's integrity. But each of the three countries has powerful interest groups that seek ways to sidestep or sideswipe NAFTA. These groups tend to represent agricultural groups or industries that fear competition and can use their political leverage to compel the government to offer it some protection. Such groups represent a range of agricultural

---

58. "Mexico Wins Trucking Ban Dispute," *Houston Chronicle*, 30 November 2000.

59. Philip Shenon, "Teamsters May Stall Bush Goals for Mexican Trucks and Trade," *New York Times*, 30 July 2001.

60. Todd Drennan, "Where the Action's At: The U.S.-Mexican Border," US Department of Agriculture, Washington, photocopy (1999).

interests in the United States (sugar, fruit and vegetables, and softwood lumber), in Canada (dairy products, magazines, and cultural "products"), and in Mexico (agriculture, petroleum, and electricity). Some of these groups succeeded in excluding their products from NAFTA entirely; others are fighting rearguard actions. The principal instrument that these groups use to impede trade is Chapter 19 of the investment-dispute mechanism dealing with antidumping and countervailing duties.

The proliferation of these claims, and the fact that they occupy nearly 90 percent of all disputes, suggest that some review of the issues is necessary. Exporters assert that these claims are frivolous and protectionist, but there are two sets of legitimate issues that reside within Chapter 19 claims and that deserve a new approach: surging exports that are due more to undervalued exchange rates than to efficiencies or new technology, and divergent regulatory structures. In the first group of issues would be included Canadian steel or hog exports; in the second set, softwood lumber. The old system is not working. The three governments have a broad continental interest in preventing any single group from trying to escape the treaty's obligations, because whenever one succeeds, it encourages others. A new approach is necessary to deal with these issues.

Beneath NAFTA: Illegal Transactions and Unilateral Reactions

A decline in trade barriers means that it is easier for businesses to buy and sell goods across the borders, but it is also easier for smugglers. Illegal transactions—drugs, money laundering, illegal arms transfers, undocumented workers—increased proportionately with the legal trade. This is the dark side or the underbelly of integration, and it poses two challenges for the governments of North America, neither one of which has been mastered. The first problem is to identify a set of procedures that could inspect, detect, prevent, interdict, or seize the illegal item *without* creating too heavy a transaction cost on the legal exchanges. One study estimated that the cost in time delays, paperwork, and other surveillance adds approximately 7 percent to the cost of cross-border shipments.[61] Because this amount exceeds most tariffs that were eliminated, one might ask whether a tariff-free border is necessarily a less expensive one.

The agenda is not new—drugs, illegal migration, illegal arms transfers, or illegal transfers of prescription drugs—but the problems of interdiction are exacerbated as other barriers come down. Many of these problems cannot be solved, but they could be better managed, and that brings us to the second challenge. Old habits die slowly, and the United States has long approached each of these problems from a unilateral direction.

---

61. Cited by Michael Hart, "Disarming the 'Undefended Border' in Order to Preserve It: Canada, the United States, and Deepening Economic Integration," Ottawa, photocopy (February 2000), 38-39.

The United States has failed to learn that unilateralism is not only ineffective in dealing with a transnational problem; it also undermines a spirit of comity or partnership, which is the essence of NAFTA and of a more effective solution. The US Congress's insistence that it grade Mexico and other drug-producing or -transit countries each year on their cooperation is demeaning and precludes a change in the relationship from paternalism to partnership. Congress has continued to treat Canada the same way. That has not changed with NAFTA, but it should have.[62]

Beyond NAFTA: Third-Country Issues

One of the arenas in which Canada and Mexico have defined their identities has been in pursuing foreign policies that were different from those of the United States. Despite disagreements, the US government understood why Canada and Mexico needed to define themselves by their distance. A tacit understanding was reached during the Cold War: Canada and Mexico would not confront the United States in areas that were of vital importance—for example, both supported the United States during the Cuban Missile Crisis in 1962. And the United States would not make a big issue out of the differences—for example, Canada's and Mexico's close relations with Cuba. This understanding worked reasonably well over the years. Mexico's policies in Central America in the 1980s angered the Reagan administration, but Congressional Democrats were pleased that those policies made possible a negotiated settlement. Canada, more recently, took the leadership in negotiating the Treaties on Landmines and on the International Criminal Court. The United States opposed both initially and was miffed at Canada's aggressiveness. But by the end, the United States not only reconciled with Canada; the Clinton administration accepted both agreements.

On the other side of the equation, Canada and Mexico have been very upset by "third-country" or "extraterritorial" applications of US policies. The passage by the US Congress of the 1996 Cuban Liberty and Democratic Solidarity Act ("Helms-Burton") was severely criticized by both Canada and Mexico for provisions that bar the executives of companies that purchased property in Cuba once owned by US citizens (including those Cubans who subsequently were naturalized) from entering the United States and which allows US citizens to sue these companies in US court. US legislation to prevent any investments or trade with Iraq and Libya also contained third-country sanctions that disturbed the United States' two neighbors.

Such differences are natural among states, even friendly ones. The issue is whether the three governments of North America can or should

---

62. Robert A. Pastor and Rafael Fernandez de Castro, eds., *The Controversial Pivot: The U.S. Congress and North America* (Washington: Brookings Institution, 1998).

continue to define themselves differently in international forums while trying to forge closer relationships. At some point, these differences might make it difficult to construct a community. Therefore, the governments might want to consult on trade and foreign policy issues more systematically than they have in the past. To the extent that they can forge common policies, the prospects for a community would improve.

Disintegrative Pressures

When Europe decided on enlargement in the 1970s and 1980s, concerns were raised about the effect on poor countries, particularly over whether integration could provoke economic oscillation, inequalities, and regional disparities. Let us address the same question for North America.

It was a sad but potent coincidence that shortly after the US-Canadian trade agreement came into effect, in 1991, Canada suffered its worst recession since the 1930s. More than 450,000 jobs were lost, dissatisfaction with free trade increased, the value of the Canadian dollar fell, and the Progressive Conservative Party lost all but two seats in a humiliating defeat in the 1993 elections. The FTA did not cause the recession, nor did it lead to the defeat by the Conservative Party. But it was harmed by the same factors that caused these two—the combination of tight monetary and fiscal policies, the overvaluation of the Canadian dollar, the US recession, and the unpopular Goods and Service Tax introduced at the time.

The Canadian debacle was bad, but the peso shock was worse. In 1995, the Mexican economy declined 6.2 percent. Because of NAFTA and the expansion of an export-oriented manufacturing sector, the impact of the contraction of the economy was very uneven. Exports grew, but the domestic side of the economy, which represented 70 percent of GDP, declined by 14 percent.[63] Although manufacturing grew by 29.5 percent from 1993 to 1998, and manufacturing exports expanded by 154 percent during that period (from $41.6 to $105.9 billion), the number of jobs for skilled and unskilled workers actually declined, and their wages suffered. Skilled workers (according to INEGI) saw a decline in real wages during this period of 13.2 percent, and unskilled workers of 17.1 percent.[64] NAFTA, as we have noted, did not cause this crisis in Mexico, except in the sense that the reduction of investment barriers might have given Wall Street more encouragement than was deserved. But the absence of a sufficiently resilient and credible foreign exchange safety net made the crisis possible.

---

63. For an excellent analysis of the impact of the 1994 crisis, see Mauricio A. Gonzalez Gomez, "Crisis and Economic Change in Mexico," in *Mexico under Zedillo*, ed. Susan Kaufman Purcell and Luis Rubio (Boulder, CO: Lynne Rienner Publishers, 1998), 37-66.

64. Tom Philpott, "Boom and Gloom: Manufacturing Rises as Wages Fall," *El Financiero International Edition*, 14 June 1999, 3.

There is some evidence that NAFTA has contributed to regional disparities—which were already quite bad—in Mexico. About half of all domestic production is concentrated in Mexico City and the states of Mexico, Jalisco (Guadalajara), and Nuevo Leon (Monterrey). On the other side of the ledger, 25 of 32 states accounted for less than 3 percent of total domestic production. After the 1994 crisis, the disparities between regions became even more pronounced. Per capita income in the southern states of Chiapas, Guerrero, and Oaxaca is 62 percent of the per capita income of Nuevo Leon—roughly proportional to Southern Europe's income in relation to the EU average. An analysis of the eight regions of Mexico by the Confederation of Industrial Chambers of Commerce (CONCAMIN), using data from INEGI, concluded that the social and economic gap between the regions has widened since NAFTA. CONCAMIN called on the government of Mexico to develop regional policies and plans,[65] but the government did not respond, in part because austerity measures *reduced* the government's spending to about 16 percent of GDP, which is by far the lowest of any OECD nation. (In comparison, Argentina's expenditures amount to about 20 percent of GDP, the US proportion is about 40 percent, and Canada's is above that.)[66]

Another analysis of the geographical impact of NAFTA on Mexico found that it "expanded the gap between Southern and Northern states."[67] That study by Tamayo suggested that the gap was due to the impact of trade and investment on faster growth in the northern states. In the southern state of Oaxaca, Tamayo finds slower growth, but no growth in areas that were bypassed by NAFTA. He also notes that the railroad and road networks ignored the southern states and reinforced the power of the rich states. He finds an interesting dynamic in which the income per capita in the South increased somewhat because of illegal outmigration, whereas the sizable inflow of labor in the North resulted in a much more modest increase in income.[68]

Another study on foreign investment by Mexico's Center for Economic Teaching and Research (CIDE) found that 90 percent of the $54 billion in foreign investment in the country from 1995 to 2000 went to just four

65. Gonzalez Gomez, "Crisis and Economic Change," 55-56; Elvia Gutierez," Disturbing Trend Haunts Economic Development: Regional Disparities Are Alarming, *El Financiero International Edition*, 31 May 1999, 15.

66. Tom Philpott, "Cash Strapped: Tax System Flounders in Neglect," *El Financiero International Edition*, 5 July 1999, 3.

67. Rafael Tamayo-Flores, *The Differential Impact of International Integration on Local Economies: How Are Lagging Mexican Regions Performing?* Documento de Trabajo AP-77 (Mexico City: Centro de Investigación y Docencia Económicas, 2000), 21.

68. Rufino Tamayo, "Mexico in the Context of the North American Integration: Major Regional Trends and Performance of Backward Regions," *Journal of Latin American Studies* 33 (2001): 377-407. The rising income per capita was due to fewer people.

states—three in the North (Monterrey, Nuevo Leon, and Baja California) and one in the West (Jalisco). Conversely, six southern states received about 0.7 percent of the investment.[69] Luis Ernesto Derbez, Mexico's economy minister, estimated that during the 1990s, the export-oriented North grew at an annual rate of 5.9 percent, while the South barely grew at 0.4 percent.[70]

Income inequalities in Mexico are far more severe. Using its standard-of-living measurements, the World Bank estimated that in 1996, "roughly two out of every three Mexicans were poor, and one in three was extremely poor." Moreover, the 1994 crisis reversed the 10 percent reduction in poverty that Mexico had achieved in the previous decade.[71]

Canada's trade dependence on the US market increased from 75 percent in 1990 to 86 percent in 1999, and it also widened disparities between its provinces.[72] Newfoundland has been dependent on a declining fishing industry, and its per capita income is only about two-thirds of Ontario's. Unlike Mexico, however, Canada has an extensive system of transfer payments (welfare, social security, and federal tax transfers to provincial governments) and regional policies (development grants and subsidies) that together have narrowed differences in income and employment opportunities between the provinces.[73] The problem of volatility is more and more focused on the Canadian dollar, and the question is whether a unified currency with the United States would mitigate the swings.

Like Canada, the United States has an elaborate system of federal transfers that reduces the differences between the states. In addition, labor mobility is very high in the United States, as is evident from the large movement of people in the past two decades to the South and Southwest and the economic growth in those regions.[74] Both federal transfers and the labor movement smooth the disparities between regions.

From the early 1970s until 1993, the gap between rich and poor in the United States widened, and questions were raised as to whether this was

69. "NAFTA Heightens North-South Divide," *Latin American Weekly Report*, 5 April 2000, 4.

70. Henry Tricks, "Free Trade Still Rules in Mexico," *Financial Times*, 27 February 2001, 6.

71. Marcelo M. Guigale, Olivier Lafourcade, and Vinh H. Nguyen, *Mexico: A Comprehensive Development Agenda for the New Era* (Washington: World Bank, 2001), 13.

72. Hufbauer and Schott, *North American Economic Integration*, table 2, 5; Department of Foreign Affairs and International Trade, *Opening Doors to the World*.

73. See Michael Howlett, Alex Netherton, and M. Ramesh, *The Political Economy of Canada: An Introduction*, 2d ed. (Oxford: Oxford University Press, 1999), 107-08, particularly table 4 on provincial per capita incomes and transfers, and 309-11 on the government's regional development measures.

74. In one year, about 16 percent (43 million) of Americans moved from one home to another. This has remained relatively constant since the 1950s. Most move within the same state, although 6.4 million move to a different state. US Department of Commerce Bureau of the Census, "Moving Rate Among Americans," *News*, 19 January 2000, http://www.census.gov/Press-Release.

a consequence of increased dependence on trade. Most studies attributed the widening gap to technological improvements and disparities in education. The thesis that trade widened the gap between rich and poor was impugned by data in the mid-1990s. Between 1993 and 1998, as trade began to ascend, the income gap began to close. Family incomes in the lowest quintile rose at an annual rate of 2.7 percent, slightly faster than the 2.4 percent rate recorded by the top quintile. Similar evidence can be found in the broadly based growth in earnings since 1994. Moreover, of the new jobs created in the 1990s, 81 percent paid wages above the median. Finally, the proportion of Americans living in poverty declined from 15.1 percent in 1993 to 12.7 percent in 1998.[75]

So the evidence on the diverging effects of integration is mixed, but not inconsistent with what was learned from the European Union. The strongest economic power in North America experienced the least effect. The weaker countries suffered the most volatility, although this was also due to mistaken macroeconomic policies. The widest disparities in income and between regions was in the weakest country. Canada's policies—and, of course, those of the United States—demonstrate that income transfers among regions can mitigate these disparities and lift the country as a whole. That offers an important lesson for Mexico.

Coalescing Pressures

Governments that adopt public policies similar to those of their neighbors usually do so for two reasons—to improve competitiveness or to experiment with a better idea. As trade expands, and investment and jobs move in both directions, governments become more sensitive to their level of competitiveness. The principal way this concern plays out in the national debate is through taxes. Canadian taxes have been substantially higher than those in the United States, and businesses have long complained about that. As the conservative opposition began to gain support in Canada for its tax-cutting philosophy, in the fall of 2000 Prime Minister Chrétien gained Parliament's approval for a sharp reduction in taxes and then called for general elections, which he won.

During the health care debate in the United States in 1993-94, both those who wanted a universal system and those who opposed one men-

---

75. *Economic Report of the President 2000* (Washington: US Government Printing Office, 2000), 26-28. A Congressional Budget Office report suggests that the distribution of income among households grew more unequal between 1979 and 1997, but the tax code—particularly after the rise for upper-income levels in 1993—ameliorated that. The top 20 percent of households paid 57 percent of all taxes in 1979 and 65 percent in 1997. See Richard W. Stevenson, "Study Details Income Gap Between Rich and Poor," *New York Times*, 31 May 2000. Jagdish Bhagwati argues that trade may actually have reduced inequality in the United States. See his *The Winds of the Hundred Days: How Washington Mismanaged Globalization* (Cambridge, MA: MIT Press, 2001).

tioned the Canadian National Health system as an example. In that way, the policy of one country enters the debate in another. Still another example is gun control laws. Canadians have long expressed pride in their society's low level of violence as compared with the United States, and both Canadians and many Americans have attributed this to Canada's more restrictive gun control laws. In a study of Vancouver and Seattle—cities only 140 miles apart, but across a national divide—crime rates were similar in all respects except homicide. The risk of being killed was 65 percent higher in Seattle than in Vancouver, and the reason was the prevalence of handguns, which caused five times as many deaths in Seattle as Vancouver, where gun control laws were quite strict.[76] The irony is that a new conservative party emerging from the western part of Canada sought to repeal the restrictive gun control laws, believing that the right to own a gun so often asserted in the United States was one that they also wanted. They lost the election badly, and the 1998 Gun Control Act was implemented rigorously.

Nations rarely adopt the exact same policy of their neighbor, but groups within a democratic nation might very well seek ideas from across the border and insert it into their national debate. The federal experiment, in brief, can expand in a North American community.

The most expensive purchase of public policies, of course, occurred by Mexico. Salinas and his successors were well aware that their government's protectionist policies had led to economic stagnation and social injustice. They did not need to look to Asia for a model; they could have looked north of their border. They did not need to replicate the model of Canada or the United States, nor would it have been desirable to do so, but the government accepted the broad outlines of a deregulated, privatized, export-oriented democratic state.

Missed Opportunities

Despite the enormous growth of trade and investment in North America—and the consequent increase in the movement of goods and services—investment in transportation and infrastructure connecting the countries has lagged. The result is evident between Canada and the United States, but mostly on the Mexican-US border, where long lines—in both directions—spew increasing pollution and generate higher transaction costs. The problem is that Mexico invested in extravagant and often poorly designed toll roads during the Salinas administration (1988-94). These 23 roads charged such high tolls that few used them. After the 1994 peso crisis, they went bankrupt, and the government had to assume their debt of $7.7

---

76. John H. Sloan, Arthur Kellerman, Donald Rey et al., "Handgun Regulations, Crimes, Assaults and Homicide: A Tale of Two Cities," *New England Journal of Medicine* (1988), 319, cited in a study that elaborated on the causes of violence in the United States by Derek Bok, *The State of the Nation* (Cambridge, MA: Harvard University Press, 1996), 228-30.

billion.[77] To pay off its own mounting debt, Mexico has had to reduce its investment in infrastructure from a level of about 10 percent in the 1980s to less than 2 percent in 1998. As a result, every means of transportation—roads, rail, air, and ports—is beset with serious problems.[78]

The privatization of rail lines has permitted some new investments in Mexico, and the Canadian national railway proposed merging with one of the largest railroad companies in the United States. Instead of consulting with its Canadian and Mexican counterparts on how such a merger would relate to a continental plan on railway transportation, the US Surface Transportation Board simply imposed a 15-month moratorium on this and all rail mergers.[79]

None of the three countries has developed national plans for infrastructure and transportation, let alone North American plans. As we have seen, Mexico and the United States have been fighting over whether to permit their trucks to drive into their neighbor's territory. They have spent little or no time negotiating uniform standards on safety, inspections, braking systems, weights and dimensions of trucks, or limits on the time spent driving. To compound the problem, their regulatory agencies do not consult with each other.

*   *   *

There are many other areas in need of serious "North American" consideration. The three governments could negotiate a larger "swap" arrangement with Mexico and possibly Canada to prevent a run on their currencies. They could negotiate long-term programs on immigration, energy, competition policy, and a plan to reduce disparities within the entire area. These ideas will be developed in the next two chapters.

The brief review above of the challenges leads one to conclude that the problem with NAFTA is not what it was designed to do, but what it omitted. A North American Community is emerging at the social and economic level, but the governments are not leading. Indeed, most leaders in the three countries seem either fearful of or uninterested in the forces of integration that are reshaping the continent.

---

77. Jeff Ruster, *A Retrospective on the Mexican Toll Road Program (1989-94)* (Washington: World Bank, 1997), 1-3, http://www.worldbank.org/html/fpd/notes/125/125ruste.pdf; Economic News and Analysis on Mexico, "Federal Government Acquires 23 Financially Troubled Toll High Highways from Three Engineering Companies," Dow Jones Interactive Library, 3 September 1997.

78. World Bank, *Comprehensive Development Agenda for Mexico: Synthesis* (Mexico City, 2000), 1.

79. Anthony DePalma, "U.S. Regulators Impose 15-Month Moratorium on All Rail Mergers," *New York Times*, 18 March 2000, B1, 2.

5

A North American Community: A Proposal to Deepen NAFTA

> What the highway builders of North American regionalism perhaps need most is a few good surveyors who can take the lay of the land and give the highway engineers, as well as the future drivers, a feeling for what lies ahead.[1]
> —Charles F. Doran

Canada, Mexico, and the United States do not view themselves as parts of a region in the way that France and Germany view themselves as part of the European Union, but the idea of a European identity did not spring up fully formed in 1957. Indeed, even today, although most everyone living in France or Germany views themselves as French or German, they do not feel that they compromise their national identity by also viewing themselves as European.[2] Despite the differences in origins and paths between the two organizations, Europe's experience with integration during the past 40 years yields lessons that can facilitate the development of a North American Community.

The first, perhaps most important, lesson is that the European Community has succeeded because, like all great experiments, it began with an idea—that Europe could prosper only if it remained peaceful, which would only be possible if its sovereign states combined in a new cooperative entity. That idea was written into the preamble to the Treaty of Rome,

---

1. Charles Doran, "Introduction" to *A New North America: Cooperation and Enhanced Interdependence*, ed. Charles F. Doran and Alvin Drischler (Westport, CT: Praeger, 1996), xii.

2. Gary Marks, "Territorial Identities in the European Union," in *Regional Integration and Democracy: Expanding on the European Experience*, ed. Jeffrey A. Anderson (Lanham, MD: Rowman and Littlefield Publishers, 1999), 69-91.

and it has been repeated and expanded in subsequent treaties to inspire the people of Europe to embark on a great journey.

In contrast to Europe, North America is more market-driven, more resistant to bureaucratic answers, more pragmatic, and more respectful of national autonomy. Despite these differences, however, North America can learn from Europe on the importance of defining goals that inspire a unity of purpose and on the necessity of establishing institutions that can help translate these goals into cooperative policies. After identifying these goals and organizations, this chapter will offer three proposals: on infrastructure and transportation, trade policy, and macroeconomic policy coordination and the possibility of a common currency. These represent the spine (transportation) and the limbs (trade and finance) of a North American Community. In the next chapter, we will develop specific plans for customs and immigration, energy, regional development, and education. These issues are illustrative of the range of issues that a North American Community could address. We will then discuss the question of how North America should move from a free trade area to a Community of nations and peoples.

This proposal for a North American Community represents a formidable leap for three governments that have not even begun to look across the chasm, let alone consider jumping. In chapter 7, we will examine each government's reservations, and we will ask three questions: Are the plans developed in chapters 5 and 6 feasible? How can the governments be reorganized to increase the prospects for a partnership? And can the fears about the erosion of sovereignty be overcome? Remarkably, we will find that the public in all three countries is significantly ahead of its leaders—that in fact they are ready to consider more serious steps toward political union, provided that their quality of life would improve. Let us, however, start at the beginning.

In the Beginning:
Revising the North American Preamble

In comparison with the lofty declaration in Europe's founding treaty, the preamble to the NAFTA Treaty is written more like a business contract. The three governments resolved, in the NAFTA preamble, to "create an expanded and secure market ... reduce distortions to trade ... [and] enhance the competitiveness of their firms ..." In response to criticisms raised by unions and environmentalists, the negotiators inserted a pledge at the bottom of the preamble to enforce environmental laws and workers' rights, but the tenor of the language did not change. The governments acted as if they were three large corporations signing a contract to permit their businesses free rein to produce and trade cheaper and better goods.

The governments shortchanged their people by defining the North American relationship solely by commerce. The leaders should return to the drawing board and sketch a vision of the future and of North America's place in it. They have much with which to work. North American society is changing in ways that reflect a convergence in values and interests. Migration has melded all three countries, making Canada and the United States more genuinely multinational and also somewhat more like Mexico. Residents of North America visit each other's countries more than they travel anywhere else in the world. Cities, states, and provinces are becoming partners. Professional societies hold North American conventions. Canada's Museum of Civilization, the US Smithsonian Museum, and Mexico's Museo de Arte collaborated in early 2001 to create "Panorama: The North American Landscape in Art," an online art show exhibiting 300 landscape paintings by artists of the three countries.[3] Society—not government—is in the lead. It is now time for governments to articulate a modern definition of North America that goes beyond dismantling trade barriers and provides direction and added impetus to construct a North American Community.

What makes NAFTA unique in the world is the integration of a developing country with two industrial ones. This experiment is important not just for the people of North America, but for the rest of the world, because a central challenge of the 21st century is how to integrate developing countries into the modern world economy. So the issue for North America is how to assure that the integration is successful and becomes a model worth emulating by other regions. Can a framework of policy coordination be established that can anticipate and solve problems before they become sources of tension? Can it help governments view future opportunities with sufficient clarity so that they will quickly marshal their resources to seize them?

"Integration" can be defined as a process by which two or more parties come together to form a whole or a new relationship. This process usually involves exchanges of goods, people, and cultures. For integration to occur smoothly, the parties need to define the rules for the exchanges and institutions to manage and enforce the rules. Integration does not mean, for example, that the three official languages (and many "unofficial" ones) should be compressed into a single official language, but rather that the continent should permit space for all cultures and languages and offer incentives for people to learn and use each other's languages. Economically, it should mean that no region or group is excluded or left to stagnate. To the contrary, special programs should aim to lift those regions or groups so that they have a stake in their societies and in North America. With some leadership, it should not be difficult to draft a revised

---

3. See http://www.virtualmuseum.ca/panoramas.

preamble for a deeper NAFTA, because it can build on norms that have roots in all three countries. Those norms should include:

- respect for cultures, religions, and languages;

- a spirit of inclusiveness, openness, and reciprocity;

- a commitment to democracy, the fundamental rights of the individual, and the rights of individuals to associate with others in groups;

- support for a free market as the best mechanism to produce goods and services, but tempered by the obligation of the Community to assure that the distribution is not unjust, that disparities are reduced among peoples, nation-states, and regions, and that everyone has an equal opportunity to achieve his or her potential;

- the aim of achieving a wider Community in North America, one that respects the differences among peoples and nation-states and encourages experimentation among groups or states, but also one that provides incentives to approach collective problems with a common approach; and

- a commitment to fostering the free, unfettered movement of goods, services, capital, and eventually people, but also to assuring public security and the cooperative, coordinated enforcement of laws by officials of the three governments.

These ideas represent a rough outline of some of the goals that a deeper North American Community might pursue. Each norm or goal requires a fuller exposition, but let me here elaborate on the last one. Although the three countries were only getting used to the idea of a free trade agreement, Mexican President Fox proposed a common market with free movement of labor as well as goods, services, and capital. This is a bold idea, and not one that can be implemented anytime soon, and Fox has said as much. *But he is right to sketch a future picture of the trilateral relationship*, because this picture lifts the thoughts of those working on different bilateral or trilateral issues and helps people understand that the issues that concern them are related to each other—as they are. The precise nature of their relationship does not need to be decided now; indeed, the Europeans, who have been wrestling with these issues for 50 years, are still debating them and remain far from a consensus.

Nonetheless, what is lacking in North America is a picture of the future given by our leaders, and that is what the idea of a "Community" is intended to evoke. The governments should discuss this concept at both conceptual and practical levels. Over time, one hopes that the two levels will converge in forming a Community.

A consensus on general principles can provide a framework to guide the talks on specific policies. However, the proper way to define North

American goals would be through summit meetings of the three leaders, and ultimately through an assembly of the people's representatives.

North American Institutions

If the European Union's mistake was to establish too many institutions, NAFTA made the opposite mistake of failing to establish any that were serious. To grasp problems that are transnational or international, member states of a free trade area have two options: they can react to one crisis or dispute at a time, or they can establish an organization with the capacity to manage or solve problems before they become crises. NAFTA has adopted the first option, and we have seen its limits.

Before proposing new organizations for NAFTA, however, it is worth recounting why they do not exist. In most cases, strong countries tend to resist international organizations because they do not want to be constrained and because their relative power is greater in a bilateral context. This explains the reluctance of the United States,[4] but in North America, the two weaker countries, Canada and Mexico, have been equally cautious, albeit for a different reason. They believe that they could better pursue their interests in a bilateral context.

The historical evidence does not confirm this belief in bilateralism. Rather, it shows that most disputes take a long time to be resolved, and often leave the overall relationship worse than before. It would be far better to handle such disputes in a neutral, rule-based forum. This actually insulates nation-states from their own interest groups, while giving the groups a chance to petition for claims. Some recognize the power of this idea. Hart, a Canadian trade negotiator, analyzed the dispute-settlement mechanism and concluded that "the new, more binding procedures have helped the management of Canada-US relations," and that a rule-based mechanism is "highly desirable . . . for the smaller, less powerful partner."[5] Yet the leaders themselves are either reluctant to accept the need for organizations outside the trade area, or they simply lack the understanding or imagination to create them. And there is yet *another* powerful reason for *trinational* organizations: *They would permit NAFTA to be something more than the sum of two bilateral relationships.*

---

4. US policy in the 20th century has alternated between a narrow definition of its interests, when it views international organizations as constraints, and a more visionary approach, when it helped establish critical international institutions: the IMF, NATO, the OAS, the United Nations, the World Bank, and the WTO. See Robert A. Pastor, "U.S. Foreign Policy: Divided by a Revolutionary Vision," chap. 6 in *A Century's Journey: How the Great Powers Shape the World*, ed. Robert A. Pastor (New York: Basic Books, 1999).

5. Michael Hart, "The Role of Dispute Settlement in Managing Canada-U.S. Trade and Investment Relations," in *Canada Among Nations 2000: Vanishing Borders*, ed. Maureen Appel Molot and Fen Osler Hampson (New York: Oxford University Press, 2000), 107, 113-14.

The hesitation has some redeeming value. The EU experience teaches us to be wary of creating new bureaucracies. They grow, particularly in times of crisis, but rarely shrink, even though their time may have passed. The antidote, however, is *not* anarchy, but rather to carefully establish organizations with a clear need and mandate, a small staff, and a "sunset provision" of, say, 10 years, which would lead to a phaseout in the absence of a deliberate decision by the governments to extend its lease.

The first such institution to be established should be a North American Commission (NAC). It should be led by 15 distinguished individuals, 5 of whom would be appointed by each of the leaders of the three countries, for a fixed term. Together, they would select a chair, who would alternate, say, every 2 years. It should be staffed by a mix of civil servants and independent professionals designated by the three countries. Its mandate would be to develop a plan for the integration and development of North America.

This preliminary plan—or rather the outline of such a plan—should be developed within 6 months to serve as the agenda for the three leaders at a summit meeting. The plan should begin with a carefully crafted list of goals—along the lines of the revised preamble described above—together with a range of options for achieving these goals. In addition, the NAC might choose one sector—say, transport and infrastructure—and propose a plan. The three leaders, together with representatives from the national legislatures, should respond to the NAC's recommendations and then meet every 6 months to review progress toward its implementation. The NAC should supervise working groups and the NAFTA commissions on labor and the environment and instruct them with precise, operational objectives.

The NAC should have two offices to help prepare sectoral and continental proposals: an Office of North American Statistics to collect data from the three governments and research organizations, and a North American Planning Office to analyze the data. Working with appropriate ministries in the three governments as well as with universities and research centers, the NAC should draft papers on ways to improve cooperation and facilitate integration. It should also consider an explicit "regional policy" to reduce disparities within North America.

Lacking a planning body, the three governments were not prepared to respond effectively or quickly during the peso crisis in December 1994. Without a group whose job is to think about the interrelationship of issues, each government—or, more precisely, each ministry—would continue to deal with one issue at a time and fail to see the relationship between uneven development in Mexico and immigration and drug trafficking to the United States. The North American Commission should also serve as a catalyst for the three countries to coordinate selected domestic, foreign, and trade policies.

The NAC also should educate the public on the existence and potential of the region and seek to instill a sense of regional identity. It should try to alleviate anxieties about integration among certain groups and devise policies that respond to NAFTA-related problems. It should provide funding to establish Centers for North American Research and Studies in all three countries. These would be similar to the 10 European Union Centers that the EU funds in the United States. The NAC should also serve as the center of a network of NGOs, business and labor groups, and partnerships between cities and states or provinces and universities.

The North American Commission, in brief, would be very different from the European Commission. Instead of a large, supranational executive, managing the continent's affairs, the NAC would be lean, independent of the governments, and advisory to the three leaders and legislatures. Each leader would continue to rely on his own staff and Cabinet to prepare for meetings and manage relations. The NAC would provide a North American agenda and perspective, encouraging the leaders to take into account the other countries and to contemplate future opportunities and problems. Nor would the NAC be pulled into the business of proposing a tripartite industrial policy when no country is interested in one. But one hopes that over time, and as the three governments become more comfortable with the NAC, that they might delegate more responsibility and seek its advice more often.

Establishing such a Commission will require an act of statesmanship and a recognition that a quasi-independent advisory body is the only way for the three leaders to be drawn toward a common long-term agenda. But there are three other options. The first and most likely is the status quo because many leaders would be reluctant to establish a Commission, which they could not control. But the status quo is an ad hoc bilateral bureaucratic response, such as occurs regularly on immigration and drugs between Mexico and the United States, or on border management between Canada and the United States. This approach, however, tends to produce a narrow, short-term product.

The second approach would rely on a private commission of distinguished individuals established under the auspices of nongovernmental institutes in the three countries. The advantage of such a private commission is that it would be free to propose new ideas; the disadvantage is that it would be unlikely to engage the three leaders in the same way as an organization that they choose to establish.

The third approach would be a classic intergovernmental organization (IGO), a group established by the three governments, managed by its civil servants, and wholly responsible to the three governments. The model would be the European Commission, and it would report to the governments and have supervisory authority over NAFTA affairs. There are assets and liabilities to such an IGO, and in the long-term, this approach might be inevitable and desirable. But the leadership in the three governments do not appear to want to proceed down this path at this time, and a compelling case could be made for developing a new and different kind of system to respond to the unique needs of North America. The question, then, for the prime minister and two presidents is whether they want to raise "North America" to a new level and try to create a legacy that will shape future generations of North Americans. If the answer is "yes", then they need to establish a responsible, semi-autonomous, agenda-setting North American Commission to propose and monitor a plan.

The second organization should be a North American Parliamentary Group (NAPG), which would be composed of legislators from the Canadian Parliament, the Mexican Congress, and the US Congress. In fact, forming this organization only would require merging and revitalizing two existing parliamentary groups. In 1960, the US Congress established the US-Mexican Inter-Parliamentary Conference, and a few months later it did the same with Canada. These groups have met periodically since then, but they remain separate. As such, they reflect the dual-bilateral character of North America. If the three governments commit to North America, it would be logical to merge these two bodies.[6]

The NAPG would broaden the horizons of all three legislatures, but US border-state legislators, who have concentrated on US relations with either Mexico *or* Canada, would probably profit the most from the introduction of a third perspective. There are already some signs of interest by legislators in joining the two perspectives and groups. At the 40th Annual Meeting of the US-Canadian Inter-Parliamentary Group in Quebec in 1998, Val Meredith, a Canadian Member of Parliament from British Columbia, was asked to prepare a report on "Trade Corridors." She took the mandate seriously and explored not just US-Canadian border issues but also those between the United States and Mexico. The report analyzed the costs of not having a continental transport system and offered recommendations on what the three governments should do.[7]

Any serious attempt to coordinate policies on North American issues inevitably collides with the federal structures of the three governments. In Canada and the United States, and increasingly in Mexico, subnational governments have substantial power and autonomy. For that reason, the North American Parliamentary Group should set up "federal task forces" on different issues, involving provincial (and state) premiers (and governors) and legislators. Assuming that the NAPG concludes that a "North American Transportation Plan" is necessary, then each country first will

---

6. For an elaboration of this proposal, see Robert A. Pastor and Rafael Fernandez de Castro, eds., *The Controversial Pivot: The U.S. Congress and North America* (Washington: Brookings Institution, 1998), chap. 8.

7. See Val Meredith, M.P., *Trade Corridors: A Report to the Canada-U.S. Inter-Parliamentary Group* (Ottawa, 2000).

need to establish uniform procedures, and that will require gaining agreement among the states.

Another idea would be to organize groups from different regions of the country. There is already a Binational Association of Western Governors and Premiers from the United States and Canada, which began meeting informally a decade ago and now meets annually.[8] Governors from both sides of the US-Mexican border have also been meeting regularly. Both groups should be encouraged to meet with the NAPG as well as with the NAC to exchange ideas and concerns.

The third institution should be the Permanent North American Court on Trade and Investment. This would also involve upgrading the existing dispute-settlement mechanism. As we have seen, dispute panels have worked well, but they are running into problems due to their ad hoc nature. Because panelists are not well paid, it has proven more and more difficult to locate expert panelists who do not have a conflict of interest. Moreover, the case law that has accumulated during the past decade requires an investment of time that few people without a conflict of interest would have. That is why the time has come to establish a permanent court and appoint judges for extended terms. The court must also make its proceedings public, particularly on NAFTA Chapter 11 suits, because of the controversy that has swirled around corporate claims that affect environmental or other public policies. Some narrowing or clarification of the scope of Chapter 11 is also needed to reestablish the credibility of the panels and to prevent the erosion of environmental rules.

A fourth set of organizations would involve meetings of cabinet ministers. Since the late 1970s, each new administration in Mexico and the United States gave a new name to binational cabinet meetings. Initially, these meetings oriented ministers with domestic portfolios, but each then pursued his or her own agenda. Most viewed the binational commission meetings as they did cabinet meetings—as diversions from their work. This problem was compounded with the dual bilateralism of North America. These meetings might be more effective if the North American Commission were to set an agenda and to organize them.

One additional idea to promote a North American identity—or at least a sensitivity to the other countries' perspectives—would be to exchange personnel from the executive branch of each government and staff from the legislatures for tours of 2 or 3 years. To the extent that each government begins to look at the others as strategic partners rather than as objects of fear or suspicion, officials might begin to view their work in other governments' ministries as natural and as an opportunity to explore areas of cooperation.

---

8. "What Border? Together Canadians and Americans Are Redefining the Nature of Their Common Frontier," *Time/Canada*, 10 July 2000, 22-28.

A North American Plan for Infrastructure and Transportation

If the purpose of NAFTA was to reduce transaction costs in doing business between the three countries of North America, then it has failed. The reduction in the tariff barriers has been exceeded by the increase in costs due to delays at the border and bureaucratic impediments and duplications at both borders. "Crossing the border," concludes a May 2000 report by a Canadian member of Parliament, "has actually gotten more difficult over the past five years." The causes are twofold. "While continental trade has skyrocketed, the physical infrastructure enabling the movement of these goods has not." And second, the bureaucratic barriers that confront cross-border business make the infrastructural problems seem "minor in comparison."[9]

There are 64 different jurisdictions in North America that set regulations for trucks, and a study undertaken by the three governments under the auspices of the NAFTA Land Transport Standards Subcommittee concluded that "there is no prospect of developing complete consensus within North America on a common set of truck weight and dimension limits."[10] The announcement by senior officials that an agreement on a subject as important as the safety of trucks was impossible among the three countries is stunning. The elected leaders should have been embarrassed and would have been, if anyone had been paying attention.

The cost of failing to set uniform standards is exorbitant in terms of safety and cost. Ignoring the different regulations could lead to the deterioration of roads and bridges and endanger drivers and pedestrians. Or truckers could obey the rules, and that would mean that a truck could not travel between Canada and the US-Mexican border because it would be impossible to comply with dozens of incompatible rules.[11] Heavier, long-combination trucks that are popular in Canada and Mexico, for example, are not permitted on US highways.

The problems are actually more severe within the countries than between them. Double-trailer trucks traveling south on the midcontinental corridor from the Dakotas are not permitted in Iowa, and the Oklahoma-

---

9. Meredith, *Trade Corridors*, 8, 7, 10.

10. NAFTA Land Transportation Standards Subcommittee, Working Group 2, "Harmonization of Vehicle Weight and Dimension Regulations within the NAFTA Partnership," photocopy (October 1997), 2. The authors' frustration, if not parochialism, was evident in their comment that "there is no other field of public policy which is more complex than truck size and weight limits" (p. 1). For the number of jurisdictions, see p. 35. There are 51 state jurisdictions (including Washington, DC) in the United States; and 12 provincial ones in Canada; only Mexico has a single set of rules. For this section on transportation, I am especially grateful for the research assistance and papers prepared by Ben Goodrich and Mary Scott Pearson.

11. Meredith, *Trade Corridors*, 11.

based tractor semi-trucks weighing 40,825 kilograms are not permitted in Texas. And it is not just weight limits that prevent trucks from moving from one jurisdiction to another, but also truck configurations (height, width, number of axles). Moreover, the differing standards on sulfur content of diesel fuel can affect truck ignition systems, engine performance, and maintenance.[12]

On the border, the cost of delays is quite steep. The Canadian Trucking Alliance calculated that for every minute that all trucks are held at the border, an additional Cn$8 million is added to the direct costs of cross-border shipping. With an average delay at the most frequently used border crossing between Canada and the United States of about 20 minutes, that means additional costs of roughly $160 million.[13] The wait at the US-Mexican border is much longer, and the "drayage system" described in chapter 4—under which containers might be transferred seven times—adds a substantial hidden cost to commerce.

Subcommittees of NAFTA working groups have already prepared books of statistics on the roads, railways, seaports, and airports of all three countries, together with the number of vehicles, the amount of investment, and the description of the standards and regulations applied within each country. The data are impressive, and reflect, as we have come to expect, a major imbalance within North America. In 1996, Mexico had a total of 12.4 million vehicles, of which about two-thirds were cars and one-third were trucks and buses. Canada, with a population of one-third of Mexico's, had 17.2 million vehicles, of which about three-fourths were cars. The United States had 210 million vehicles, of which 68 million were light trucks and 7 million were commercial vehicles.[14] To put it another way, Mexico's fleet of vehicles was roughly comparable to that of Texas, whose population is one-fifth of Mexico's; and Mexico's highway network (242,000 kilometers, with only 49,000 of those classified as main or paved roads) is comparable to that of Kansas, which has just 5 percent of Mexico's population.[15]

From a policy and resource standpoint, the number of overlapping jurisdictions is such that none of the three countries has a national infrastructure and transportation plan, let alone a continental one. The United

12. Barry M. Prentice and Mark Ojah, "NAFTA in the Next Ten Years: Issues and Challenges in Transportation," Transport Institute, University of Manitoba, paper presented at the NAFTA in the New Millennium Symposium, University of Alberta, Edmonton (24-25 May 2001).

13. Meredith, *Trade Corridors*, 9.

14. US Department of Transportation, Statistics Canada, and Instituto Mexicano del Transporte, *North American Transportation in Figures*, BTS00-05 (Washington, 2000), table 12-1.

15. William R. Black, "North American Transportation: Perspectives on Research Needs and Sustainable Transportation," *Journal of Transport Geography* 5, no. 1 (1997), 12-19.

States has invested the most money at the national level, particularly in the past decade with two major laws—the Intermodal Surface Transportation Efficiency Act of 1991, which authorized $150 billion for 6 years, and the Transportation Equity Act for the 21st Century (TEA-21), which authorized $217 billion through 2003. The latter law included a Coordinated Border Infrastructure Program, which allocated about $140 million for both borders.[16] Canada did not have a national investment strategy for its roads since the construction of the TransCanada highway in the 1950s and 1960s. In 1997, the government determined that it would need Cn$16 billion in improvements just to meet the minimal engineering standards on its national highway system.[17] That figure was clearly out of reach, but in response to the US TEA-21 program, the Canadian Parliament in February 2000 decided to allocate $400 million for strategic highway infrastructure—starting in 2002.[18]

Mexico, of course, has the fewest and worst roads and infrastructure. After more than a decade of austerity programs, and a toll road system that went bankrupt, public investment in infrastructure investment fell from more than 10 percent of GDP in the early 1980s to less than 2 percent in 1998.[19] Mexico's private sector analyzed the country's infrastructure and concluded that it needed 34,000 more miles of highways, the expansion of 18 airports and a new one in Mexico City, and significant investments in telecommunications and energy. The total cost was estimated at about *$250 billion.* They hoped a substantial amount of the funds could be raised by the private sector.[20] This is wishful thinking, particularly because the country does not yet have a functioning banking system. The government, however, succeeded in privatizing both the railroads and the airports, and both are more efficient than ever before. One challenge is to build and maintain the roads to connect all the transportation modes.

The good news is that much of the data have been collected, and considerable research and analysis has been done. The overall objective was defined with clarity and conciseness by Meredith: "To ensure our continued economic growth, there is a need to plan, implement and

---

16. See Surface Transportation Policy Project, *Changing Direction: Federal Transportation Spending in the 1990s*, Executive Summary, March 2000, 5. Also see http://www.istea. org/guide/guideonline.htm.

17. Cited in Prentice and Ojah, "NAFTA in the Next Ten Years," 7.

18. Department of Foreign Affairs and International Trade of Canada, *Canada-U.S. Partnership: Building a Border for the 21st Century* (Ottawa, 2000), 37.

19. Marcelo Giugale, Olivier Lafourcade, and Vinh H. Nguyen, eds., *Mexico: A Comprehensive Development Agenda for the New Era* (Washington: World Bank, 2001), 2.

20. Isabel Becerril and Jaime Hernandez, "Big Needs: $250 Billion Investments Will Be Required for Infrastructure," *El Financiero International Edition*, 22 March 1999, 3.

finance a safe, seamless, integrated continental transportation system."[21] Although her mandate was only to examine the US-Canadian border, she insisted, quite properly, that Mexico should be an active participant, and that the provinces and private and nongovernmental groups should have a stake in the plan. The three governments should negotiate a *common set of safety standards* and *uniform regulations on weight and dimension*. As the NAFTA subcommittee noted, this is not as easy as it appears, but it is also not as difficult as is claimed. Design engineers in all three countries are well trained; their assessments seem to be based on different judgments as to the risks of damage to the trucks, roads, and particularly the bridges. This judgment is, in turn, related to the age of the roads in their country and the cost of investment. To a certain extent, it is also related to the weather. (In the northern climes of Canada, the spring thaw is a particularly fragile time for roads, and therefore the provinces set lower weight standards for trucks.) The engineering studies have been completed. The specific steps should be as follows:

- First, the three national governments should each develop uniform regulations on weight, safety, and configuration of trucking for each nation (perhaps allowing for a few exceptions in special areas, e.g., the Arctic) and then negotiate uniform standards for North America with the other governments.

- Second, the governments should agree to eliminate "cabotage" restrictions, which usually take the form of customs duties on the vehicle or prohibitions on the employment of nonresident drivers. These restrictions are pure protectionism, designed to discourage truckers from working across the border.

- Third, the governments should plan and finance new highway corridors on the Pacific Coast and into Mexico.

- Fourth, the regulatory agencies of the three governments should negotiate a plan that would permit mergers of the railroads in a manner that would serve the interests of the three countries. High-speed rail corridors should be considered between Canada and the United States.

- Fifth, the three governments should begin collaborating on inspections for immigration and customs. (This essential task will be developed in the next chapter.)

Another barrier that needs to be overcome is money. The cost of investing in infrastructure in Mexico is very high, considerably beyond Mexico's current capacity. The World Bank proposed an "infrastructure fund, per-

---

21. Meredith, *Trade Corridors*, 7.

haps in partnership with an international investment bank."[22] This idea will be developed in the next chapter.

Before too long, overland trade within North America will confront a barrier manned by bureaucrats and mined by flawed or inadequate infrastructure. This wall can be dismantled and demined only by a concerted effort of the three leaders. "If the 1990s were the decade of the free trade agreements," writes Meredith, "then the first decade of the 21st century should be the decade of the transportation agreements."[23]

Trade Policy—Within and Without

The proposed North American Commission ought to draft two papers on trade issues for the three leaders: an internal agenda and an external strategy. The first agenda would cover the trade issues that were either unresolved by NAFTA or have emerged since the agreement. It should also outline the steps that are needed to move the agreement to the next stage—that of a customs union. The second paper would explore the costs and benefits of the three governments adopting a unified approach to trade negotiations with other countries and the WTO.

The trade and investment barriers that remain in North America are the ones that were most difficult to negotiate. They have not become easier, but they have become more controversial. Among the issues that need to be addressed are uniform (or compatible) standards and labeling for products and processes; health and environmental standards, particularly for agriculture (genetically modified food, additives); harmonization of licensing requirements for professionals; coordination and harmonization of competition policies and other regulatory policies, which have cross-border effects; and coordination of inspections of agricultural goods. In some cases, harmonization is neither practical nor desirable, because of varying living standards and administrative capabilities. Instead, it might be better to seek to eliminate incompatible standards, rules, or labeling. With regard to government procurement, Hart estimates that *only* 25 percent of government contracts in Canada and the United States are subject to real competition, and it is less in Mexico.[24]

Agriculture remains the most difficult area for all three countries because of extensive government involvement and subsidies. In 1996, the US Congress passed a farm bill to remove government subsidies to its farmers. At the same time, the United States put increasing pressure on Europe to eliminate its farm subsidies, which averaged $40-50 billion a

22. Giugale et al., *Mexico*, 405.

23. Meredith, *Trade Corridors*, 13.

24. Hart, "Role of Dispute Settlement."

year. Then, the global market was glutted, and as the value of the US dollar increased, US crops were crowded out of many markets. The US government reinserted itself into the rural economies. By 2000, US farm subsidies totaled $28 billion.[25]

Mexico continues to protect its corn and seeks to limit imports from the United States of high-fructose corn syrup; the United States protects its sugar and vegetables; Canada, its dairy products. Canadian companies can harvest softwood lumber at very low prices set by the government, and US timber companies complain that the price represents a subsidy. In 1996, under threat of US suits, the Canadian government "voluntarily" restricted its exports. That agreement expired in March 2001, and US companies immediately requested countervailing duties of 78 percent on lumber imported from Canada.

None of the governments has shown much interest in trying to come to grips with the broader issue of how farming should be managed in North America in a manner that is fair to the farmers in all three countries and not too costly to the taxpayer. Moreover, for trade to be fair, Canada will have to deal with its monopolistic marketing boards, and the United States with its extensive subsidies to poor rural areas. Lacking the funds, Mexico cannot compete in the game of subsidies.

The softwood lumber issue will be argued in courts and trade panels by legions of lawyers; the victim could very well be the dispute-settlement mechanism. The alternative is for the two, or preferably three, governments to address the underlying problem—which is the unevenness of regulatory schemes. In the case of lumber, roughly 90 percent of the forests are owned by the provinces that sell the lumber to Canadian companies at very low fees, whereas in the United States, perhaps as much as 90 percent of the forests are owned by large and small private firms, and the price is set in the marketplace. This means that the price of US lumber has been much higher than that of Canadian lumber.[26]

One solution would be to privatize Canadian forests. A second would be for the US government to nationalize the private forests. Acceptance of the other's regulatory and ownership system would solve the problem, but neither is feasible. A third idea would be to allow all private foresters, including foreigners, to bid freely on the timber in the Canadian forests. This might lead to a higher price for Canadian lumber, and if so, it would

---

25. See Timothy Egan, "Failing Farms Learn to Profit from Wealth of U.S. Subsidies," *New York Times*, 24 December 2000, 1, 16; and Edmund L. Andrews, "No Agreement on Reducing Europe Farm Subsidies," *New York Times*, 27 February 1999, B1, 2.

26. See Patti Bond, "Canadian Timber Deals to Be Probed," *Atlanta Journal-Constitution*, 25 April 2001; Anthony De Palma, "Lumber Dispute Threatens U.S.-Canada Ties," *New York Times*, 28 March 2001; and Jimmy Carter, "A Flawed Timber Market," *New York Times*, 24 March 2001, A27.

solve the problem, at least for a time.[27] Given the expanse of British Columbia's forests, this formula, however, is unlikely to lift the price to US levels, and the only US buyers of timber would be large logging firms. Small farmers would still be hurt. Still, a fourth solution would be to replicate the 1996 voluntary export restraint agreement with two modifications: allow the stumpage fee price in Canadian forests to rise gradually, and permit exports of timber from Canada to increase marginally each year. This would encourage an adjustment by both markets.

A significant element of the timber problem—and, for that matter, many other trade problems—is due to foreign exchange rates. As long as the Canadian dollar sells for about two-thirds (65 cents) of the US dollar, Canadian exports will remain cheap, and a surge is likely to have dangerous effects, evoking threats of countervailing duties or antidumping from the United States. If the currencies were in better alignment, protectionist pressures would diminish. In the next section, on macroeconomic policy coordination, we will explore several ways to address this underlying issue.

The "trade remedies" of countervailing duties and antidumping (CVD/AD) have been the source of many trade-related problems within NAFTA and with the other US trading partners. Indeed, one reason for the fiasco at the 1999 WTO talks in Seattle was the Clinton administration's refusal to consider these issues. Whether or not one agrees that CVD/AD are legitimate subjects for global trade talks, it seems improper not to discuss them with our NAFTA trading partners. The truth is that both Canada and Mexico have also begun to use these remedies, and therefore this might be the best moment to consider negotiating a formula for disarmament.

Beyond the internal trade issues, should the three governments of North America adopt a common approach to negotiating the Free Trade Area of the Americas or with the WTO? It would not be easy to reach agreement on a unified trade policy, and it might take some time. However, once the three governments agree to a common external tariff and a customs union, they would have traveled a good distance toward defining common interests in trade policy as they relate to the rest of the world.

Since NAFTA came into effect, Mexico has negotiated nine free trade agreements and Canada has completed three bilateral agreements and is negotiating others. The United States, for its part, has approved preferential trade regimes for the small Caribbean Basin countries and the weak governments in Sub-Saharan Africa, but Congress has not granted the president authority to negotiate on a fast-track basis, and this has inhibited definitive negotiations with Latin America for the Free Trade Area of the Americas.

---

27. I am indebted to Gordon Giffin for this idea. Conversation in Atlanta, 1 June 2001.

This haphazard process is frustrating when it is not completely counter-productive, but the question is whether the three governments would not be better served with a common approach. The disadvantage is the one inherent in any international obligation—that is, it constrains choice. For Canada and Mexico, which are concerned about their increased dependence on the US market, it is understandable that they would want to diversify their trading relations with other important countries. This should not bother Washington. There is a *second issue*—how to deal with countries like Cuba and Libya—in which the three countries have markedly different policies. Assuming that it would be more difficult to reach a meeting of the minds on these issues, these countries or issues could simply be exempted from the rest of the agreement.

The advantage of a unified approach, however, is that it would give North America leverage and credibility. Canada and Mexico both have established their autonomy and effectiveness in international forums, and the United States, of course, as the largest trading power in the world, has its own influence. Together, they assemble the perspectives of the three tiers of the international trading system—the highest level; the mid-level for advanced market economies; and what Jeffrey Garten refers to as the "big emerging markets." To the extent that all three governments can integrate their approaches, they could, in effect, act as a surrogate of the entire international system. And the benefit therefore would accrue not just to them, but to all, because—as the world saw in Seattle—the World Trade Organization with its 142 members may have reached the size at which negotiations prove extremely difficult, if not impossible. If North America can negotiate these problems, their formula might be adopted by the WTO.

Macroeconomic Policy Coordination and the "Amero"

As an increasing amount of trade among the three countries is done with the US dollar, and as other countries in the Americas adopt the dollar or peg their currencies tightly to it,[28] some businesspeople in Canada and Mexico also have begun to propose adopting the dollar. Most political leaders, however, are either opposed or show little interest.

At a discussion of this issue in 1998, Thomas Courchene, a Canadian economist, explained to Paul Martin, his country's finance minister: "With so much trade going to the United States, we simply cannot tolerate the

---

28. Panama has used the dollar since 1903; Argentina has pegged its peso to the dollar. Ecuador adopted the dollar in February 2000, El Salvador in January 2001, and Guatemala in May 2001. In the most incongruous case of all, Cuba has more and more used it as their currency.

degree of exchange rate variability we've had over the last decade and a half." Martin responded vehemently: "That is not what NAFTA is all about. NAFTA is a trade agreement. It is one thing to contemplate a united Europe consisting of some 20 odd countries—a number of which are of equal size. It's quite another to contemplate that in terms of North America where you would have one very large dominant country and two much smaller ones." John Kirton of the University of Toronto agreed: "There's no way Canadians would go for it as a matter of symbolism, sovereignty, and a matter of history." Courchene insisted on the need to discuss the issue, given the cost of exchange rate variability to the Canadian economy, but he conceded that it might be impractical at the current time, even in the United States: "Americans love to devolve sovereignty to the markets. But not to anybody else."[29] This captures the sounds of a debate that has just begun.

The current US position on "dollarization" for other countries is neutrality.[30] One could argue that is not a bad approach. If the United States were to promote the dollar vigorously as the single currency, our two neighbors would probably react as negatively as they did when the United States first proposed free trade agreements. As Hart put it: "The combination of US chauvinism and Canadian paranoia dictates than any initiative must emanate from Canada."[31] The same argument applies to Mexico. It would be better if the two governments approached the United States first, but it would also increase the prospects for success if the United States were prepared to be flexible in its response. The law requires that US monetary policy should not be diverted from its task of assisting the US economy, but officials could offer to discuss privately its ramifications with counterparts in Canada and Mexico.

Dollarization, of course, is only one way to adopt a common currency. Because it raises sensitivities about sovereignty, one might usefully return to the original question regarding its purpose. Those countries, such as Argentina and Ecuador—which have linked or replaced their currency for the dollar—have done so because they were traumatized by hyperinflation, or feared financial volatility. In that sense, the dollar is intended to serve a role similar to that of the gold standard—as an anchor that

29. Norma Greenway, "Is a 'North American Dollar' the Best Option for Canada? Finance Minister Quickly Dismisses Idea of Single Currency for Continent," *The Ottawa Citizen*, 8 August 1998.

30. See the testimony by US Assistant Treasury Secretary Edwin M. Truman to the Senate Banking Committee, 8 February 2000. He incorporates remarks made previously by Treasury Secretary Lawrence Summers. Truman said: "We do not have a view on whether dollarization is advisable in general."

31. Hart, "Role of Dispute Settlement," 24.

prevents political leaders from overspending, or as protection against being buffeted by gale-force financial winds.[32]

There is a second reason to consider a common currency that more nearly corresponds to Europe's decision to adopt the euro. When countries experience a high rate of integration, and trade liberalization is already advanced, the exchange of currencies can become a serious transaction cost. For Canada and Mexico, which export about a third of their output to the United States, dollarization, according to Bergsten, ought to be considered seriously to minimize the costs of trade.[33] Although neither Mexico nor Canada has experienced hyperinflation, both have suffered from foreign exchange costs and crises. The peso crisis of December 1994 shrank Mexico's economy so much that even after 4 consecutive years of 5 percent annual growth, it still had not fully recovered. And Canada has witnessed a continuous, generation-long depreciation of its currency against the US dollar. The question posed by Gibson, a Canadian commentator, is whether there is "a way of ending the pattern of significant long-term decline that has been the fate of the Canadian dollar over the past generation with the subsequent international erosion of Canadian wealth."[34]

At a theoretical level, the benefits and costs of dollarization are relatively clear-cut. Advocates judge that the principal benefit for the country adopting the dollar would be financial stability. But foreign investment would also probably increase; the cost of borrowing would decline as access to the dollar market widened; the cost of doing business and trade would decline as firms used a single currency and did not need to hedge against other currencies; fiscal discipline would be steadier; and, to the extent that inflation were reduced, the lives of the poor would improve.

Opponents of dollarization argue that governments would lose sovereignty, seigniorage (the profits from printing money), and a "shock absorber" in times of crisis (in the event of a decline in the prices of commodity exports, a rise in interest rates, or the disappearance of investor confidence). A government might keep its prices stable, but it would deny itself a tool to combat recessions and unemployment. Indeed, a major concern of dollarization is that a government would transfer its power to respond to its own business cycles to the United States, whose Federal Reserve is mandated by law to set interest rates only in response to US

---

32. The costs of being tied down may be very high, as Argentina discovered in 1999-2001.

33. C. Fred Bergsten, "Dollarization in Emerging-Market Economies and Its Policy Implications for the United States," testimony before the US Senate Finance Committee, 22 April 1999.

34. Gordon Gibson, foreword to *The Case for the Amero: The Economics and Politics of a North American Monetary Union*, by Herbert Grubel, Critical Issues (Vancouver: Simon Fraser Institute, 1999), 2. See also "Cheap Dollar Is Making Canada the Land of the Spree," *New York Times*, 1 August 1999, 11; and James Brooke, "Is the Dollar Leaving Canada Feeling Drained?" *New York Times*, 13 November 1999, B1.

economic cycles.[35] Of course, Congress could expand the mandate of the Federal Reserve to take into account the economic cycles of its two North American neighbors, and it could establish two new Federal Reserve districts in Mexico City and Toronto.[36]

An alternative would be to establish a new currency. That, of course, is the point of the euro, and that is the essence of a proposal developed by Grubel in a paper for the Simon Fraser Institute in Vancouver. He makes the case for a North American Monetary Union with a central bank and a common currency, which he dubs the "amero."[37] The board of governors would be chosen by the three governments in proportion to their country's population and income. The mandate of the Central Bank of North America would be similar to that of the European Central Bank—to maintain price stability rather than full employment—but it would respond to the economy of the continent rather than just of one nation. The amero would be equivalent to the US dollar, and the Canadian and Mexican currencies would be exchanged at the rate that they are then traded for the US dollar. In other words, at the outset, prices, incomes, and wealth in all three countries would be unchanged, and the power to manage the common currency and earn profits from printing it (seigniorage) would be roughly proportional to the existing wealth of the three countries. The United States would share some of its decision making, and its goals would be continental rather than just national prosperity, but it would remain as economically dominant as today.

Grubel's main arguments are directed at a Canadian audience. He believes that flexible exchange rates "have contributed to poor economic performance," price instability, and lower incomes in Canada. A common currency, in his view, could lower long-term interest rates, expand trade, and enhance productivity in Canada without compromising cultural sovereignty and political independence. He acknowledges that the United States "has less to gain" from the union than do Canada and Mexico, except that it would benefit considerably "from having more stable and

---

35. For a full discussion of these issues, see Andrew Berg and Eduardo Borensztein, *The Pros and Cons of Full Dollarization*, IMF Working Paper WP/00/50 (Washington: International Monetary Fund, 2000); Ricardo Hausmann, "Should There Be Five Currencies or One Hundred and Five?" and Jeffrey Sachs and Felipe Larrain, "Why Dollarization Is More Straitjacket than Salvation," *Foreign Policy* (Fall 1999); Federal Reserve Bank of Atlanta, "Responding to Global Crises: Dollarization in Latin America," *EconSouth* 1, no. 2 (1999); and Robert Mundell, "Threat to Prosperity," *Wall Street Journal*, 30 March 2000, A30. Mundell, a Nobel Prize winner for his concept of the "optimal currency," writes: "The biggest danger to world prosperity arises from wide swings, not based in any economic fundamentals, in the exchange rates of these three [dollar, euro, yen] currencies." He argues for a single world currency and central bank, but in the interim, combining the currencies and managing them better.

36. I am indebted to Fred Bergsten for this idea.

37. Grubel, *Case for the Amero*.

prosperous countries as neighbors." This is a significant proposal, but also one that will take substantial time for the elites and the public to digest and consider seriously.

Grubel's argument has resonated in Mexico, where his paper was adapted, translated, and published as a book,[38] but it will be very hard for Americans to give up the dollar even for an instrument that is its equivalent in everything but name. The strongest argument in favor of the idea is that it is "fair" in the US sense of that term; that is, it does not alter the relative power equation in North America, but it provides space for our neighbors to participate in decision making. That is the essence of the idea that Woodrow Wilson and Franklin D. Roosevelt captured in the international organizations that they designed.[39] That is why, in the long term, one would be mistaken to dismiss this idea, even while recognizing that it stands little chance of acceptance any time soon. In the long term, the amero is in the best interests of all three countries.

There are other options. The most likely course is inaction. As trade expands, businesses in Canada and Mexico are more and more using dollars. Foreign currency deposits—almost all US dollars—in Canadian banks have ballooned from 27 percent of total deposits in 1995 to 52 percent in 1998. In other words, Canadian banks hold more US dollars than Canadian dollars on deposit.[40] Similarly, a poll in May 1999 asked Mexicans whether they wanted to have US dollar accounts in their country, and 86 percent responded positively, although they were more ambivalent about replacing the peso with the dollar.[41] Over time, it is possible that so many Canadians and Mexicans will use dollars that "de facto dollarization" might save their political leaders from having to make a difficult decision.

In the short term, however, complacency with the status quo is unwise; there have been too many abrupt crises in Mexico and too much creeping deterioration in Canada. At the minimum, the three central banks should share more information and expand their swap arrangements to help each other in the event of a crisis. The United States has had a swap

---

38. Herbert G. Grubel, *El Amero: Uno Moneda Comun para America del Norte*, adaptacion para Mexico y actualizacion por Manuel Suarez Mier (Mexico: CIDAC y Cal y arena, 2001).

39. For an elaboration of this thesis, see Robert A. Pastor, ed., *A Century's Journey: How The Great Powers Shape the World* (New York: Basic Books, 1999), especially chapter 6 on US foreign policy.

40. Eric Beauchesne, "Greenback Is Shoving Loonie Aside," *The Ottawa Citizen*, 13 July 1999. See http://www.ottawacitizen.com/national/990629/2548950.html. This percentage may be high. The Bank of Nova Scotia and the Canadian Imperial Bank of Commerce, two of Canada's six largest banks, reported that 37 percent and 41 percent, respectively, of their deposits were in dollars in 2000. (I am indebted to Michael Chriszt of the Federal Reserve Bank of Atlanta for this information, 14 June 2001).

41. Julia Preston, "Mexico Measures Identity in Dollars," *New York Times*, 16 May 1999, 16.

arrangement with Mexico since 1941, in which the US Treasury through the Exchange Stabilization Fund (ESF) provided injections of dollars at critical moments to stabilize the Mexican peso. There is little evidence that this exercise succeeded, in part because the amounts were quite small.[42]

In April 1994, Canada, Mexico, and the United States negotiated a little-noticed North American Framework Agreement (NAFA), which included low-level consultations and a swap arrangement involving the US Treasury and Federal Reserve, the Bank of Canada, and the Central Bank of Mexico. The agreement had to be renewed annually, and the amount was paltry. NAFA only contained $6.8 billion—$3 billion from the Fed, $3 billion from Treasury's ESF, and $800 million from Canada. When the peso crisis struck, NAFA was much too small to have any impact. In the end, the United States had to assemble a $55 billion rescue package, of which $20 billion came from the ESF. NAFA was extended for 1 year, the Canadian contribution was increased to $2 billion, and the Bank of Mexico agreed to set aside $3 billion for it. That nearly doubled the fund to $11 billion, but that amount was still trivial as compared with the magnitude of the capital flows in and out of Mexico each year.

It is true that as long as Canada and Mexico have flexible exchange rates, the buffer fund does not need to be that large. But the intensity of integration among the three countries is such that the size of the fund is as important for psychological as for economic reasons. There was some recognition of that fact when the Mexican government negotiated a standby arrangement with the IMF in advance of the 2 July 2000 elections for $16.9 billion—just to help it through the transition.[43]

Whether the governments discuss the amero or dollarization or beefing up the swap arrangement, they should explore ways to mitigate the financial volatility that endangers all three economies. That may mean high-level and routine consultations and, to the extent possible, coordination of their macroeconomic policies. Eventually, the governments should adopt disciplines that could reduce the divergence in inflation, interest rates, and fiscal balances. Absent such steps, movement toward a unified

---

42. See Anna G. Schwartz, *From Obscurity to Notoriety: A Biography of the Exchange Stabilization Fund*, NBER Working Paper 5699 (Cambridge, MA: National Bureau for Economic Research, 1996). The ESF was established in 1934 to bring stability to the currency markets. Schwartz discovered that Mexico had the longest record of ESF agreements, but she doubts that these or the ones with other governments have succeeded in stabilizing the markets: "The message of the loan packages seems to be that mismanaged countries have a friend at the ESF, which will arrange a rescue" (21). The Federal Reserve also had an arrangement with Mexico since 1967. I am indebted to Ted Truman for his comments on this section.

43. Secretario de Hacienda de Mexico, "Mexico Sends a Letter of Intent to the IMF," 15 June 1999, http://www.shcp.gob.mx/english/iro/. The letter also includes a reference to NAFA. For the agreement's extension, see http://www.federalreserve.gov/fomc/minutes/20000516.htm.

currency might actually exacerbate the financial differences. At the outset, such consultations might involve periodic meetings of senior budget and financial officials of all three governments. In a North America defined by a genuine partnership, a joint statement by these senior officials could have a positive effect on a government whose policies were veering off course toward a bloated fiscal deficit or an appreciating currency.

6

A North American Community: Sectoral Plans

Many of the challenges facing the three countries of North America are related to or entangled with each other. The relationship between legal and illicit trade is obvious: if you facilitate the first, you also get more of the second. If you try to impede illicit traffic, you also delay legal trade. The relationship between migration from Mexico and income disparities between that country and its northern neighbors is also clear. Until the disparities are reduced, the flow is likely to remain at a high level. There is also an insidious link between special interests trying to evade NAFTA's obligations and the spirit of partnership implicit in the agreement. The more governments succumb to special pressures the less likely they will maintain a good relationship or preserve the integrity of the agreement.

The failure to understand the relationship between these issues condemns the three countries to repeat old dysfunctional patterns of relating to each other. In this chapter, we will explore new "North American" ways to deal with old problems like customs and immigration, energy, regional development, and education. These issues have a curious relationship. Unless customs and immigration are managed more efficiently, the costs of doing business across the border will rise. Mexicans and Canadians have long been concerned about US immigration policy, whereas the United States has raised the energy issue with both governments. Instead of a trade-off, the two issues seem stalemated. Instead of confronting these issues head-on, I propose an alternative, Zen-like strategy of solving them by concentrating on a separate problem—regional development. After examining each issue, I will suggest priorities for a strategy to lift NAFTA and put it on the road to a North American Community.

Customs, Enforcement, and Immigration: The Border and the Perimeter

Along both borders, the three governments inspect vehicles, question travelers and migrants, and try to ferret out criminals, terrorists, and drug traffickers. It is very hard to judge the effectiveness of these operations, although it is quite easy to see the consequences when traffic slows at the border, or when one government acts unilaterally to stop traffic. The question is whether there is a more effective way to manage traffic.

Since 1993, the United States has more than doubled the size of its border patrol, more than tripled its budget for the Immigration and Naturalization Service (INS), and used the new funds to build more fences and sturdier barriers than ever before.[1] How can one measure progress? If border guards seize more illicit goods, is that a sign that the problem is getting worse or that interdiction is getting better? There is a similar problem with regard to illegal migration, but there are also some signs that the effort is having some effect. The border patrol, according to the *New York Times*, "all but shut down the routes along the traditional border jumping towns of San Diego, El Paso, and Laredo, Texas." As a result, fewer migrants are taking more dangerous routes through the deserts of Arizona, and an increasing number of migrants are losing their lives— 491 in 2000—to dehydration in the desert, freezing in the mountains, or shootings by angry ranchers. The border patrol arrested 272,397 people in the Tucson area in 1997, but that number tripled by 2000 before more border agents and better technology were sent there. As a result, in the early months of 2001 there were 25 percent fewer apprehensions in the same area. A second sign that the crackdown was working was that the price paid to the "coyote" (smuggler) for the illegal trip increased from $650 in 2000 to $800 in 2001.[2] Some believe that this crackdown actually increased the illegal population in the United States, because migrants who had previously gone back and forth are more reluctant to return. Moreover, the United States pays a price for its stringent border enforcement in its relations with Mexico. President Fox, more than his predecessors, has insisted that Mexicans—whether in his country or in the United States, legal or not—be treated respectfully and equally. He has described immigrants as "heroes."

Beginning in August 2000 with his meetings with George W. Bush and Al Gore, Fox alerted the United States that the issue of immigration would be among his highest priorities. In February 2001 in Guanajuato,

---

1. Carnegie Endowment for International Peace and Instituto Technológico Autonomo de México, The U.S.-Mexico Migration Panel, *Mexico-U.S. Migration: A Shared Responsibility* (Washington: Carnegie Endowment, 2001), 7.

2. Charlie LeDuff, "A Perilous 4,000 Mile Passage to Work," *New York Times*, 29 May 2001, 1, 16.

Presidents Fox and Bush agreed to set up a high-level group led by their foreign ministers and attorneys general to make sure that immigration would be "an orderly process that guaranteed humane treatment of migrants." The binational panel considered issues of border safety, temporary-worker programs, legalization of undocumented Mexicans, expansion of permanent migration, and regional economic development. On 22 June 2001, the cabinet secretaries issued a joint communiqué proposing cooperative strategies to warn Mexicans of the danger of crossing the border, to provide better searching for and rescue of those who are endangered, to cooperate to prevent the smuggling of migrants, and to initiate a pilot program of nonlethal weapons use by the US border patrol.[3]

These policies represented substantial changes by each government. In previous years, when the United States had asked for help in stopping the illegal flow of people, Mexico said its Constitution precluded discouraging its own citizens from leaving. But under Fox, the government has established a Grupo Beta force of border agents, whose mission is to discourage illegal migration and arrest people-smugglers. Moreover, the government has instituted a tough advertising campaign warning people of the dangers.[4] The US government also has made concessions, instructing its border patrol to be sensitive to illegal migrants and to consider using nonlethal weapons.

The United States has fewer border-related immigration problems with Canada than with Mexico, but there are some. Congress passed Section 110 of the Immigration Act of 1996, which requires the INS to keep track of everyone leaving the country as well as entering it. Because of strong protests from Canadians, who feared that this would cause even worse traffic delays, the United States temporarily suspended implementation of this provision. Many groups on both sides of the border joined and succeeded in modifying that provision with the INS Data Management Improvement Act of 2000, which improves tracking of border crossings without increasing documentary requirements.

There is one way to reduce simultaneously the delays at the border and the tensions among the governments regarding border traffic. *The three governments should develop common forms and a single "North American Customs and Immigration Force."* This force would be composed of immigration, customs, and law enforcement officials from all three countries. They would be trained together in a North American professional school, and instead of working on both sides of each border, they would work together on the border. This would reduce by at least half the paperwork and the delays. The force should also be used on the perimeter of North

---

3. See Eric Schmitt, "Measures Aim at Violence Along Border," *New York Times*, 24 June 2001, 15.

4. Susan Ferriss, "Mexico Bets Fear Can Curb Migration: Videos Describe Border's Risks," *Atlanta Journal-Constitution*, 11 July 2001, A6.

America, where illegal goods and drugs are most likely to enter. Terrorists and fugitives would no longer have a safe haven; law enforcement officials would be able to track them in all three countries. There are no simple answers to stopping drugs and money laundering, but such a force could permit these problems to be managed better with a positive effect on the trilateral relationship.

There are many other ways to manage the border problem, and there are experiments under way on the US-Canadian border that also could be applied on the southern one. In October 1999, President Clinton and Prime Minister Chrétien launched the Canadian-US Partnership to find new ways to facilitate trade and travel while enhancing security. All of the relevant agencies on both sides of the border met and devised systems to reduce the number of in-transit cargo inspections by half, to share intelligence on illegal migration, and to establish an Integrated Border Enforcement Team to battle smuggling and money laundering. The two governments established a Commercial Vehicle Processing Center in Fort Erie, Ontario, where trucks can assemble in a staging facility and complete the paperwork necessary for US customs without holding up traffic on Peace Bridge. They use a "pre-arrival and processing system" that gives carriers a unique barcode for each commercial invoice and permits them to fax these codes to Canadian or US customs. A longer-standing experiment is the "Intelligent Transportation System," which permits information to be relayed electronically to transponders. The problem with this system, however, is that each jurisdiction uses a different electronic system, so once again the first problem for Canada and the United States is to establish a national system before they can collaborate on a binational or North American system.[5]

An Uncommon Immigration Policy

Fashioning a common immigration policy is an entirely different matter than managing the flow of people across the border. Let us begin with the easier case of Canada and the United States, because the standard of living in both countries is comparable. Both are multicultural societies with the most liberal immigration policies in the world. The two systems are slightly different. The United States gives preference to family reunification as the main criterion for entry, whereas Canada emphasizes skills and education.[6] But both governments' policies are converging—the

---

5. Department of Foreign Affairs and International Trade of Canada, *Canada-U.S. Partnership: Building a Border for the 21st Century* (Ottawa, 2000), 15-42.

6. In 1998, e.g., of 660,000 immigrants to the United States, 72 percent were family-sponsored and 12 percent entered because of skills. In contrast, of 200,000 immigrants to Canada, 27 percent were family-sponsored, and 57 percent entered because of skills. See Barry Newman, "In Canada, the Point of Immigration is Mostly Unsentimental: It Tackles Labor Shortages By Scoring Education, Youth Ahead of Family," *Wall Street Journal*, 9 December 1999, 1, 12.

United States is allowing more skilled and wealthy migrants, and Canada is considering more family reunifications.

One NAFTA objective that should apply to all three countries would aim to use travel to nurture a sense of community. This could be done by expanding the "NAFTA visa" program and adapting it into a North American passport. Professionals and businesspeople who travel often in North America could apply for and receive such passports. The passport would not only be an appreciated convenience for frequent travelers, but it might also be viewed as a valuable symbol of an emerging North American identity. As such, it would create its own demand, and the three governments should respond by expanding the supply—making more people and occupations eligible.

Between Mexico and the United States, the immigration agenda is much wider and more problematic. In travels in the United States in July 2001, Fox made the case for a comprehensive expansion and legalization of migration, and Foreign Minister Castañeda spoke to a National Convention of Hotel and Restaurant Workers on 18 July, expressing his solidarity with their efforts to allow 3-4 million undocumented Mexican workers in the United States to earn permanent legal residency. He indicated some willingness to consider a temporary-worker program, provided it assures workers of their rights, and urged the United States to accept "the whole enchilada" of proposals.[7]

Let us consider these issues after examining the data. For the past 40 years, the flow of Mexican legal and illegal migrants to the United States has far exceeded that of any other country or groups of countries. On the average, every year for the past two decades, more than 180,000 Mexicans have immigrated legally to the United States, representing nearly 25 percent of total legal immigration from more than 100 countries (see table 4.3). In addition, in recent years, the United States has permitted about 55,000 temporary workers from Mexico under the H1 A and B programs.[8] So, on the level of legal immigration, Mexico is by far the largest source. This also applies to illegal migration, although it is harder to know the numbers. The INS estimated that about 5 million illegal migrants were living in the United States as of October 1996, of which about 60 percent (3 million) were from Mexico, with an annual cumulative flow of about 200-300,000 people. A more recent INS estimate in June 2001 was of 6.5-

---

7. Eric Schmitt, "Bush Aides Weigh Legalizing Status of Mexicans in U.S.," *New York Times*, 15 July 2001; and Steven Greenhouse, In U.S. Unions, Mexico Finds Unlikely Ally on Immigration, *New York Times*, 19 July 2001.

8. See LeDuff, "Perilous 4,000 Mile Passage," 1. He cites a figure of 4.5 million illegals. The Carnegie-ITAM report cites 5-6 million illegals, of whom 60 percent were from Mexico. For the annual estimates on the flow of illegals, and the data on temporary workers, see B. Edmonston and J.S. Passel, *Immigration and Ethnicity: The Integration of America's Newest Arrivals* (Washington: Urban Institute, 1994).

7.5 million illegal migrants; 60 percent of that would be 4-4.5 million Mexicans.[9] Based on the Current Population Survey of the Census Bureau, a study by the Center for Immigration Studies estimates that nearly 400,000 legal and illegal Mexican immigrants arrived in the United States each year from 1998-2000.[10]

Five sets of issues need to be examined in constructing an effective immigration policy and agreement. First, how can migration be made safer, legal, and more orderly? Second, who benefits from an open border or from more migration? Third, should Mexico (and Canada) receive special preferences for larger numbers of permanent legal residents, rather than other countries? Fourth, should there be an expansion and modification of the temporary-worker program? And fifth, should there be a "legalization" or "regularization" program for illegal Mexican workers in the United States at this time?

Making Migration Safe and Legal

Both countries' interests would be served far better by an approach that tries to legalize and humanize the movement of people within clear restrictions and with effective enforcement. How can this be done?

Fox and Bush have already taken some steps to defend the human rights of undocumented workers and to discourage illegal migration. The US president should also instruct federal law enforcement authorities to work with border-state governors to ensure that Mexican migrants— whether legal or illegal—are treated humanely. Any violations of their human rights should be prosecuted swiftly by federal courts, if states are hesitant to do so. The Mexican president ought to instruct Grupo Beta to step up its efforts to arrest "coyotes" on the border and to ensure that punishment is appropriate and publicly known. Every unfortunate incident should be publicized, so that Americans learn that they should treat Mexicans respectfully and so that Mexicans learn the danger of an illegal trip to the north. The crime of smuggling people should be a federal crime in both countries.

The June 2001 communiqué between the two governments acknowledged substantial progress along these lines, including preventing Central Americans from transiting across Mexico, but more needs to be done to discourage the flow and to demonstrate to Mexico that the United States demands fair and humane treatment of all Mexicans.

---

9. For the 1996 estimate, see US Department of Justice, Immigration and Naturalization Service, *1998 Statistical Yearbook of the INS* (Washington, 2000), 236-39. For the more recent estimate of the INS, see Jim Yardley, "For Aspiring Americans, New Hope and Worry," *New York Times,* 21 July 2001, 1, 9.

10. Steven A. Camarota, *Immigration from Mexico: Assessing the Impact on the United States* (Washington, DC: Center for Immigration Studies, 2001), 8.

Who Benefits from an Open Border or More Migration?

The conventional wisdom is that because of a large population, high unemployment, and even higher underemployment, Mexico benefits more from migration, particularly because of the large amount of remittances, and that the United States does not benefit from Mexican migration to the United States. This would explain why Mexico is the *demandeur* on the immigration issue, and the United States is the reluctant suitor. But there is substantial evidence to question this conventional wisdom. Mexicans are concerned about economic loss due to the brain drain—the increasing numbers of university-educated emigrants—and Americans benefit from inexpensive Mexican labor. The cost-benefit analysis grows more complicated the more one examines the phenomenon, but let us start with the most extreme example—an open border—to try to understand the implications of migration for both countries.

If the border were open, and public opinion polls are to be believed, Mexico would witness a massive exit. Seventy percent—or 70 million people—have said they would emigrate to the United States if they thought they would benefit economically.[11] No one expects that many Mexicans to pick up and leave, but if just 15 million people—double the number of illegal migrants in the United States today—left, the consequences would be devastating for both countries, especially Mexico. The magnitude of remittances to Mexico would increase dramatically, but so too would the percentage of the population dependent on those remittances.

The central Mexican state of Zacatecas has long been one of the principal sources of migration to the United States. An analysis by the Autonomous University of Zacatecas estimated that the state received about $1 million in remittances each day, more than the national government spent in the state. The mayor, however, was distressed that assembly plants had to close because a lack of young workers, and farms needed to import labor from poor southern states. "The people can make more money by staying at home and waiting for a check from the United States, so more of them do not work," said one farmer.[12] *With an open border, Mexico could become the first absentee welfare state.*

Even if there were hints of a serious relaxation of the border in the years ahead, that also could affect the national psychology in Mexico in deleterious ways; workers would spend more time planning to leave Mexico than working to invest there. As long as the ratio in incomes

---

11. Ronald Inglehart and Miguel Basañez, "World Values Survey/USA and Mexico," 2000. I appreciate Dr. Basañez sharing the survey data. See chapter 7 for an extensive discussion of this issue.

12. Ginger Thompson, "Migrant Exodus Bleeding Mexico's Heartland," *New York Times*, 17 June 2001, 1,6.

between the United States and Mexico ranges from 4 to 30, the incentives to migrate will be compelling.[13] Until that differential can be reduced by about half—and, under very optimistic projections, that could take 30 to 40 years[14]—a deliberate decision to relax US immigration laws would have serious adverse consequences for Mexico's economy.

The effect of such a relaxation on the United States would depend on the state of its economy. But leaving that factor aside, the likelihood is that a new large wave would congregate in existing Mexican-American communities—in Southern California, Texas, and Chicago. The social tensions that would accompany such a large shift in population might very well lead to clashes among ethnic groups.

If open borders are ruled out, would a marginal increase in immigration benefit the Mexican economy? Many surveys have found that those who emigrate to the United States are not only among the most enterprising Mexicans, they also usually leave jobs. Their journey is not motivated by the need for work, but by the wage differential. While their income in the United States is likely to exceed their income in Mexico, the relevant equation is whether their remittances exceed their productivity if they remained in Mexico. That is not known, but it does not appear to be an open-and-shut case that emigration helps the Mexican economy. In the short term, however, emigration may provide a critical social escape valve for Mexico, but the economic costs and benefits for the sending and receiving countries might be the reverse of what many think. Migration might impede the development of the sending country while assisting in some ways the receiving country.[15]

The effects of migration in both countries, however, are not uniform. There are some in each country who benefit, and some who do not. This is particularly true of illegal migration, which tends to involve a much higher percentage of unskilled workers. Unskilled or illegal migration benefits US employers (who can pay less for fearful, exceptionally motivated workers) and the relatively well-off in the United States, at the cost

---

13. George J. Borjas, "Mexico's One-Way Remedy," *New York Times*, 18 July 2000. Borjas estimates that the wage differential between manufacturing jobs in the two countries is a factor of 4, and between a manufacturing job in the United States and a farming job in Mexico is 30. For an alternative view that economic integration is more important in promoting migration than wage differentials, see Douglas S. Massey, "March of Folly: U.S. Immigration Policy after NAFTA," *American Prospect* (March/April 1998).

14. Gary Clyde Hufbauer and Jeffrey J. Schott, *NAFTA: An Assessment* (Washington: Institute for International Economics, 1993), 24-25.

15. In the mid-1980s, I directed a study for the World Bank and the Inter-American Development Bank on the implications for the sending countries of the Caribbean Basin, including Mexico, of immigration to the United States, and concluded that the receiving country benefited more economically than the sending country. See Robert A. Pastor, ed., *Migration and Development in the Caribbean Basin: The Unexplored Connection* (Boulder, CO: Westview Press, 1985).

of the unskilled native born. Borjas estimated that almost half of the gap in wages between native-born high school dropouts and other workers— a gap that widened in the period 1985-95—was due to competition with unskilled immigrants.[16] The illegal Mexican workers compete against 11.7 million adult native-born workers who lack a high school education. During the 1990s, unskilled jobs shrunk by 400,000, and the increased competition led to a decline of real wages of 7.2 percent by high school dropouts who work full-time. The impact fell disproportionately on African-Americans, and the same study shows that consumers do not benefit from price reduction.[17] Although the AFL-CIO now supports additional migration, a labor economist who surveyed the relationship between migration and employment during the past 200 years found that wages have increased and unionism has thrived when immigration declined.[18] To summarize, migration's affect seems to be the opposite of conventional wisdom: the receiving country benefits more than the sending country. The affluent in the receiving country benefits the most and the poor pay the highest price.

One other dimension needs to be incorporated into the analysis: the social-psychological. A critical priority for the new Mexican government is that the United States show respect for and protect the rights of the Mexicans living in the United States. This is what sets Fox apart from his predecessors, and why legalization is such an important goal. But Fox may need to decide whether it is more important to gain respect by Americans or to persuade the United States to permit larger numbers of Mexican immigrants. It is possible that these two distinct issues are mutually reinforcing. The more Mexicans there are in the United States, the more influence Mexico could have. But there may be a trade-off between the two goals—respect and numbers—because many Americans fear being overrun by large numbers of Mexican immigrants. (This issue is developed in the next chapter in the section titled "Subterranean Fears.") It might be easier to secure respect for Mexicans in the United States if Americans felt the latest wave was not just the beginning of a tsunami. If so, both governments might need to make a choice.

Should There Be Preference for North American Migrants?

The United States has never found an easy way to define criteria or set limits for immigration. Congress took 20 years to pass the first immigra-

---

16. The estimates are from Borjas' book, *Heaven's Door*, in this case summarized by an editorial in the *New York Times*, "Hasty Call for Amnesty," 22 February 2000.

17. Steven A. Camarota, *Immigration from Mexico: Assessing the Impact on the United States* (Washington, DC: Center for Immigration Studies, 2001), 21-28. See pp. 22-23 for a summary of other research that confirms these conclusions.

18. Vernon M. Briggs, Jr., *Immigration and American Unionism* (Ithaca, NY: Cornell University Press, 2001).

tion bill in 1921, and it took more than a decade to pass the 1986 immigration law imposing employer sanctions and permitting amnesty for illegal workers. The decisions on who and how many are permitted to enter are, in essence, decisions about national identity. And in a multicultural, immigrant country like the United States, this raises formidable problems.

Fox argues that as a country of "North America," Mexico (and implicitly, Canada) ought to have a special preference for immigration. That is the thesis of this book—there is a "North America," and we need to find appropriate ways to translate that preference into policy. This approach has been endorsed by a Joint Panel of Experts from Mexico and the United States, which also made many other recommendations, including wholesale amnesty for undocumented workers, a dramatic expansion of the temporary-worker program for Mexicans, coordinated strategies to crack down on illegal migration, joint building of a viable border region, and strengthening the Mexican economy.[19]

Of course, Mexico, as we have seen, already receives many more legal visas and larger numbers of temporary workers each year than any other country, and Canada also is less constrained than almost any country. But the issue is whether these "informal" preferences should be translated into law. An alternative approach—one comparable to that on dollarization—is to simply let the numbers increase by indecision, to let Mexico and the United States adjust to a more fluid movement of people and cultures, just as the two countries are slowly adjusting to the integration of their economies. If the three governments decide to deepen North America, then immigration preferences should be a part of that deepening, but the United States will face additional pressures from the Caribbean Basin countries, which have long sought similar preferences, as well as from other countries in the world, to do for them what it promises Mexico.

Should the United States Consistently Enforce "Employer Sanctions" and Expand a Temporary-Worker Program?

The United States needs to decide whether to enforce its laws against undocumented workers or expand the temporary-worker program. The existing policy is based on an arbitrary and uneven enforcement of the employer sanctions law. When the labor market in the United States was tight, and unemployment was low, as was the case in 2000, the INS relaxed its enforcement within the country. When unemployment increased, it enforced the law.[20] This is not the way a country based on the rule of law should behave, and it sends the wrong signal to Mexico.

---

19. Carnegie Endowment and Instituto Technológico Autonomo de México, *Mexico-U.S. Migration.*

20. See two in-depth reports by Mark Bixler in the *Atlanta Journal-Constitution* on how Georgia's farmers were assisted by members of Congress and senators to urge the INS to

In early January 2001, US Senator Phil Gramm led a delegation of his colleagues to Mexico and was persuaded by President Fox to press for a guest-worker program to end illegal migration and to provide Mexican workers in the United States with basic rights.[21] This is no longer as implausible an option as it was a few years before, when Gramm himself stopped the passage of such a bill. The major shift was not by Gramm, however, but by the AFL-CIO, which had been the principal bulwark against any relaxation of immigration restrictions. Republicans would prefer an expansion of the existing temporary-worker program, which ties the worker to the employer for a fixed period of time. Mexico would prefer to give rights to temporary workers to find jobs anywhere in the United States and to have the option to apply for permanent-resident status after that. Consistent with the principles of an emerging North American Community, the United States should strengthen its laws against illegal migration and expand and modify its temporary-worker program to provide more rights for these workers.

Should Illegal Migrants Be Legalized or Given Amnesty?

At its meeting on 16 February 2000, the AFL-CIO announced its support for amnesty for illegal migrants and an end to most employer sanctions. This was a startling "Nixon-goes-to-China" turnabout. The reason for the shift was that the Hotel and Restaurant Employees Union viewed illegal migrants as candidates to expand its membership, and the other unions wanting to expand their numbers, expressed their solidarity.[22]

The main argument for "legalization" is that the people who are in the United States are hardworking and generally law-abiding. "Legalization" removes the possibility of their exploitation. Employers know they can take advantage of these workers because the workers cannot complain to the legal authorities. And their children and spouses live in permanent fear of being deported or arrested.

To understand the hypocrisies wrapped around illegal migration, it is useful to note that it is in everyone's short-term interest, but in no one's long-term interest. It is in the short-term interest of workers, because they can earn more money in the United States than at home; of employers, because they get employees who work harder for less; of Mexico, because

---

relax their enforcement during harvests. Mark Bixler, "Onion Growers, Allies Urge INS Not to Dig too Deep," 7 May 2000; and "Illegal Immigrants at Risk When Economy Weakens," 5 March 2001. The INS maintains tight enforcement at the border; the only place it loosens its enforcement is within the country.

21. Susan Ferriss, "Legal Guest-Worker Plan for Mexicans to Be Pushed," *Atlanta Journal-Constitution*, 11 January 2001, 4.

22. Steven Greenhouse, "Labor Urges Amnesty for Illegal Immigrants," *New York Times*, 17 February 2000.

of the remittances and the escape valve; and of the United States, because these workers fill an important economic gap with cheap labor. But in the long term, the costs exceed the short-term benefits: illegal migration allows exploitation of and discrimination against workers; Mexico loses entrepreneurial individuals; and the poor in the United States are forced to compete for lower wages and working conditions than most native-born workers would accept. Most important, illegal workers undermine the rule of law because they are outside the legal system. That is why the laws against illegal migration should be enforced—not ignored—regardless of the state of the economy. If the United States needs workers, they should be accepted legally.

But what of those who are already here? Should they be legalized? When Congress previously granted amnesty to 3 million illegal aliens in 1986, it coupled that with strong employer sanctions and promised not to give amnesty again. Since then, the number of new illegal workers in the United States has more than doubled.

The strongest arguments against legalization are that it rewards those who broke the law; it penalizes those who obeyed the law; and it therefore undermines existing immigration laws. Every day, Mexicans wake up early or stay overnight to get in line around the US Embassy in Mexico City for a legal visa to the United States. People often have to wait for weeks, and some for years, to get a visa, and many never receive one. Illegal workers have, in effect, cut in line to get into the United States. Actually, they have paid no attention to the line—or the rules. If the United States chooses to give the lawbreakers a visa at the expense of the law-abiding ones, it will be sending the wrong message to Mexico. One could argue that a single grant of amnesty—as occurred in 1986—after 60 years was an appropriate and justified response to the buildup of illegal workers, but if the United States repeats this exercise every 15 years, who will pay attention to the immigration law?

Moreover, it would be difficult politically and technically to implement a program just for some Mexicans. And to legalize all 7 million or more would probably be considerably more than the US body politic could absorb, particularly in a year of a stagnant or declining economy.

A number of proposals have been offered for more limited amnesty. Illegal aliens could be given temporary-worker status. Over time, those who qualify by length of residency or employment history could apply to become permanent residents. Eventually, they could apply for full citizenship. The purpose would be to transfer those who are here illegally into legal channels. In principle, this is a much better proposal than wholesale amnesty, but it still poses two hard questions. Can it be implemented in such a nuanced way, or is this merely a face-saving path toward broader amnesty? And second, does not this approach still signal to the many Mexicans, who are patiently obeying the US immigration law and applying for visas through the US Embassy, that they are foolish to follow US laws?

It is essential to legalize the flow of migrants, but the question remains: How? If there is a need for more workers, then the United States should expand and modify the temporary-worker program. But we need to understand clearly the risks. After Europe's guest-worker program turned sour, one scholar commented: "We invited workers, but people came." The meaning was that the Europeans thought the new workers would be "guests," staying just as long as the economy needed them. They turned out to be people, who brought families or married, and set down roots.

In the case of the United States, one need only look at public opinion polls on migration since the great second wave of migration began in 1965. The results show conclusively that the United States tolerates migrants when the economy is doing well; and it becomes angry and restrictive when the economy declines.[23] In the summer of 1993, just before the United States embarked on its longest economic expansion, a national poll by *Time* magazine found a public that resented both legal and illegal migration and welcomed laws to reduce legal and stop illegal migration.[24] The temporary-worker program, in brief, is rarely temporary, and often leads to serious social tensions. Therefore, before embarking on this course, the United States should be wary of this history, and Mexico also needs to think hard about what it wants and needs. If Congress chooses to expand the temporary-worker program, it should make it sensitive to the rhythms of the US economy and protective of the rights of Mexican workers. Previous programs did neither.

The politics of "legalization" turned upside down in the United States in a single year. In 2000, no serious political figure would offer such a proposal, but by the summer of 2001, both political parties in Congress were competing to apply it to an ever-wider circle of undocumented workers. What happened? President Bush expressed interest in responding to the agenda of President Fox in part because he understands the importance of Mexico and in part because he sees "legalization" as a path toward gaining influence with future Hispanic voters. For the same reason, many of the Democrats have decided to support it. Whether those expressions of support translate into a new law or provoke a reaction in "Main Street America" that defeats the law and reverses the new sensitivity to Mexico remains to be seen.

---

23. For a table of public opinion polls on immigration from 1965 to 2000, see http://www.gallup.com/poll/indicators/indimmigration.asp.

24. Bruce Nelan, "Not Quite So Welcome: As Reflected in a *Time* Poll, The Public Mood Over Immigration is Turning Sour Again," *Time*, Fall 1993, 10-16; see also Seth Mydans, "A New Tide of Immigration Brings Hostility to the Surface, Poll Finds," *New York Times*, 27 June 1993, 1, 14.

Assembling an Immigration Package

A gradual assimilation of cultures is the best long-term path for the United States and for North America, but to accomplish that goal, we need to take steps to protect the immigrants when the economy declines. This means that we need to prepare the population for a new way of looking at Mexico and the new migrants in our midst. Nongovernmental organizations are helping the new migrants, and 45 Mexican consulates in the United States actively work with the immigrants to help them understand and assert their legitimate rights in their communities.[25] More important, US leaders must help the country to understand that we are part of a larger entity—called North America—and that this obligates us to behave toward our neighbors in different ways than we have in the past. President Bush understands this point, because when he was governor of Texas, he insisted that Texans treat Mexico with respect. Translating that point into a national policy will not be easy, but it is essential.

Immigration to the United States has been the glue that has been slowing binding the countries of North America. At the outset of the 21st century, the US Hispanic population was about 35.3 million people, or 12.5 percent of the total population. About 60 percent were of Mexican origin, and if illegal or temporary migrants were included, that would rise to about 75 percent of the Hispanic population.[26] This movement of people is the human dimension of an extraordinary integration process that has been under way for decades, but has begun to accelerate in the past 10 years. It is incumbent upon all three governments to articulate a conception of North America that people will understand and that will help them appreciate their neighbors more and fear them less—whether they are across the border or in their communities.

Consistent with these principles, the three leaders should declare their hope that in the long term, the people of North America should be permitted to move freely in a common market. However, as long as the disparities in income between Mexico and its two northern neighbors are as wide as they are today, any significant relaxation of immigration controls would be contrary to the interests of the region. Still, there are four initiatives that could and should be taken immediately.

First, the three governments should agree to expand the "North American visa" and to institute a "North American passport" for people who do frequent business in the three countries. One hopes that the demand

---

25. See "Mexican Consuls Interpret Safety Measures," *Atlanta Journal-Constitution*, 15 January 2001, B3.

26. Betsy Guzman, "The Hispanic Population: Census 2000 Brief," (Washington: US Department of Commerce, Bureau of the Census, 2001), 1-2; and Roberto R. Ramirez, *The Hispanic Population in the United States: Population Characteristics* (Washington: US Department of Commerce, Bureau of the Census, 2000), 1.

for such a "passport" would increase, and that the three governments would gradually expand the supply to new categories of professionals and other workers.

Second, Congress should legislate a "preference" for permanent resident visas for citizens from Mexico and Canada. The profile of the new immigrants should reflect a convergence with Canada's policies so that over time a unified policy might be possible.

Third, the United States should expand and modify its temporary worker program for Mexicans so as to permit them to have expanded rights to move between jobs and apply for permanent residence status. But those who make the decision on the numbers should be sensitive to the swings in the US economy.

Fourth, the United States should commit to enforce its immigration laws humanely but consistently, and it should work with Mexico to arrest "smugglers" and discourage migration from and through Mexico.

A North American Energy Plan

When the negotiations on NAFTA began in 1990, Mexican President Salinas proposed that immigration and the free movement of labor should be a part of the agreement. US President George H. W. Bush rejected that idea as a "nonstarter," reflecting a widespread fear in the United States of being overrun by Mexican immigrants. Then, when Bush proposed including energy, Salinas dismissed that in equally strong terms. The exclusive ownership of Mexico's oil, gas, and natural resources was a legacy of Mexico's revolution, written into their Constitution and their national psyche. Salinas realized that trying to change the Constitution on this issue would provoke a firestorm.[27]

It was therefore with a trace of déjà vu, not to say irony, that the two issues would return to the negotiating table at the beginning of the Fox and the second Bush administrations. For reasons having to do with the growing importance of immigration in the minds and lives of Mexicans, Fox proposed this issue first, and Bush agreed to a high-level commission to study it. Bush—a Texas oilman whose first 6 months in office coincided with a California energy crisis that threatened to become a national one— naturally looked to the substantial energy resources of his neighbors as a possible solution to the US problem. Fox knew that his country also had a serious set of problems related to energy, and perhaps thought initially that trilateral negotiations might make his decisions easier.

---

27. For the nondiscussion of these two "sacred cow" issues—immigration and energy— see George W. Grayson, *The North American Free Trade Agreement: Regional Community and the New World Order* (Lanham, MD: University Press of America, 1995), 82; and Frederick W. Mayer, *Interpreting NAFTA: The Science and Art of Political Analysis* (New York: Columbia University Press, 1998), 116-19.

Bush may not have been aware that Mexico had been importing natural gas and oil products from the United States. Demand in both the United States and Mexico for natural gas greatly exceeds supply. In Mexico, 9 of 10 new power-generating units built in recent years use natural gas, and so demand for gas increased by about 5 percent each year since 1995. Energy analysts estimate that Mexico's demand for gas will continue to increase even faster until 2020. Unfortunately, supply is increasing at the rate of 1 percent. Because Mexico has severe problems of fiscal austerity and an energy sector managed by two notoriously inefficient state-owned behemoths, the country did not have the funds to expand its production.

Mexico's reserves of oil and natural gas are substantial, but funds for investment are scarce because the government relies on Pemex, the national oil company, for as much as 30 percent of its annual revenues, and the Federal Electricity Commission is compelled to charge very low prices. To just meet its own demand, not even that of the United States, Mexico (according to World Bank estimates) would have to invest approximately $10 billion each year for the next 10 years. This is roughly equivalent to the amount spent for health, and the government does not have it.[28]

Although he understands the problem, Fox also recognizes the political constraints that make it so difficult to solve. That is why he was compelled in his inaugural address to make two unequivocal promises—first, that "the Federal Electricity Commission will not, I repeat, will not be privatized, nor will any of its assets be sold," and second, that "Pemex will continue as the exclusive property of the nation."[29] Although US oilmen would like to purchase Pemex or its oil reserves, they realistically know that they need to find an alternative approach.

The World Bank has offered numerous recommendations to meet Mexico's domestic needs while adapting to its political realities, and Fox has been trying several of them. Instead of privatizing the state-owned companies, he has appointed private-sector leaders to their boards and wants to promote efficiency, honesty, and competition by developing a framework of transparent regulation and legal certainty. Only in that way will Mexico be able to attract the magnitude of private investment it needs. This may involve production-sharing agreements in which the state maintains ownership and control, but private companies are able to recover the costs of exploration and receive a share of the profits.

---

28. For an extensive and insightful analysis of Mexico's problems in the energy sector and recommendations on ways to deal with them, see Marcelo Giugale, Olivier Lafourcade, and Vinh H. Nguyen, eds., *Mexico: A Comprehensive Development Agenda for the New Era* (Washington: World Bank, 2001), 10-11, 357-76.

29. Embajada de México en Estados Unidos de America, "Vicente Fox Inaugural Speech," Washington, photocopy (1 December 2000), 16.

The three leaders established a North American Energy Working Group, which convened in June 2001 to set an agenda that included pipeline construction, cross-border power transmission and regulation, and research into new technologies. Because Canada and the United States have exceedingly complicated and decentralized regulatory policies on energy, but also a substantial share of the power residing in the provinces or states, meshing regulatory approaches—as California and Washington discovered—will be no easy matter even within each country, let alone among all three. Still, a proposal to coordinate policies advanced by Ralph Goodale, Canada's Minister of Natural Resources is a positive and constructive one, which is why it is distressing that the Canadian minister was severely criticized in his country for proposing it. "We're being panicked by the Americans with their so-called energy crisis; it's more Canadian sovereignty down the drain," said Albert Pratt, who wrote a very critical report of Canadian energy policy entitled *Energy: Free Trade and the Price We Paid*. His argument was that as a result of NAFTA, Canadians are now paying world prices for energy, and that amounts to an increase of almost six times in the level of natural gas prices in 1998.[30]

Energy, in brief, remains a very sensitive symbolic issue in all three countries, but particularly in Canada and Mexico. If some of the poison in this issue could be extracted through a respectful, cooperative plan, it could facilitate the emergence of a North American Community. If it is handled poorly, then the leaders will pay the political price and the countries will find it more difficult to cooperate on other matters.

A North American Development Fund

In contemplating a "regional" development policy for North America, let us recall certain lessons from the European Union. First, sustained growth remains the most effective way to reduce disparities, and national policies are at least as important as the Union's regional policies. That is why Ireland did so much better than Greece, although it received a third as much aid. Second, the Single Market and foreign investment may have contributed as much to the development of the poor countries in southern Europe as aid. Third, regional aid helped in significant ways—encouraging governments to maintain good macroeconomic policies, targeting bottlenecks in the economy, and multiplying investments. Of all regional aid projects, the two most effective ways to stimulate growth and reduce disparities were infrastructure and education. Fourth, as disparities declined, so too did emigration from poor to rich countries.

---

30. Linda Diebel, "U.S. Seeks to Control Our Energy: Critics," *Toronto Star*, 10 March 2001.

From these lessons, and from the experience of North America, the leaders of the three countries should consider establishing a North American Development Fund to promote regional development. The fund first would concentrate on investing in infrastructure to facilitate the integration of poor regions into a single North America, and second would establish community colleges in poor regions.

When the European Union first decided on a regional policy, its funds were scarce, but with each enlargement, the Union expanded the resources for poor regions to the point at which the sheer magnitude of investment helped lift some and gave a sense of community to all. These resources were significant from both the direction of the donors—0.045 percent of EU GDP—and that of the recipient—2-4 percent of GDP. To put real numbers alongside those percentages, 0.045 of US GDP would be about $400 billion, and 2 percent of Mexico's GDP would be $10 billion. It is not hard to judge the reaction in the US Congress if the president requested an aid program to Mexico of $10 billion each year for the next 10 years— let alone what the response would be if $400 billion were mentioned. The American people and Congress are unlikely to consider such a request at this time, regardless of how good an investment it would be.

The president needs to frame the issue so that Americans understand the vital interests that are at stake. Americans have always risen to a challenge when their leaders have explained it clearly and in a compelling way. There is no national interest greater for the United States than to help lift all of North America to a new level of prosperity and social justice. The president should use an example and offer a specific proposal.

The example would be Ireland. EU funds for Ireland had a special impact because they arrived in 1989 when there was a substantial backlog of projects and infrastructural needs. That is exactly where Mexico is today. Soon after President Fox was elected, senior World Bank officials presented him with detailed memoranda, outlining his country's problems and proposing solutions.[31] To establish a strong macroeconomic foundation, Ernesto Zedillo had to restrain his government's expenditures so severely that the government stopped investing in the future. Overall, public infrastructure investment declined from more than 10 percent of GDP in 1994 to less than 2 percent in 1998. The Bank estimated that Mexico would need $20 billion a year for the next 10 years just to close the country's widening infrastructure gap.[32] The Bank judged that the private sector would invest in the energy sector under the right

31. Many of these memoranda were subsequently published in Giugale, Lafourcade, and Nguyen, *Mexico*. Interview with Olivier Lafourcade, director of the World Bank office, Mexico City, 1 December 2001.

32. Giugale, Lafourcade, and Nguyen, *Mexico*, 2, 11.

conditions, but only governments or development banks could provide the funds for infrastructure.

The United States has a very practical interest in helping Mexico obtain these resources. Without this investment, Mexico cannot come near to fulfilling its development potential, with the result being an increase in migration, crime, corruption, and difficult relations. The funding, however, could jump-start the Mexican economy to begin to reduce the gap with its northern neighbors. It could do much more, if deployed in a strategic fashion.

To reduce geographical disparities within Mexico while lessening pressures to emigrate, *the best approach would be to improve the road system from the US border to the center and southern parts of the country.* Because of foreign investment, the northern border economy is booming. The expansion has been so rapid that the system cannot cope. The land, water, and air "are thick with industrial and human waste." More than 1 million Mexicans have moved to the border from the center and southern parts of Mexico in the past 5 years, and the reason is that the factories on the border pay nearly triple the Mexican minimum wage. Of course, at $4 a day, that wage still cannot compete with the hourly wage across the border, so the annual turnover rate of labor in border factories approaches 100 percent.[33] US firms do not like to invest in the border area because of the pollution and the inefficiencies associated with such a high turnover rate, but they invest there rather than in the country's center because the roads from the border to the center are so bad.

If roads were built or improved from the border to the center, investors would locate there, for three reasons. First, the center and south of the country—Oaxaca, Zacatecas, Michoacan, and Guanajuato states—have the highest rates of unemployment, and indeed are the principal sources of immigrants to the border and the United States. Second, the wage level is much lower in these areas, and the workers are no less educated than those on the border. Indeed, they are often the same workers. Third, the region is not the polluted, cramped border. The government has incentive systems to encourage investors to locate there, but the problem is a lack of infrastructure—roads, electricity, and the like. *Build the roads, and investors would come, and immigration levels and disparities in income both would decline.*

President Fox has proposed a Puebla-Panama Corridor to connect Puebla, a city southeast of the capital, with the countries of Central America. Senior officials of the international development banks pledged to help Mexico build roads and infrastructure in the nine poorest southern and eastern states of his country to connect to the seven countries of

---

33. Ginger Thompson, "The Dividing Line: Misery on the Border," *New York Times*, 11 February 2001.

Central America. On 22 June 2001, Fox signed the agreement with his Central American counterparts for a 25-year plan to promote infrastructure, education, and health. Many of these Mexican areas have few or no roads, and so such a development project would have a profound effect on the region—even more so if those roads were connected to new ones coming from the border. Although most of the investment would be targeted on infrastructure, some of it should be allocated to establishing community colleges in poor regions. (In the next section, I will develop this proposal.)

The amount of investment would be relatively small as compared with the return. And prosperity in Mexico benefits the United States in numerous ways, not the least being that for every additional dollar of imports that Mexico buys, the United States sells about 80 cents. Nevertheless, it might take some time to build a consensus for a partnership strategy, because even if President Bush decided to try to persuade Congress to approve it, Congress would undoubtedly saddle the new program with so many conditions that it would undermine the premise and purpose of the structural funds, which is to build a unique partnership in North America.

Therefore, let me propose an intermediate option while the leaders of the three countries begin to construct the kind of relationship that will make such a program seem a wholly natural extension of their summits and of a new North America. Since the establishment of the World Bank, Mexico has been its third largest recipient of loans—169 loans totaling $30 billion. Only India (having received $52 billion) and China ($33 billion) have obtained more. In June 1999, the World Bank Board decided to direct $5.2 billion to Mexico during the next 2 years to improve social conditions for the poor, strengthen public-sector reforms, and reinforce macroeconomic stability. In its report on Mexico in 2001, the Bank affirmed that it would maintain a project pipeline worth about $1.5 billion a year. Mexico has also received more loans from the Inter-American Development Bank—160 loans totaling $12.2 billion—than any other country.[34] These loans have gone to a wide range of projects, but none of them have addressed the question: How could the funds best facilitate the integration of North America?

If Canada, Mexico, and the United States all agreed that half of the loans from these two institutions during the next 5 years—say $1.5 billion—would be devoted to answering the question of integration (through infrastructure and education), the two development banks would probably respond positively, particularly because the precedent (integrating a developing country into a regional agreement with industrial countries)

---

34. The figures from the World Bank and the Inter-American Development Bank are from their Web sites.

has global significance. A cost-benefit analysis of various sectoral plans might demonstrate how far a relatively small amount of investment could go in furthering Mexico's development, particularly because the private sector would play a large role. Under those circumstances, all three countries might devote a substantial amount of call-in capital or foreign aid to implement the plan—of building better roads and bridges across the borders and into central and southern Mexico, of modernizing railways, and so on.

It would neither be necessary nor desirable to establish a new bureaucracy to undertake these projects. A special coordinating office in the World Bank could work with the Inter-American Development Bank and other institutions to mobilize the funds, supervise the bidding, and oversee the projects. It might be useful for the North American Development Bank to work with the two major development banks, but the NADBank does not have the capability or the experience to manage these projects, and its mandate is different. The North American Commission proposed by this book would not manage the projects, but it would be involved in preparing the broader picture of how these investments would contribute to the goal of a more integrated North America.

While helping Mexico to integrate its poor and rich regions, the development fund's managers might very well discover the best approach to the troubled border area as well. During the past 30 years, almost every administration in Mexico City and Washington has promised to develop the border. All failed. Whether the border economy expanded or contracted, the political system could not cope. Since NAFTA, the border has exploded with new investment that has burdened the system way beyond its capacity. A development program that aimed to build up the center of the country would relieve the border of some of its congestion, and it would permit a better-managed system. The border then could become more of a commercial and transit station rather than a manufacturing platform that rises and sets in short order depending on the demands of the US public or of a particular company. As with the European Union, North America should use the development funds to help Mexico make the decisions—for example, on fiscal reform—that they need to approve to modernize their economy.

To enlist support from the donors—the United States and, to a lesser degree, Canada—Americans will need to be persuaded that this investment will alleviate their concerns about Mexico and advance their interests. If a plan relates the various interests of the United States—stemming drugs and illegal immigrants, expanding trade and development—then the prospects of supporting such a venture would increase.

Although much of the infrastructure and the universities would be built in Mexico, Canada and the United States also have considerable infrastructure problems. The increase in trade has slowed traffic in Texas going to the border and led to numerous accidents. Congress allocated $700 million for NAFTA-related highway and infrastructure improvements, but apparently only a small portion was allocated to Texas.[35]

To help forge a regional identity, a case could be made that some "North American" projects should be built in Canada and the United States and advertised, as the European Union does, as North American Community Projects. Historically, one of the reasons why there has been so little US public support for foreign aid or for international organizations is that Americans never see the projects and the offices that manage them. That could be corrected if the projects and offices were also in the United States as well as in the two other countries most visited by Americans, but the lesson from Europe is to keep these offices and projects small and symbolic and save the funds for where they are needed.

Would Canada contribute? A decade ago, or even 5 years ago, the answer would probably have been "No." But in recent years, Canada has played an increasing role in Latin America, and it has singled out its relations with Mexico for special priority. There is no doubt that Canada could not—and would not want to—contribute as much as the United States, but just as with Salinas' original proposal, they probably would not want to be left out of any new North American project.

To be effective, the development fund would need a clearly designed plan and a pipeline of money for an extended period. Mexico's needs exceed the capacity—or, more accurately, the political will—of its neighbors. The World Bank estimated that it needed $20 billion a year for a decade just for infrastructure. This is roughly equivalent—in current dollars—to what the United States delivered to Latin America through the Alliance for Progress during the 1960s. The United States would need to contribute only a small proportion of those funds as call-in capital, which would allow the World Bank to borrow the remainder. It is hard to conceive of a more worthy investment, but only the president could convince the American people of that.

A North American Education Plan

The 1990s brought a consensus that education is key to economic development. The problem is in finding the right formula to improve a country's educational system, and that approach has to be different in Canada and the United States than in Mexico.

In the European Union, the two most effective "regional policy" investments were in infrastructure and higher education. Specifically, the Union helped establish regional community colleges in the four Cohesion coun-

---

35. Robert Bryce, "A Texas-Size Tie-Up: Traffic from Trade Agreement Has Created a Lone Star Nightmare on Interstate 35," *U.S. News and World Report*, 25 October 1999, 36.

tries, and these colleges served as magnets for education and development in poor areas. Is such a strategy relevant to Mexico?

Mexico has made substantial gains in education during the past two decades. Students are now required to complete 9 years of school. Enrollment has soared to more than 80 percent at the primary level; for the first 3 years at the secondary level, enrollment increased from 31 percent in 1970 to 66 percent in 1997. Educational expenditures increased from 7.8 million pesos in 1970 to 118 million pesos (both in current pesos) in 1997.[36] Mexico's educational problems are similar to those in many parts of Latin America. The quality of education is much poorer in the rural areas and the dropout rate is higher, although there have been improvements in the past decade. Its level of spending for education is relatively high for a developing country, but Mexico, like much of Latin America, devotes a disproportionate amount to higher education for a small number of people. Funding of elementary and secondary schools has been inadequate.[37]

The major educational challenges for Mexico in the 21st century, according to an OECD report, are "equity, quality, and educational pertinence."[38] In many ways, Mexico's level of economic and educational development is comparable to Portugal's or Spain's in the early 1980s, and the EU strategy with some adaptations might make sense for Mexico.

Portugal and Spain, with EU help, established small colleges in rural provinces. These colleges served as magnets that attracted professionals from more advanced regions, and they also radiated their influence into the wider rural community, helping to upgrade their education. Although there have been many explanations for the dramatic progress made in Iberia since the mid-1980s, when Portugal and Spain joined the EU, still one needs to marvel about the expansion of educational opportunities (table 6.1). From 1985 to 1995, the proportion of students in higher education in Spain increased from 29 to 48 percent; and in Portugal, from 12 to 39 percent; but in Mexico, it declined from 16 to 15 percent. By 1995, all high school-age students in Portugal and Spain were in school, whereas only 61 percent of Mexicans were there.

---

36. Sergio Medina, *Human Resources and Population in Mexico at the Dawn of the 21st Century: A Regional Perspective* (Amsterdam: Thela Thesis, 2000), 100-04; World Bank, *Country Assistance Strategy for Mexico* (Washington, 1999), 7.

37. Nancy Birdsall, Nora Lustig, and Lesley O'Connell, "The U.S. and the Social Challenge in Latin America: The New Agenda Needs New Instruments," in *The United States and the Americas: A Twenty-First Century View*, ed. Albert Fishlow and James Jones (New York: W.W. Norton, 1999), 93-94.

38. Organization for Economic Cooperation and Development, *Review of National Policies for Education: Mexico Higher Education* (Paris, 1997), 47. This conclusion was supported by studies by the World Bank and the Inter-American Development Bank.

Table 6.1 Comparing development and education in Mexico, Portugal, and Spain

Country	GDP dollars, PPP basis			Enrollment/tertiary education (percent)			Enrollment/ secondary education (percent)		
	1985	1990	1995	1985	1990	1995	1985	1990	1995
Mexico	5,306	6,408	7,222	15.9	14.5	15.3	56.5	53.3	61.2
Portugal	7,209	11,238	13,774	12.3	23.2	38.8	57.3	67.4	111.0
Spain	8,433	12,914	15,412	28.5	36.7	47.8	98.5	104.1	122.1

PPP = purchasing power parity

Source: World Bank, World Development Indicators 2000 (CD-ROM).

As occurred in the Iberian Peninsula, poor regions in Mexico would benefit from community colleges that placed emphasis on technical and computer training. These colleges could attract investment and upgrade secondary school teaching in the vicinity, and they could partner with an extremely well-developed community college system in the United States. If funding were provided to Mexico for community colleges on the condition that the government systematically reduce the proportion of funding for universities and increase it for secondary schools, then an investment in community colleges would yield a double dividend. The failed attempt to institute tuition in the National University in Mexico City shows that it will be difficult to gain consent for a reallocation of educational resources, but that might be easier if Mexico's poor regions had more of a stake in the change.

An Alliance for Higher Education and Enterprise in North America was established in 1998 under the auspices of the North American Institute (NAMI), a nongovernmental group based in New Mexico and led by former Canadian Senator Jack Austin. The mandate of the alliance is to facilitate strategic partnerships among universities, community colleges, and businesses in all three countries. With the support of the three governments, NAMI could help develop "North American Community Colleges" in the poor regions of Mexico.[39]

An equally serious, if not greater, problem is illiteracy or low levels of education in the rural areas. Here, community colleges could reap a third dividend if their students were required—in lieu of tuition—to spend a semester working in the remote areas on a "literacy crusade."[40]

---

39. David Crane, "NAFTA Lacks a Sense of Community," Toronto Star, 23 August 1998.

40. I am grateful to Ted Gerber for suggesting a variation on this idea.

Greater Than the Sum of Its Parts:
A Strategic Package

When President Fox proposed the idea of a common market after his election, he took quite a leap. An intermediate point between a free trade area and a common market is a customs union—a free trade area with a common external tariff. This would be no small feat, particularly because Canada and Mexico have negotiated so many other free trade agreements.

Nonetheless, a decision to move NAFTA to a customs union in 5 years would yield real benefits for the three countries. The difficulty stems from the divergent external tariffs and nontariff barriers between Mexico on the one hand and Canada and the United States on the other. The advantage would be to discard the very elaborate but inefficient "rules of origin" procedures that are required under NAFTA. One procedure for achieving this step would be to harmonize tariff levels to the lowest level maintained by one of the three countries. It is fortunate that Mexico first proposed the idea, because its adjustment is likely to be the most difficult. This would also prove to the Canadians that their fear was unfounded that Mexican participation in a free trade area would impede progress toward a customs union.[41]

The step after a customs union is a common market, and that is far more difficult, because it involves the free movement of labor. Most of the people on the periphery of the United States would like nothing better than to travel freely to the United States. This is understandable, because the process of trying to enter the United States can be demeaning and is always time consuming and frustrating. From the US perspective, the problem is obvious: Each year, the United States has a lottery for 40-55,000 immigration visas, and the number of applications range from 7 to 20 million.[42] One has better odds in Las Vegas, but this does not deter the applicants. This is all the more reason why the intermediate steps on migration discussed above need to be part of the broader discussion of how the three countries can make the transition toward a common market. And it is useful to keep in mind that the European Community incorporated transitional periods of 7 years after Greece, Portugal, and Spain joined it before their workers would be permitted to travel freely to the rest of the Community.[43]

The North American policies outlined above—for infrastructure and transportation, trade, macroeconomic coordination, border enforcement,

---

41. Michael Hart, "Disarming the "Undefended Border" in Order to Preserve It: Canada, the United States, and Deepening Economic Integration," Ottawa, photocopy (February 2000), 60.

42. US Department of State, Report of the Visa Office, 1997, http://www.ins.usdoj.gov/graphics/aboutins/statistics.

43. Judy Dempsey, "Brussels Sets Out Migration Options," *Financial Times*, 8 March 2001.

immigration, energy, regional development, and education—are illustrative of the range of sectors that are in need of continent-wide consideration. A trinational perspective opens one's eyes to new, creative ways to deal with old problems. And more important, a trinational approach diminishes the possibilities of paternalistic behavior, which has proven so destructive of bilateral relations in the past.

In a relatively short time, Fox opened a debate on North America that had been almost mute since the passage of NAFTA. The Canadians are watching the dialogue between Mexico and the United States, but they have not become engaged, and are unlikely to do so, unless they feel that something will happen. Many issues are on the table, and the prospects for trade-offs are real. Bush clearly wants to be responsive to Fox because of Mexico and because of the growing importance of the Hispanic community in the United States, but he also does not want to ruin his own agenda or capsize his party. Senator Phil Gramm, a Republican from Texas, vowed that any legalization program would have to pass "over my cold, dead political body."[44] And Gramm's view is not unrepresentative.

A *Time* magazine poll shows that the American people know that Canada and Mexico are very important and that Mexico has a huge impact on US politics (50 percent), the economy (64 percent), and culture (65 percent). But when asked whether they wanted it to be easier or harder to cross the border into the United States from Canada, 15 percent of the American people said it should be easier, and 21 percent harder. From Mexico, 15 percent of Americans wanted it easier, and 53 percent harder.[45] Americans are not ready to tear down the fences. Indeed, they seem to be sitting on the fence on the issue of Mexico. The principal subterranean anxiety of Americans regarding their neighbor to the south is immigration (see next chapter), and yet public opinion surveys also show that Americans—and also Canadians and Mexicans—are prepared to accept a North American union, provided "cultural identity" is not threatened.

The Bush administration might be tempted to assemble a minimal package to respond to Mexico and different constituent groups, but that would be shortsighted. Rather, this is the time to forge a program that responds to long-term goals and priorities. The key to the new relationship lies in establishing a North American Commission and in the three leaders deciding to define a framework of cooperation within which to negotiate each of these issues and sectors. Absent such a concept and lacking an institution to apply it, the old habits will stay.

Fox has pressed the immigration issue so persistently, and with so much credibility, that the United States is paying attention, and wants to

---

44. Cited in Eric Schmitt, "Bush Aides Weigh Legalizing Status of Mexicans in U.S.," *New York Times*, 15 July 2001.

45. *Time*, 11 June 2001, 46.

be responsive. But the question is whether immigration is *the* issue. This issue is very difficult for the United States and is not central to Mexico and the relationship, it is a surrogate for two other goals: respect within the rule of law and development aimed at reducing disparities.

The development fund proposal that was outlined above needs to sit at the center of the package. Fox himself has said: "We should work hard to create opportunities for Mexicans and their families so that they will stay in Mexico."[46] But Mexico does not have the capital to create the infrastructure that would permit it to narrow the gap with its northern neighbors. Canada and the United States have the opportunity to do for Mexico what the European Union did for its four poor partners—to lift it up to the industrial world. In addition, Canada and the United States need to identify ways to tell Mexico and the Mexicans in their communities that they are respected as partners. That might involve a special immigration preference, a new program for temporary workers that protects their rights and gives them the option of seeking permanent residence, and a North American passport.

The design of the North American Community borrows ideas and experience from the European Union, but it is a unique model that relies more on the market and less on bureaucracy, more on pragmatic solutions to sectoral problems and less on grand schemes of confederation. Still, if the three governments of North America can define a common approach, they will give the middle-class developing countries hope that there is room for them in the industrial world.

---

46. He has often made this comment. A recent statement is in "Activities of President Fox on the Last Day of His US Tour," 17 July 2001, http://www.presidencia.gob.mx/.

7

Is a North American Community Feasible? Can Sovereignty Be Transcended?

The sad truth of North America is that very few leaders of Canada, Mexico, and the United States have ever entertained a serious discussion of North American goals or plans, as outlined in the previous chapters. A lack of imagination is only a small part of the reason for this absence of debate. The three governments are not organized to approach North American issues, and officials in each government prefer to deal with problems by themselves or bilaterally. An even more important reason why these ideas have not been discussed is the complex set of fears and prejudices that lurk deep in the souls of the three countries. This dark side sometimes overwhelms the hopes that each country has toward its neighbors; more often, it simply leads to deadlock, leaving the relationship static, working on one issue, two countries at a time. The anxieties stem from similar sources: unknown language, unfamiliar culture, prejudice, or fear of domination because of size, power, or numbers.

Some Americans think that if its government relaxes its border controls, Mexicans would overrun it from the south, and terrorists and drug dealers might infiltrate across its northern border. Some Americans think the Mexican political system is hopelessly corrupt and that there is nothing to be gained by a closer relationship and much that could be lost. Few Americans who do not live close to their northern border pay much attention to Canada, and Canadians and Mexicans pay little attention to each other. It is hard to see each other over the expanse of the United States. "The one relationship that overwhelms all the others," said Canada's former ambassador to Washington, Raymond Chrétien, "is the one with the United States of America."[1] Canadians are preoccupied with

1. Cited in *Time/Canada*, 10 July 2000, 27.

Americans, who they feel can be arrogant and condescending, but also disinterested and sometimes disarmingly friendly. Some Canadians also fear if they eased their border restrictions, they "would be inundated with American fugitives, firearms, and drugs."[2] The Mexican view of the United States is similar to that of Canada; they are irritated by the imperious, unilateral approach to so many issues. Added together, it is not hard to see why the three governments settled for a narrow definition of NAFTA and have reservations about deepening the relationship.

The problems that beset North America today, and the opportunities that await the region, however, cannot be addressed effectively unless the three—or at least two—begin to organize themselves around a concept like "community." Let me offer examples on the two issues—drugs and immigration—that continually disrupt US-Mexican relations because both are handled unilaterally and in a patronizing fashion by the United States. The truth is that drugs constitute a far more serious threat to the national security of Mexico than of the United States. The reason is that the amount of drug money available to corrupt the Mexican political system is such that its president can never be sure who works for him and who works for the drug traffickers. To have the United States annually grade his government on its performance, as required by US drug laws, is not only unhelpful in stopping drugs, but also is demeaning and generates mistrust when it does not provoke resistance. In other words, if a partnership is necessary to cope with drug trafficking, then a unilateral certification process is counterproductive to that goal. If the problem is defined as a shared one, then joint teams should solve it, and the spillover effects on the rest of the relationship would be positive.

Why has this been so difficult? US officials have shared sensitive intelligence with senior Mexican officials in the past, and they later learned that the Mexicans passed it—for a fee—to the drug traffickers. The simple way to cope with such a betrayal is to distrust all Mexican officials, but such an approach is a cul-de-sac. So the answer to past problems is caution and precaution, but it should not be to cease cooperation. Indeed, the new Fox administration proved that patience was the wiser course. It assembled a new team to work with US government officials, and that team has shown itself worthy of being trusted. This new level of cooperation has permitted the most effective operations against drug traffickers that either side had seen in many years.[3]

Illegal migration from Mexico increased sharply after the peso crisis, and Congress reacted by doubling the personnel in the INS.[4] The US

---

2. See Val Meredith, M.P., *Trade Corridors: A Report to the Canada-U.S. Inter-Parliamentary Group* (Ottawa, 2000), 8.

3. Tim Weiner, "Mexico's New Anti-Drug Team Wins the Trust of U.S. Officials," *New York Times*, 18 July 2001.

4. Mirta Ojito, "Once Divisive, Immigration Is a Muted Issue," *New York Times*, 1 November 1998, 28.

government must enforce its immigration laws, but in the long term, there is only one way to inhibit immigration, and that is to narrow the difference in income between Mexico and the United States. On the basis of the premise of community, the three countries of North America could work to raise wages and reduce pressures for migration. That will not occur easily or soon, but programs aimed at reducing this disparity need to be undertaken without delay.

Let us explore, in turn, why the three governments have been uncomfortable with trilateralism; how the governments could reorganize better to address North American issues; what are public attitudes in the three countries and whether traditional arguments of sovereignty can be overcome.

Why Trilateralism Is Contrary to Habit but Essential

To the extent possible, the three governments should work together to try to fashion continent-wide or trilateral responses to issues, recognizing that some issues might not lend themselves easily to such an approach. Nonetheless, the policies that emerge from trying to incorporate the interests of all three countries are likely to be fairer and more effective than if each government acts alone.

Of course, this is not the way the three governments approach most issues. The United States, as the most powerful and paradoxically insular of the three, faces a constant temptation to act unilaterally, although this infuriates its neighbors. The number of examples is legion, and every administration repeats the mistake. Why?

There are three reasons. First, the structure of the US government is such that Congress plays a critical and independent role in making US policy, but its entire incentive system is aimed at meeting local needs. There may be no institution that has more power to affect the globe and less awareness of that fact than Congress. Therefore, it should come as no surprise that Congress not only resists any international obligations, but also presses the Executive Branch to take actions that serve a partial interest at the expense of the national interest.

The second reason is that the Executive Branch itself is ill-equipped to retrieve its historical memory and apply it in a way that would avoid repeating past mistakes. One is not surprised when this occurs when a new administration takes office, but these are not the only times the government stumbles. US foreign and civil service personnel are rotated so frequently that at any one time the career officers might be just as green as their new superiors.

The third reason is psychological, and it derives from American power and the feeling of "exceptionalism." The combination explains why

Americans do not feel a need to consult or take into account other views. This trait is what our neighbors call "arrogance," a not inappropriate word.

Beyond the American temptation of unilateralism, *the other obstacle to moving toward a trilateral approach is the Canadian and Mexican preference for bilateralism.* This is also a perfectly natural reaction by two countries that can barely see each other over the giant elephant that sleeps or stampedes between them. Moreover, each country sees its "North American" problem as unique, and many of those problems are, in fact, different. For example, the drug, immigration, and border problems look very different on the northern border of the United States than on the southern border. There is some debate as to the principal cause of the difference—whether it is the greater economic disparity between Mexico and the United States or cultural differences. But "culture" is not static or immutable; it has changed markedly in the past three decades because of immigration, improved communications, and travel.

It is precisely because the cultural gap has narrowed, while the economic gap has not, that a trilateral approach would be more effective in framing the future relationship. To the extent that the three governments employ their distinct perspectives but also think like North Americans, they will be more likely to locate a fair and reciprocal policy. For example, on drugs, if Canadian officials could join Americans and Mexicans on drug raids in the three countries, all three would soon appreciate both the similarities of their problem as well as the differences. Through such joint approaches, the three countries might find it easier to devise more effective policies and more genuine partnerships.

Reorganizing the Governments

NAFTA represents a fundamental shift in the relationship of the three governments, but none have fully incorporated or adapted to that new relationship. One reason is that the governments are organized to respond to and pursue the old agenda, one issue at a time by an agency whose principal responsibility is to assist a local constituency. All three governments should reorganize themselves more effectively, not just to advance their national interests but also to respond to the proposed North American Commission and to North American issues. Because of the asymmetric nature of the relationship, Canada and Mexico have always given highest priority to their relationship with the United States. In July 2001, Canada reconstituted the office responsible for the bilateral relationship so that its staff would also be responsible for Mexico and therefore able to see the North American connection.[5] Mexico might want to do the same.

---

5. Interview with Michael Kergin, the Canadian ambassador to the United States, and Jon Allen, who will be the first director-general for North American affairs in the Ministry of Foreign Affairs and International Trade, Washington, 20 June 2001.

The most important governmental reorganization needs to be done by the United States. Its existing system is excessively compartmentalized, with each agency defining its own approach to a problem. The result is that each interest often holds the entire relationship hostage. The US Drug Enforcement Administration—angry that one of its agents was tortured and killed in the mid-1980s in Mexico—sent a team into Mexico to kidnap a doctor who was allegedly involved in the murder. The State Department was not informed; the Mexican government was furious; and several years later, a US judge released the doctor for insufficient evidence. The US government privately promised that it would not do anything like that again. But a decade later, several agencies of the US government lured some Mexican bankers to California, where they were arrested in a grand money-laundering scam called Operation Casa Blanca. In his inaugural address, President Fox pointed to both incidents as the kind that would make it impossible to have a close relationship with the United States. But unless the US government fundamentally changes the way it approaches its neighbors, these incidents will continue to recur.

In June 1998, US Secretary of State Madeleine Albright undertook the first department reorganization for North American issues but it was so inadequate that it was almost laughable. She moved the Office of Canadian Affairs out of the European Bureau and into a newly constituted Bureau of Western Hemisphere Affairs. The reorganization had two flaws. First, the Office for Canada and the one for Mexico report to *different* deputies. This defeats the whole point of trying to build up a capability to understand and analyze the trilateral relationship. Second, the two office directors and the Bureau are all located at too low a level to get the attention of the domestic Cabinet officers, who do most of the business on Canadian and Mexican affairs.

There are two models for dealing with the bureaucratic problem—one based at the State Department and one at the White House. If the State Department is going to oversee North American affairs, it needs to establish a position at the rank of undersecretary of state and staff it with a person of independent stature. That person needs to obtain the authority from the president and the secretary of state to relate to domestic Cabinet secretaries as equals, because they are the ones with the most responsibility in the different compartments of US policy toward Mexico.

The second model would place the position in the White House and appoint an adviser to the president for North American affairs. The position would be comparable to the special envoy of the Americas, a post created by President Clinton for his former chief of staff, Thomas M. McLarty, but the advisor on North America would play a more substantive role as coordinator. The adviser should chair a Cabinet or sub-Cabinet-level council to manage those issues, and he or she should report to the president after getting concurrence from the national security adviser and economic adviser.

The US government should have learned from decades of handling Canadian and Mexican issues that it is simply not organized to deal effectively, constructively, and imaginatively with either relationship. There is a bias in the way the government is organized that leads it to adopt again and again a segmented, parochial perspective rather than to see the connections between the issues and project a continental strategy to advance US interests. A strong secretary of state might be able to manage the process, but it would make more sense for it to be managed in the White House by a senior advisor to the president.

Alternative Approaches to Sovereignty

Even if the leaders were convinced to adopt a trilateral approach, and they reorganized their governments accordingly, they would need to cope with the long-standing argument against collective action—"sovereignty": We will not accept an international initiative, because it constitutes "interference in our internal affairs." None of the three governments is immune to this argument. The Mexicans, of course, championed this warning for decades, and the Canadians insisted on exempting "culture" and information from NAFTA to safeguard its national essence from foreign ideological pollution. The United States, the principal creator of the most important international institutions in the 20th century, should be taking the lead in establishing North American organizations. But in recent years, many American leaders have sounded like third-world populists. The US Senate has refused to ratify or even consider numerous international conventions, and in 2000, the then-chairman of the Senate Foreign Relations Committee, Jesse Helms, went to the United Nations to warn the Security Council not to interfere in US internal affairs. So "sovereignty" is not just a tactic that Mexicans use; it is one that is used by leaders in all three countries.

The truth is that the concept of "sovereignty" is one of the most widely used, abused, and least understood terms in the diplomatic lexicon. Leaving aside the debate on its juridical meaning, and instead examining how it has been defined in practice, one soon realizes that it barely resembles its old self. Europe, the site of the birth of the multistate system in the 17th century and of its most violent struggles in the 20th century, also was the first to look beyond the original definition. In an address in 1962, Jean Monnet, the leader of the European unity movement, marveled at how much had changed in a relatively short time. "Today," he said, "people have almost forgotten that the Saar was ever a problem and yet from 1919 to 1950, it was a major bone of contention between France and Germany. European unity has made it seem an anachronism. And today, at French invitation, German troops are training on French soil."[6] The frigid issue of sovereignty was melting.

Within North America, no one understood the transformation of the meaning of sovereignty better than Mexican President Salinas, whose country had long used the "defense of sovereignty" as a shield to protect its ruling party and exclude influence from its northern neighbor. Still, Salinas woke up one morning in the spring of 1990 and realized that the shield was *harming* Mexico, *not* protecting it. In his third message to the Mexican Congress, he explained: "Historically, nationalism has responded to an external threat. Today, that threat has become the prospect of remaining outside, at the margins of the worldwide integrationist trend . . . To fail in that challenge would be to weaken oneself."[7]

In 1980, Mexico rejected US proposals to reduce tariffs or modify its foreign investment law as constituting interference in its internal affairs. By 1990, Mexico invited US proposals in this area. In 1990, Mexico regarded efforts by the international community to monitor its elections as interference in its internal affairs. By 1994, Mexico invited international observers. In the 1970s, Mexico's ambassador to the United States was instructed to avoid the White House and Congress and present formal messages to the Department of State. Two decades later, Mexico launched one of the most intensive and expensive lobbying campaigns Washington has ever witnessed, blanketing every member of Congress and collaborating with the White House to persuade the United States to approve NAFTA. In an assessment by a Mexican scholar, this last shift—from diplomatic niceties to a no-holds-barred public relations campaign—was characterized as "the beginning of the end of the discourse of sovereign democracy."[8] The boundary of sovereignty—the line separating internal and external affairs—had been moved.[9]

The harder question is whether a Community—a political entity that could transcend traditional conceptions of sovereignty—exists or even is possible in North America. Karl Deutsch wrote that as states become

---

6. Jean Monnet, "A Ferment of Change," in *The European Union: Readings on the Theory and Practice of European Integration*, ed. Brent F. Nelsen and Alexander C-G. Stubb (Boulder, CO: Lynne Rienner Publishers, 1998), 23.

7. Cited in Guadalupe Gonzalez and Stephan Haggard, "The United States and Mexico: A Pluralistic Security Community?" in *Security Communities*, ed. Emanuel Adler and Michael Barnett (Cambridge: Cambridge University Press, 1998), 314.

8. Jorge Chabat, "Mexico's Foreign Policy after NAFTA: The Tools of Interdependence," in *Bridging the Border: Transforming Mexico-US Relations*, ed. Rodolfo de la Garza and Jesus Velasco (Lanham, MD: Rowman and Littlefield, 1997), 43.

9. For an extensive discussion of the many issues swirling around "sovereignty," see Joyce Hoebing, Sidney Weintraub, and M. Delal Baer, eds., *NAFTA and Sovereignty: Trade-Offs for Canada, Mexico, and the United States* (Washington: Center for Strategic and International Studies, 1996).

more integrated, they begin to develop a sense of "community," which he defined as an assurance "that they will settle their differences short of war." Adler and Barnett build on this idea and define a "pluralistic security community as a transnational region comprised of sovereign states whose people maintain dependable expectations of peaceful change."[10] Gonzales and Haggard test whether this definition applies to Mexico and the United States, and they conclude that the relationship falls short because of a lack of trust and common identity.[11] They reach this conclusion after reviewing the swings in the relationship after the 1940s. Despite determined efforts by Presidents Franklin D. Roosevelt and Manuel Avila Camacho to press their countries toward a new level of respect, Gonzales and Haggard believe that "collaboration remains segmented and the extent of mutual confidence limited." In short, no community.

Shore, however, explored the long-term relationship between Canada and the United States, and concluded that the two countries had become a "community," and the main reason was that the long (5,000-mile) border was not defended. That fact became a "powerful trust-generating mechanism: the longer the two sides refrained from arming, the more trustworthy they appeared to one another." That, plus their reaction to the wars in Europe, created the basis for a "shared North American identity."[12]

Of course, the US-Mexican border has been demilitarized almost as long as the US-Canadian border, so other factors explain the difference. Some obvious candidates are shared language and culture between Canada and the United States and the sharp differences in political development, social class, and language between Mexico and the United States.

The most serious omission in the otherwise perceptive essay by Gonzalez and Haggard was their failure to examine public opinion. Do the people of each country think a community exists in North America? Although we do not have as precise survey data on this subject as one would like, there are numerous polls from which one can splice an answer.

Fertile Soil for a North American Identity

As Europe became more integrated, many people began to change the way they identified themselves. Germans did not give up their citizenship, but roughly 30 percent of them (and of most of the other nations) became

---

10. Adler and Barnett, Security Communities, 3, 30.

11. Gonzalez and Haggard, "U.S. and Mexico," 295.

12. Sean M. Shore, "No Fences Make Good Neighbors: The Development of the U.S.-Canadian Security Community," 1871-1940, in Adler and Barnett, Security Communities, 333-35.

"as attached to the EU as they are to their own country."[13] Marks analyzed public opinion in Europe and concluded that people were adopting multiple identities: that their attachments were "mutually inclusive," not exclusive. In Canada, Mexico, and the United States, the three publics do not see themselves as "North American," but that should come as no surprise because the idea is still so novel. A related problem is that the term "Norteamericano" is currently the Mexican word for a US citizen. If the term is to apply to the citizens of all three countries, Mexicans will first need to become comfortable applying it to themselves.

An analysis of public opinion surveys suggests that the public in all three countries is open to the idea of being part of a larger unit. This conclusion emerges from answers by the public in each country to the following four sets of questions: (1) Are the attitudes of people in each country toward family, government, and the economy similar or different? Is there, in other words, a cultural unity or divide among the three peoples? (2) Does the public in each of the countries view the others as friends or enemies? (3) How does each view NAFTA? (4) And how does each view the prospect of growing integration? Under what conditions might the people of each country want to combine into a North American entity?

Convergence of Values

Under the direction of Ronald Inglehart of the University of Michigan, scholars conducted the World Values Survey evaluating the values and attitudes of people in about 43 countries. Miguel Basañez of Mexico and Neil Nevitte of Canada joined Inglehart to do surveys of the three countries of North America in 1981, 1990, and 2000. Rather than documenting cultural differences, they found a convergence of values among the people in the three countries in 12 of 16 key domains. For example, people in all three countries more and more emphasize independence and imagination in child rearing; there is less support for state ownership of industry, and national pride is waning; church attendance rates are falling; and respect for authority is declining. This last point is particularly significant.

In most of the industrial democracies, the World Values Survey has found that people more and more question the authority of government and other institutions. Some see this decline of confidence as alarming and a trend that could lead to the erosion of democracy; others see it as a positive sign of increasing autonomy by individuals.[14] Public opinion

---

13. Gary Marks, "Territorial Identities in the European Union," in *Regional Integration and Democracy: Expanding on the European Experience*, ed. Jeffrey J. Anderson (Lanham, MD: Rowman and Littlefield, 1999), 73-74.

14. A concern about the decline in confidence in American institutions is the premise of Joseph S. Nye, Jr., Philip D. Zelikow, and David C. King, eds., *Why People Don't Trust Government* (Cambridge: Harvard University Press, 1997). The opposite premise guides Inglehart's work. See his *Modernization and Postmodernization: Cultural, Economic, and Political Change in 43 Societies* (Princeton, NJ: Princeton University Press, 1997).

surveys suggest that the "political cultures" in Canada and Mexico have undergone fundamental changes. Canadians have long been viewed as having a "culture of deference,"[15] but in the past two decades, the traditionally restrained debates in Canada became heated on critical issues like the Constitution, the independence of Quebec, the environment, and such social issues as gay rights and equality for women. Mexico's long-standing political authoritarianism had led many scholars to describe a political culture that was corrupt and coercive, and yet the past decade has seen an astonishing advance toward democracy and free elections.[16]

Indeed, there has been a convergence in North America toward similar values, also basic public policies. In all three countries, there has been movement toward political liberalization, market-based, regulatory economic policy, and more respect for the rights of groups—notably minorities and indigenous peoples—that had been marginalized. Attitudes—the civic culture, if you will—and policies converged not toward an American average but toward a different point. "North Americans," Basañez and Nevitte concluded, "have become *significantly more alike*."[17]

Trinational Perceptions

Despite suspicions that each country was said to have harbored toward one another, public opinion surveys suggest that the three peoples of North America have very positive views of each other. The Chicago Council on Foreign Relations has been doing public opinion surveys on US views of the world every 4 years since 1974. One question measures "favorability"—the warmth that Americans feel toward other countries. During the past 25 years, Americans have consistently given Canada the

---

15. In his important book, *The Decline of Deference* (North Guelph, Ontario: Broadview Press, 1996), Neil Nevitte offers a persuasive critique of the interpretation of Canadians as historically and culturally different, if not opposite, from Americans—a view most effectively developed by Seymour Martin Lipset, *Continental Divide: The Values and Institutions of the United States and Canada* (New York: Routledge, 1991).

[emphasis added]16. The literature on the political culture of authoritarian Mexico is vast, but a good summary is by Wayne A. Cornelius, Politics in Mexico, in *Comparative Politics Today*, ed. Gabriel A. Almond, Bingham Powell, Jr., et al. (New York: Longman, 2000). For an analysis of the July 2000 election and its implications for Mexico's political culture, see Robert A. Pastor, "Mexico's Victory: Exiting the Labyrinth," *Journal of Democracy* 11, no. 4 (October 2000).

[emphasis added]17. Ronald Inglehart, Neil Nevitte, and Miguel Basañez, *The North American Trajectory: Cultural, Economic, and Political Ties among the United States, Canada, and Mexico* (New York: Aldine de Gruyter, 1996). For a summary and update of the argument, see Nevitte and Basañez, "Trinational Perceptions," in *The Controversial Pivot: U.S. Congress and North America*, ed. Robert A. Pastor and Rafael Fernandez de Castro (Washington: Brookings Institution, 1998), 149 for the quote. [emphasis added]

highest favorability rating among all nations. The US view of Mexico is also very positive, just below that of Canada and the United Kingdom and on roughly the same level as some of the leading countries of Europe (Germany, France, and Italy).[18]

Roughly three-fourths of all Mexicans hold a positive view of the United States (almost the same as the percentage of Americans with a positive view of Mexico) and particularly of the US political system. More than 80 percent of Mexicans believe that the United States exercises the most influence on their country. But it is rather surprising that 67 percent of Mexicans view US influence as positive, a marked difference from the way that the elite had long portrayed the Mexican public's views. A 1998 poll showed that 77 percent of the Mexican public felt relations with the United States were good.[19]

Canadians also have warm feelings about the United States, although not quite as warm as Americans have toward them. For example, in a 1999 survey in Canada, 49 percent of Canadians viewed Americans as similar to themselves, whereas 71 percent of Americans viewed Canada as similar. When asked for a word to describe Americans, the two most frequently chosen words were "arrogant" (16 percent) and "aggressive" (8 percent), whereas Americans chose "friendly" (29 percent) most often to apply to Canadians.[20] The problem, according to several Canadian commentators, is that Canadians feel that Americans take them for granted and never take the time to learn about them. "Canadians," writes Ferguson in Maclean's, "love to be misunderstood and unappreciated—especially by big, strong America."[21] The more telling point is that 26 percent of the Canadian public would become US citizens if they could, and 25 percent of the American public expressed a similar preference for Canadian citizenship.[22]

Canadians and Mexicans have had much more contact since NAFTA than before. There are many anecdotes but few surveys to assess the relationship. Only since 1990 has Canada looked to Latin America in a serious way, joining the Organization of American States that year and negotiating free trade agreements with several countries since then. It is

---

18. Chicago Council on Foreign Relations, *American Public Opinion and U.S. Foreign Policy*. The polls have been done every 4 years beginning in 1974 and published the subsequent year. The most recent was published in 1999.

19. See Nevitte and Basáñez, "Trinational Perceptions," for a description of this and other polling, 152-57.

20. Canada's leading magazine, *Maclean's*, did an extensive survey in 1999 in both Canada and the United States, and devoted an entire issue, "Vanishing Borders" (29 December 1999) to analyzing it; see 23-25 for the polls on mutual perceptions.

21. Cited in Andrew Phillips, "Benign Neglect," *Maclean's*, 20 December 1999, 25.

22. *Maclean's*, 20 December 1999, 22.

clear that Canada has invested more economically and diplomatically in Mexico than anywhere else in Latin America.

So, in brief, not only are the three countries of North America *more alike today than ever before,* but *their people like each other more than before* or than those of most other countries. This is both cause and consequence of a gradual shift occurring in the way people in the region are identifying themselves—from their local communities to national ones. In addition, the percentage of the public that identified themselves as "North American" doubled during the 1980s, although that was only from 2 to 4 percent.[23] One possible explanation for the shift is the arrival of a younger, more cosmopolitan generation, dubbed the "Nexus," because they are more connected across borders.[24]

Views of NAFTA

During the past decade, public attitudes toward NAFTA in the three countries have traversed a rather curious path. One might expect that the convergence in values and the accelerating pace of integration would have led to a rather consistently positive view of NAFTA, but as figure 7.1 shows, all three countries traveled a roller-coaster ride on the NAFTA train. The US public was very supportive from the time negotiations began in 1991 until a year later. From then until NAFTA's approval by Congress in November 1993, public opinion was almost evenly divided. The intensive public campaign on behalf of NAFTA managed to lift the support slightly above that of the opposition. After Congress approved NAFTA, support for it rose until the peso crisis. From that point on, both support for and opposition to NAFTA plummeted for the next year, and then began to increase again—while all the time, the margin of difference remained consistent through 1997.

In the fall of 1997, the US Congress faced the question of whether to extend fast-track authority to allow the president to negotiate the expansion of NAFTA to the Free Trade Area of the Americas. A Gallup/CNN poll in August 1997 showed that 52 percent opposed and only 44 percent

---

23. Inglehart, Nevitte, and Basañez, *North American Trajectory*, 158-60. They surveyed attitudes in the three countries in 1981 and 1990 as to the principal geographical unit with which people identified: town, region, nation, North America, and world, and they found "a consistent pattern: in all three countries, there was a substantial shift from emphasis on the town . . . toward the broader geographical units." One should not exaggerate. Even though, for example, the number of Americans who identified with "North America" doubled in that period, that only went from 2 to 4 percent. Still, the shift toward "nation" was impressive in all three countries—from 20 to 30 percent in the United States, 30-40 percent in Canada, and 18-28 percent in Mexico.

24. Jennifer Walsh, "Is a North American Generation Emerging?" *ISUMA/Printemps* (Spring 2000), 86-92.

**Figure 7.1   Public opinion on NAFTA in Canada, Mexico, and the
United States, 1990-97**

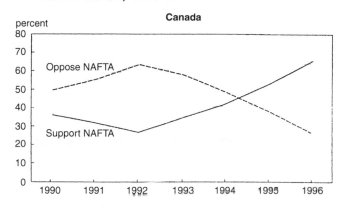

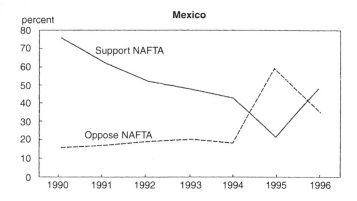

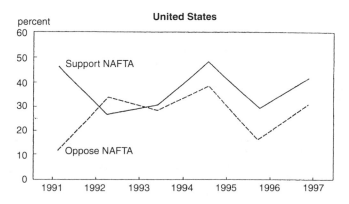

Source: Nevitte, Neil, and Basañez, Miguel. 1988. "Trinational Perceptions" in *The Controversial Pivot: U.S. Congress and North America,* eds. Robert A. Pastor and Rafael Fernandez de Castro, 158-59. Washington: Brookings Institution.

favored its extension. This was consistent with an NBC/*Wall Street Journal* Poll in November 1997, which showed 42 percent saying NAFTA had a negative impact on the United States and only 32 percent declaring a positive impact. But it was inconsistent with a Pew poll at the time, which showed that 47 percent of the public thought NAFTA was a "good thing"; and only 30 percent, that it was bad. In a poll 2 years later, on 29 October 1999, 35 percent of the US public said that NAFTA had helped the United States; 32 percent that it had hurt; and 24 percent that it had made no difference.[25]

Other surveys on trade and international issues are of help in interpreting these polls. It is also useful to recall that after the passage of NAFTA, and particularly after the peso crisis, the issue largely disappeared from the public debate. In August 1999, when people were asked in a *Washington Post*/Henry K. Kaiser/Harvard University poll whether they had heard enough about the issue to decide whether NAFTA was good or bad, 51 percent said they had not. In comparison, 24 percent said NAFTA had been good, and 20 percent thought it had been bad.[26] Pockets of constituencies remained engaged in the issue, but by and large, the US public had moved on to other issues. When asked about trade agreements in general, a substantial majority—by a ratio of more than 2:1—have expressed support, provided that the agreements are genuinely reciprocal and fair. When asked about the impact of a particular agreement, the public's response tends to correlate with the state of the economy at the time.[27]

Public opinion in Mexico and Canada on NAFTA also experienced some radical swings. In Mexico, supporters of NAFTA outnumbered opponents 5:1 when Salinas first proposed the idea, but during the next 4 years, as the negotiations dragged on, support declined. Opposition remained steady at about 15 percent of the public until 1994, when a series of crises lifted the number of opponents above the number of supporters. The two sides remained in their respective positions until the beginning of 1996, when support for NAFTA once again surmounted the opposition. The trajectory in Canada was just the opposite. Opponents outnumbered supporters from 1990 until 1994, when the economy began to grow again. Since then, most Canadians have indicated their support.

---

25. The polls are: Pew (17 October 1997) on NAFTA a good thing (47-30); Gallup/CNN (August 1997) opposing its extension (52-44); NBC/*Wall Street Journal* (November 1997) on NAFTA's negative impact (42-32); and NBC/*WSJ* (October 1999) on free trade agreements helping the United States (35-32-24). For these sites, see the *National Journal* Web site http://www.nationaljournal/polltrack/nationalissues/trade.htm.

26. Cited by Steven Kull, *Americans on Globalization: A Study of U.S. Public Attitudes* (College Park: University of Maryland, Program on International Policy Attitudes, 2000); see http://www.pipa.org/onlinereports/globalization/appendixb.html.

27. Kull, *Americans on Globalization*, International Trade, 1-4.

The swings of public opinion in the three countries need to be placed in the context of declining interest in the issue. In the elections of 2000 in all three countries, NAFTA was not an issue. Indeed, international issues faded from the debate as the candidates focused on domestic concerns. By then, all three countries had accepted NAFTA as a reality, and despite one poll in the United States that indicated that as many as 40 percent of the public would like it changed, the candidates thought it would be far better to let the issue lie quietly rather than offer any ideas for reform.[28]

A recent round of polls, however, demonstrates a curious symmetry on NAFTA. When *Americans* were asked about NAFTA's effect on themselves, 39 percent thought it had been good for the United States, and 35 percent thought it had been bad. But when Americans were asked about NAFTA's effect on Mexico, 57 percent said it had been good, and only 11 percent thought it had been bad. When Mexicans were asked, 43 percent thought it had been good for Mexico, but 47 percent believed it had been bad. In contrast, 73 percent of *Mexicans* thought NAFTA had been good for the United States, whereas only 16 percent thought it had been bad. Moving to the third corner of the triangle, a 1999 survey showed that 9 percent of *Canadians* believed they had benefited more than the United States from NAFTA (twice as high as a decade before), but 60 percent thought the United States benefited more. Only 17 percent thought both sides had gained.[29]

This is an unusual display of reverse compliments. All three peoples agree on NAFTA's effect: *The others have benefited more than they have!*

A More Perfect Union

The point of departure for our discussion of public opinion in the three countries was to explore whether a new approach toward NAFTA—one that deepened the relationship—was practical, given the strong nationalist feelings in all three countries. The assumption was that the three peoples were so different and such zealous defenders of their sovereignty that any movement toward collaboration, let alone confederation, would be resisted vigorously. The opinion polls suggest that this assumption should be relaxed, if not discarded. Still other surveys provide a more focused test of whether a new relationship in North America is possible; indeed, of whether political union is a legitimate subject for discussion.

---

28. The one poll in 1999 by EPIC/MRA was commissioned by the Association of Women for International Trade. It found that 24 percent of the American public thought NAFTA should continue; 18 percent favored withdrawal; and 40 percent wanted it changed. See the *National Journal* Web site above.

29. For Mexican and US views, see the Harris Poll in April/May 1999 (*National Journal* polltrack); for the Canadian views, see *Maclean's*, 20 December 1999, 42.

In the 1990 World Values Survey, about a fourth of the Canadian and Mexican populations were in favor of erasing the border with the United States, and nearly half (46 percent) of Americans favored eliminating the border with Canada.[30] In 2000, a survey of US attitudes found Americans still evenly divided (42-42 percent, with 16 percent not knowing) on whether to do away with the border with Canada, but more than 3:1 (72-19 percent, with 9 percent not knowing) against doing away with the Mexican border. The Mexicans agree with the Americans on this issue, though not in quite such a one-sided way. Fifty-five percent of Mexicans oppose doing away with the border with the United States, and only 36 percent favor it (with 9 percent not knowing).[31]

When Americans, Canadians, and Mexicans are asked whether they are prepared to give up their cultural identity to form one nation-state or a union, all overwhelmingly reject the proposition. But when asked whether they would be prepared to form a single country if that would mean a higher quality of life for their country, *a majority of the people in all three countries answer affirmatively*. Specifically, 56.2 percent of Mexicans favor (and only 31.5 percent oppose) forming a single country with the United States if it would improve their quality of life, and 53.4 percent favor union if environmental issues would be handled more effectively. *Joining* with the United States to establish a separate entity elicits support, but Mexicans oppose being *incorporated* into the United States. Nearly half (47.8 percent) of all Mexicans opposed being absorbed into the United States; only 30 percent of the Mexican public would be in favor of that.[32]

Forty-three percent of Canadians think it "would be *a good thing to be part of a North American Union* in ten years" (emphasis added), and only 27 percent think it would be a bad thing. Moreover, *nearly half (49 percent) think North American union is likely to happen.* As with the Mexicans, Canadians are much more willing to contemplate a union in a new North American entity than to be part of the United States. A majority (57 percent) would oppose joining the United States, whereas only 23 percent would consider it.[33] When asked whether Canada and the United States should have a common currency, the Canadian public split: 45 percent in favor,

30. Inglehart, Nevitte, and Basañez, *North American Trajectory*, 139.

31. Inglehart and Basañez, World Values Survey / USA and Mexico, 2000. I am indebted to Miguel Basañez for sharing the data and his insights and comments.

32. Inglehart and Basañez, World Values Survey.

33. Ekos Resesarch, Canada, Shifting Perceptions of Globalization and the New Economy, 21 September 2000. Ekos prepared a compilation of surveys. The ones cited were in 1999. This information is available at http://www.ekos.com.

and 44 percent opposed.[34] This suggests that Canadians are much further along than their leaders in thinking about some of the practical, but sensitive, questions of integration.

Among the US public, a relatively higher percentage favor continental political union than is true of Mexicans and Canadians. Support for union soars when the contingency options—for example, if that would mean a better quality of life—are included. In 1990, *81 percent* of Americans said they would favor forming one country with Canada *if it meant a better quality of life*, and *79 percent* agreed *if it meant the environment would get better*.[35] These numbers declined a bit in 2000, but remained relatively high—63 percent approved of forming one country if it would improve the quality of life, and 48 percent if the environment would get better.[36] When one disaggregates the data, its clear that young, wealthy Americans are readier to contemplate political union than old or poor citizens.[37]

What should one conclude from these data? First, the *majority* of the people in *all three countries* are prepared to contemplate a reconfiguration of the North American political system—*if* they can be convinced that it will produce a higher quality of life and handle problems (e.g., the environment) more effectively than is done by each country. Second, the principal motive is *economic*, the approach is *pragmatic*, and the main drawback is the fear of its effect on *culture and identity*. To the extent that people perceive their cultures to be at risk, they resist integration. Third, *young people* are more connected and ready to experiment with new political forms and so the prospects for *future* integration are likely to get better. Fourth, as Deutsch predicted a half-century ago, *more contact and trust among peoples can facilitate integration, which, in turn, can increase trust.* In disaggregating the data on a regional basis, one finds greater support for integration among those regions that have the most commerce (i.e., the southwest of the United States, the northern part of Mexico, and along the Canadian border).[38] A *clear majority* of the public in *all three countries* supports political *union*, *if* they could be convinced that it would improve their lives. *The people, in brief, are way ahead of their leaders.*

John Kenneth Galbraith, the former Harvard economist, who was born in Canada, offered a simple anecdote to indicate the power of pragmatism: "I was brought up in southwestern Ontario where we were taught that

---

34. *Maclean's*, "17th Annual Poll," December 25, 2000. The 1999 poll by *Maclean's* was consistent with that survey, showing 44 percent of Canadians believing Canada would benefit from a common currency, and 42 percent believing it would be very costly. In Bruce Wallace, "What Makes a Canadian?" *Maclean's*, 20 December 1999, 36.

35. Inglehart, Nevitte, and Basañez, *North American Trajectory*, table 6.2.

36. Inglehart and Basañez, "World Values Survey."

37. Inglehart, Nevitte, and Basañez, *North American Trajectory*, 135-48.

38. *Ibid.*, 139.

Canadian patriotism should not withstand anything more than a five dollar wage differential. Anything more, and you went to Detroit."[39] The underlying basis of a community exists. Provided people are not threatened by a loss of culture or identity, and incentives for productivity and improvements for standard of living are evident, the three peoples of North America are ready to listen to ideas on how to combine in order to accomplish those ends.

Subterranean Anxieties

Although Americans, Canadians, and Mexicans are prepared to consider a broader community in North America, one should not discount the underlying fears that impeded integration in the past and may do so in the future. Indeed, the concerns that are often raised about sovereignty may function as a mask, covering a deeper anxiety. Like most fears, the legitimate blends with the subconscious. To the extent that one can dispel the rational concerns, then perhaps one can reduce the anxieties. Let us therefore address the core anxiety for each country. For the United States, the principal fear stems from Mexican immigration. For Canada and Mexico, it is the fear of being dominated by the United States or having the latter take control of their natural resources.

Every significant wave of immigration to the United States has generated a nativist reaction, particularly if the wave comes from a country or region that had not previously sent large numbers of immigrants. In the middle of the 19th century, native Protestant Americans reacted against the wave of Catholic immigrants from Ireland and Germany. At the end of the 19th century, the arrival of Chinese immigrants led to the first "exclusion act" passed by Congress. At the turn of the century, the arrival of millions of people from Southern and Eastern Europe finally moved Congress to pass the first immigration laws (in 1921 and 1924), setting quantitative limits on immigration. The most recent wave, beginning with the 1965 immigration act, has come from the developing world, but the single largest source has been Mexico.

In a recent essay, Huntington argued that Mexican immigrants are demonstrably different. "Mexican immigration," he wrote, "is a unique, disturbing, and looming challenge to our cultural integrity, our national identity, and potentially to our future as a country."[40] These are strong words from a distinguished Harvard professor. He identifies five charac-

---

39. Cited by Michael Hart, "The Role of Dispute Settlement in Managing Canada-U.S. Trade and Investment Relations," in *Canada among Nations 2000: Vanishing Borders*, ed. Maureen Appel Molot and Fen Osler Hampson (New York: Oxford University Press, 2000), 23.

40. Samuel P. Huntington, *Reconsidering Immigration: Is Mexico a Special Case?* (Washington: Center for Immigration Studies, 2000), 6, http://www.cis.org/articles/2000/back1100.html.

teristics of Mexican immigration that makes it a unique problem: contiguity, large numbers, illegality, concentration in the Southwest, and persistence. "The really serious problem," in Huntington's view, is not immigration; it is "assimilation." And yet he acknowledges that by most indices—education, intermarriage, language—the results are "uncertain." What seems to disturb him the most is the fear that "America is moving in the direction of becoming a bilingual and bicultural society."

Much of the data, however, point in a different direction. The *Washington Post*, the Henry K. Kaiser Foundation, and Harvard University conducted one of the most comprehensive polls on Hispanics and non-Latinos ever done. The survey found that 9 of 10 Latinos who are new to the United States believe that it is important to change so they can fit into American society. Among those children born in the United States to Hispanic immigrants (the second generation), only 1 in 10 mainly uses Spanish.[41]

The fears many people like Huntington have with Mexican immigration stem from the continued high level of immigration, which skews the statistics and disguises the changes that occur from one generation to the next. Of the 35 million Hispanics in the United States, roughly half were born abroad, and they have a much lower level of education and income than those born in the United States. The *Post*/Kaiser/Harvard survey focuses explicitly on the "assimilation" issue and finds that the patterns of assimilation of past immigrant groups also apply to the new immigration from Mexico and Latin America. About 73 percent of the first generation speak only Spanish at home. Of those born in the United States, 17 percent speak Spanish sometimes at home, and only 1 percent of their children (the third generation) speak only Spanish at home. This is a far cry from a bilingual nation.

Much more interesting is the change in their attitudes from immigrant to third generation. Take the issue of "fatalism." About half of all newly arrived Latino immigrants believe it is pointless to plan for the future because they cannot control it. But by the third generation, only 18 percent believe that, which is fewer than non-Latino Americans (20 percent). Across a range of issues—even on abortion, the death penalty, declining optimism—the attitudes of the third generation of Latinos are comparable to those of the non-Latino population.

Despite the relatively low level of skills of Mexican immigrants, another study found that the second generation earns levels comparable to native-born whites.[42] The United States is a diverse blend of cultures, of which

41. Amy Goldstein and Roberto Suro, "Latinos in America: A Journey in Stages," *Washington Post*, 16 January 2000. The survey was conducted between 30 June and 30 August 1999 of 2,417 Latino adults (divided between first, second, and third generations) and 2,197 non-Latino adults.

42. Roger Waldinger, *Strangers at the Gates: New Immigrants in Urban America* (Washington: Carnegie Endowment for International Peace, 2001).

the Mexican is an important ingredient. The idea that US culture is endangered by a new wave of migration is an old one that has no more validity than it had in the past.

Canadians feared that US investors would purchase their country's major corporations. But as we have seen, the overall share of foreign direct investment in Canada owned by Americans actually declined in the 1990s. A recent analysis of Canadian views on trade and the United States concludes that a majority have come to believe that trade liberalization has a positive impact on innovation and jobs, but they are concerned about its effects on social programs and human security. Over time, Canadian views are "highly correlated with assessments of the economy"— the better the economy, the higher the support for trade. Like Americans, Canadians acknowledge that they do not know much about trade, but they do care about the swirl of issues that have been raised in the debates on trade—issues such as magazines, the environment, and beef hormones.[43] In other words, the original anxieties of the 1980s have been transformed.

The same dynamic appears to be at work in Mexico. The World Values Survey found that about 65 percent would accept the erasing of the border and 70 percent would migrate to the United States if they thought they could benefit economically. Federico Reyes Heroles, a Mexican analyst, analyzed the data and concluded with a rhetorical question: "Are we really very nationalistic?"[44] Mexico had also shed some of its anxieties.

It would be a mistake to conclude that each nation's long-standing fears of integration had simply disappeared. The differences among the nations and the asymmetry of power and wealth guarantee that each country— or, more accurately, groups within each country—will worry about the pace and the direction of integration. And if the United States behaves in an arrogant or offensive way, it will evoke a nationalistic response in its neighbors. What these data show, however, is that as a whole the *people in each country* have traveled a considerable distance toward a *pragmatic*—that is, a nonideological—*acceptance* of an *integrated community*. And they have done so with *practically no leadership*. No leader, except Fox, has dared to articulate a vision of where the community should go. That is the subject of the final part of this chapter.

The Nature of the Community: Three Options

What should a North American Community be? Should it be just a thin mechanism for consulting or coordinating policies? Or should it be a

---

43. Matthew Mendelsohn and Robert Wolfe, "Probing the Aftermyth of Seattle: Canadian Public Opinion on International Trade," 1980-2000, paper prepared for the 2000 National Policy Research Conference, Ottawa (1 December 2000).

44. Federico Reyes Heroles, *Sondear a México* (Mexico: Editorial Ocfano de México, 1995). Reyes Heroles is the brother of the former Mexican ambassador to the United States.

confederation of three states or even a unified multinational state? Let us review three basic options.

Option 1: the market approach. This option represents the status quo: Remove trade and investment barriers and cross one's fingers. This is the most likely scenario, simply because of inertia or fatigue. It is also the most problematic, in the sense that it is the least able to cope with either the windfall or the fallout from integration. The business cycle will carry the three economies through periods of growth and decline, but NAFTA will remain oblivious to distributional effects and to the many mistakes or missed opportunities described in previous chapters.

Option 2: North American confederation of nation-states. The rough equivalent of the Articles of Confederation, this option would leave most power in the hands of the three governments of North America, but they would be working together under the auspices of a weak central government to guarantee the security and prosperity of the continent. One might expect the most powerful country to propose this option, but the United States is an unusual superpower. Since the Republican Senate voted against the League of Nations in 1919, a strong element in the party has viewed international organizations and agreements as undesirable restraints on the unilateral actions of the United States. This position has sometimes been confused with isolationism or protectionism, but it is quite different. It accepts that the United States has important interests in the world that it must defend, but it views international organizations as anchors that weigh the country down and prevent it from fulfilling its proper role. This unilateral internationalism would be skeptical, if not fervently opposed, to any efforts to establish a supranational body to guide or plan the integration process. The idea of a North American Confederation is a nonstarter in all three countries, at least in the foreseeable future.

Option 3: a unified, multinational state. This option would eliminate or fundamentally change the three existing nation-states. Instead, the people of North America would elect leaders to a strong central government that would be respectful of the different cultures and languages. This option is the least likely of all.

The European Union has been considering variations on these three options since the Treaty of Rome. More than 40 years later, they have still not chosen. As it contemplates expansion to include Central and Eastern Europe, three of Europe's leaders offered very different proposals in 2001. The German chancellor proposed a federation with a strong central government—a variation on a multinational state with a more accountable European executive and a more powerful Parliament. The French prime minister responded by saying: "I want a Europe, but I remain attached to my nation." He insisted on a "federation of nation states"—a variation on the confederation. Romano Prodi, the President of the European Commission, suggested that the European Union be permitted to directly tax European citizens.[45] A choice remains on the distant horizon.

Unless President Bush embraces Fox's proposal, and Chrétien follows, the three governments of North America are likely to remain anchored to the status quo option, despite the evidence of its inadequacy. A more serious crisis than the peso devaluation and a graver threat than illegal migration may be needed before they contemplate the kinds of supranational organizations that could anticipate and prevent future crises.

In the interim, what is needed is the nurturing of a regional identity and small steps that could help the peoples of the three countries understand the need for deeper integration. Here again, it would be enlightening to reflect on the experience of Europe. In the early 1950s, Europe had its visionaries. While they were in prison in Italy during the Second World War, Altiero Spinelli and Ernesto Rossi, two antifascist leaders, drafted a manifesto for a "European Federation." Winston Churchill, the British prime minister, and Robert Schuman, France's foreign minister in 1950, also had grand ideas on how Europe should reorganize itself, but the preamble to the Treaty of Rome mentioned only "an ever closer union among the peoples" and the need for solidarity and cooperation. The exact configuration of the final Europe was not defined. Monnet, the "father of Europe," believed that the best way to move Europe toward cooperation was with small collective steps that set off "a chain reaction, a ferment where one change induces another."[46]

This is the neofunctional approach to integration, and it worked within certain limits. In an analysis of public opinion in Europe during a 15-year period, Eichenberg and Dalton concluded that "the growth of intra-EC trade has been a major stimulus to Europeanist sentiment" and that elections for the European Parliament also had a "moderately positive impact on citizen support for the community."[47] In other words, trade and elections encouraged a European identity, much as Deutsch had predicted. This is a worthy lesson for North America.

The European Union also learned that the logic of neofunctionalism was inadequate to the task of getting all the EU governments to make difficult decisions about harmonizing policy and simplifying decision making. Progress on the path toward European integration required leadership and intergovernmental negotiations at critical moments when

---

45. "Debating Europe's Future," *New York Times*, 7 June 2001.

46. Monnet, "Ferment of Change," 19.

47. Richard C. Eichenberg and Russell J. Dalton, "Europeans and the European Community: The Dynamics of Public Support for European Integration," *International Organization* 47 (Autumn 1993), 523.

Europeans feared their experiment was failing.[48] Only then did prime ministers find the strength to make the essential and difficult decisions.

For similar reasons, it would be unhelpful for North America's three leaders to decide between the three grand options—status quo, confederation, or unified state—at this time. It would be far better for them to follow Monnet's advice and move forward with small steps—the first one being the North American Commission, the next ones being sectoral plans. The surveys of opinion in all three countries point with great clarity in the same direction: The people are prepared to undertake new collective efforts if they can be persuaded that these efforts could improve their standard of living. Those are the marching orders for the three leaders: Take some risks, establish some practical organizations, and if growing integration works, take some more.

---

48. Andrew Moravcsik, *The Choice For Europe* (Ithaca, NY: Cornell University Press, 1998).

8

From a North American to an American Community: The 21st Century Challenge of Integration

Men are powerless to secure the future; institutions alone fix the destinies of nations.[1]
—Napoleon

For many years, Mexico warned its neighbors of the perils of getting too close to the United States, either politically or economically. Independence and sovereignty depended on setting clear limits on the relationship with the northern colossus. Latin American leaders did not share Mexico's history, but they understood the need to protect their nationalist flank, and so few sought close relations or risked opening their economies. When the Mexicans proposed a free trade agreement with the United States, replacing their veto on good relations with an affirmation, they opened a door through which virtually every country in the hemisphere requested permission to enter. In December 1994, President Clinton invited the hemisphere's 33 other leaders to enter the US market—although, of course, that was not the way the Summit of the Americas agreement was described. The leaders only pledged to negotiate a Free Trade Area of the Americas by 2005. Nevertheless, the agenda of the negotiations was the outline of NAFTA, and so it is not inaccurate to describe the FTAA as a widening of NAFTA. The prospects for success, however, also depended on Latin America's progress in two areas: imple-

---

1. *Imperiale Séance*, 7 June 1815, quoted in World Bank, *World Development Report 1997* (New York: Oxford University Press), 29.

mentation of economic and political reforms[2] and other free trade initiatives in the hemisphere. A few such agreements—like Mercosur—were new, but most had originated in the 1960s with the first wave of regional integration. The Andean Pact, the Central American Common Market (CACM), the Caribbean Community—these schemes had run out of steam, were fractured by national rivalries, or were wracked by civil wars. Yet in the 1990s, these old schemes were not just dusted off; they were invigorated and transformed.

Let us first describe the development and progress of these subregional trade agreements. Next, we will explore whether it would be wiser to deepen NAFTA or widen it to the FTAA and whether the sequence matters. Then we will shift from the hemispheric implications to the question of how these talks will affect the next round of world trade negotiations. We will conclude the chapter by returning to North America and making the case for overcoming inertia and constructing a Community that will illuminate a path for rich and poor countries alike.

The Trend toward Integration

NAFTA was not the ignition switch that started the other integration movements in the Americas, but it did put wind in their sails. The regional schemes were products of similar causes and circumstances. Most of the countries of Latin America had undertaken structural economic reforms in the mid-1980s in response to the debt crisis. All were compelled to take the same medicine—restore fiscal discipline, privatize state-owned corporations, maintain a realistic exchange rate, and reduce barriers to trade and investment. As a result, average tariff levels declined in Latin America from more than 40 percent in the mid-1980s to 12 percent in the mid-1990s, and trade raced ahead—averaging 12 percent annual growth for the period 1990-97.[3] Intraregional trade grew considerably faster than extraregional trade in the 1990s, and this was due to the rebirth of subregional trade agreements.

The Andean Community, originally established in 1969 as the Andean Pact, negotiated a four-country free trade area by 1993 and a partial customs union between three members (Colombia, Ecuador, and Venezuela) 2 years later. Peru agreed to join in 1995, and by 2000, the free trade area was largely complete. In addition, the presidents established the

---

2. For a thorough analysis of the status of the economic and political reforms undertaken by individual Latin American and Caribbean governments as a prelude to successful negotiations for a Free Trade Area of the Americas, see Jeffrey J. Schott, *Prospects for Free Trade in the Americas* (Washington: Institute for International Economics, 2001).

3. Inter-American Development Bank, Department of Integration and Regional Programs, *Integration and Trade in the Americas* (Washington, 2000), 2, 7.

Andean Presidential Council, which meets regularly, they strengthened the Andean Court of Justice, and they pledged to establish a common market by 2005.[4] Intraregional trade grew by an annual average of 18 percent in the 1990s, three times faster than the region's trade with the world.

The Caribbean Community (CARICOM), founded in 1973 with 13 members, subsequently expanded to include Haiti and Suriname. With a combined gross product of $20 billion, and a population of 6 million (excluding Haiti), the Caribbean governments remain vulnerable to economic shocks from the world market or large neighbors. Nonetheless, beginning in the 1990s, they took steps to open their economies. They implemented a free trade area and made considerable progress toward a common external tariff (CET) and a single market. CARICOM's free trade agreement with the Dominican Republic came into force in January 2001, and it signed an agreement to enhance commercial links with Cuba in July 2000. On 18 May 2000, President Clinton signed the US-Caribbean Basin Trade Partnership Act, which provides the same free access to the US market in apparel that Mexico had received because of NAFTA. Intraregional trade in CARICOM in the 1990s grew at an annual rate of 12 percent, which was double the rate of the region's trade with the rest of the world.

The Central American Common Market was probably the most successful economic pact in the developing world in the 1960s and early 1970s, but civil wars and tensions between the countries halted its progress by 1980. In 1993, the countries signed the Protocol of Guatemala, which reaffirmed their goals of a customs union and a common market. But they also pledged to implement a low common external tariff. In 2000, they achieved their goal of a CET of 0-15 percent. At the same time, Guatemala and El Salvador formed a customs union and decided to collect tariffs together. The other countries are negotiating to join. CACM also negotiated free trade agreements with Canada, Chile, the Dominican Republic, and Mexico. Intraregional trade increased by 15 percent a year in the 1990s, 20 percent faster than their trade with the world.

The most spectacular advance in subregional integration occurred among historical rivals in the Southern Cone. Argentina and Brazil joined with Paraguay and Uruguay in 1991 to establish Mercosur, or the South American Common Market. Tariffs were dismantled according to the schedule that they initially approved, and a CET of 0-20 percent was in place by January 1995. This represented a very sharp reduction in protection for the area—from an average tariff of 41 percent in 1986 to less than 13 percent in 1999. By 1997, the governments had negotiated an agreement for the free movement of capital and services.

---

4. For a good update and analysis of each trading scheme, see *ibid.*, 28-54.

Perhaps because of the region's closer ties to Europe, Mercosur defined itself in terms that went beyond just economic cooperation. They agreed to develop together regional infrastructure in transport, energy, and telecommunications. And in 1998, the four countries signed a Declaration on Workers' Rights and a separate agreement to support democracy, human rights, and a "peace zone." The Mercosur countries have also negotiated associate membership with Bolivia and Chile, and are consulting with the Andean Community. Although Mercosur has been tested by the financial crisis in Brazil and rising unemployment in Argentina, it has continued to expand and deepen economic cooperation. The member governments have reached a sectoral agreement on automotive trade, and they are negotiating ways to harmonize immigration policies (through a Mercosur passport and greater workforce mobility), financial statements and statistics, and macroeconomic coordination. Most important has been Mercosur's extraordinary growth of intraregional trade—averaging 19 percent a year during the 1990s, almost three times higher than the rate of growth of their world trade.

Before the economic opening and invigoration or creation of regional trade agreements, Latin America had found its position in the international economy deteriorating. But in the last decade of the 20th century, Latin America halted its decline and began to improve its position. The region's growth in trade (10.8 percent in value terms) significantly exceeded that of the world (6.6 percent).[5]

The expansion and strengthening of these subregional agreements was due not just to a convergence of economic policies among Latin American governments but also to two equally powerful currents—democracy and globalization. Since the mid-1970s, when the military governments in Ecuador and Peru pledged to transfer power to civilians in free elections, Latin America gradually moved toward democracy. By the 1990s, every country in the hemisphere, except Cuba, had competitive elections judged by all parties and the international community as free and fair. Although democracy's roots were shallow and fragile in numerous countries, that fact promoted greater democratic solidarity among the civilian presidents and reinforced the trend toward economic cooperation. At the same time, the restoration of democratic rule brought to power new leaders who learned a lesson from Asia's exceptional economic progress and export-promotion strategies. Those countries in Asia and elsewhere that were most open to globalization tended to grow faster and reduce poverty more than those that protected their economies. For all these reasons, the new subregional trading efforts are much more serious than previous ones. Although it is still too soon to know whether they will culminate in free trade areas, customs unions, or common markets—let alone a

---

5. *Ibid.*, 9.

Free Trade Area of the Americas—they have already made substantial progress. If they can accept the NAFTA version of the *acquis communautaire* (the changes in national policy required for membership in the European Union), then Latin America might permanently secure their trade, economic, and democratic reforms.

The Road to the Free Trade Area of the Americas

After the 1994 Miami Summit, the hemisphere's trade ministries began to document existing trade policies and regulations of each country and organize a comprehensive database. At the Santiago summit in 1998, the leaders officially launched trade negotiations and organized them in nine negotiating groups that reflected the chapters of the NAFTA agreement: market access; agriculture; government procurement; services; investment; intellectual property; subsidies, antidumping, and countervailing duties; competition policy; and dispute settlement. In addition, the governments established other committees on business facilitation, electronic commerce, civil society, and smaller economies. The trade ministers produced a bracketed text of a draft agreement for the Third Summit of the Americas in Quebec in April 2001, and the leaders there reaffirmed their commitment to conclude negotiations for an FTAA by January 2005 and complete ratification by the end of that year.

US government officials pointed to the list of committees and meetings as signs of progress, though there was little. The only real progress in trade liberalization occurred outside these negotiations—in the implementation of existing subregional agreements and the proliferation of bilateral and plurilateral free trade arrangements. Since 1992, Latin American governments have negotiated 18 trade agreements with each other. Even more significant was that the five agreements negotiated before 1995 were narrow, in the sense that they sought to eliminate only tariffs and nontariff barriers. After NAFTA, however, all 13 agreements went beyond tariffs and nontariff barriers to include numerous NAFTA issues, including harmonization of policies on services, intellectual property rights, and competition policies.[6] In that sense, NAFTA redefined the trade agenda. This progress, however, was outside the FTAA. Why were there no serious discussions within the many FTAA committees, despite the pledges of participating governments? There are several reasons.

First, as trade barriers declined, inefficient industries began to suffer in all countries. The rich countries feared cheap imports, and the poor countries feared competing against more advanced countries. Firms that

---

6. *Ibid.*, 46-48, for a list of the agreements and a description.

are fearful are more motivated to influence the political process, and the prevalence of democratic institutions throughout the Americas made it easier for them to shape policy. Second, Brazil, with about half of South America's population and gross product, wanted time to consolidate Mercosur and extend it to the other South American countries. Toward this goal, President Fernando Cardoso summoned his counterparts from every country in South America to a summit in Brasilia in September 2000 to establish a South American Free Trade Agreement that would negotiate with NAFTA on the basis of greater equality. Most South American governments wanted to expedite, not slow the process, but their options were limited. Third, Canada and Mexico were not eager to share their exclusive access to the world's largest market, and after the passage of the Caribbean Basin Act, the nations in the Caribbean and Central America were in less of a hurry as well. The fourth reason, however, is pivotal for explaining the lack of genuine progress toward an FTAA: the US president was unable to obtain fast-track negotiating authority from Congress, and without a clear sign that the United States was prepared to commit itself to costly trade-offs, no other government wanted to make premature sacrifices.

What was the problem in the United States? The Congressional elections in 1994 not only brought the Republicans to power in Congress, but they polarized the two political parties, particularly on trade. The Republicans became more laissez-faire—rejecting any labor or environmental agreements, though they had accepted them a year before in NAFTA—and the Democrats became more reliant on labor unions and thus less interested in free trade. President Clinton was not able to build a bridge across this chasm. President Bush announced in Quebec in April 2001 that "trade-promotion authority" was a high priority, and Robert Zoellick, the president's trade representative, set to work to cobble together a coalition in Congress to approve a bill.

Brazil, with its dominant position in South America, raised legitimate questions about several protectionist tactics, such as the use of countervailing duties by the United States and other countries. A successful FTAA will need to respond to these concerns, and this is likely to occur because Brazil and the United States will cochair the last stage of the negotiations. Despite the need to take into account the concerns of Brazil, one should keep in mind the relative economic weight of Brazil and Mercosur as compared with the United States and NAFTA (see table 8.1). The gross product of all the Americas in 1998 was roughly $10.8 trillion, of which the United States accounted for $8.2 trillion, or 76 percent. Canada and Mexico add another 9 percent to the total, giving NAFTA a towering 85 percent of the market of the Americas.

Although it is the second largest economy in the Americas, Brazil accounts for only 7 percent of the total market, and its exports are less than 4 percent of the hemisphere's total exports. Two-way trade between Brazil and the United States was $30 billion in 2000; with Mexico, it was nearly $250 billion. More than 60 percent of all US exports to Latin America went to Mexico in 2000. In brief, Latin America needs the US market much more than the United States needs Latin America's.

There is another way of looking at the trade data, however. In 1999, US exports to its two neighbors were $253.5 billion, roughly 40 percent above its exports to the 15-nation European Union, and more than 3.5 times its exports to China and Japan (see table 8.2). If one adds the rest of the Latin American market, US exports climb an additional $55 billion, making it double the EU market and more than 4 times that of China and Japan. South America constitutes a small supplementary market for US goods at this time; the question is whether the FTAA would expand that market, as NAFTA did for Mexico. Although South America has made important progress in reducing its protectionism in the last decade, it remains one of the most protected middle-income regions of the world. If Brazil received the same trade treatment as Mexico, and if it lowered its trade barriers to the level of Mexico's, then US-Brazil trade would have tripled to about $86 billion in 2000, according to calculations by Schott and Hufbauer.[7] The FTAA could contribute to the internationalization of the Brazilian economy, much as NAFTA did for Mexico, and it could represent the fastest-growing market for US goods.

From a narrow economic perspective, the United States does not have an immediate or compelling need to complete the FTAA—or, for that matter, to deepen NAFTA. The motive for doing so would be to take advantage of future potential. A deeper NAFTA would facilitate the competitiveness of the North American economy; it would, if designed properly, accelerate equitable growth in Mexico and eliminate unnecessary tensions and transaction costs among the three countries. A wider NAFTA would mean an expanding market. Together, they could give additional ballast to an emerging democratic and prosperous hemisphere.

Widen or Deepen?

Which should come first? Should Canada, Mexico, and the United States deepen NAFTA, or should they give priority to widening it to the rest of the Americas? The Europeans chose to widen the European Community beyond the original six countries before they deepened it, and they found that each stage of deepening became progressively harder. It took Europe several decades of trial but mostly error to get to the point where a single currency was possible, and even today, several members have not

---

7. Jeffrey J. Schott and Gary C. Hufbauer, "Whither the Free Trade Area of the Americas?" *The World Economy* 22, no. 6 (August 1999), 765-82.

Table 8.1 Basic indicators for the Americas

Group or country	Population, 1998 (millions)	GDP (billions of dollars) 1980	GDP (billions of dollars) 1998	Exports (billions of dollars) 1983	Exports (billions of dollars) 1998	Imports (billions of dollars) 1983	Imports (billions of dollars) 1998
North America	396	3,198.5	9,202.7 (85 percent of all)	371	1,287.20	401.3	1,478.8
United States	270 (68.2)	2,709 (84.7)	8,210.6 (89.2)	256.7 (69.2)	914.9 (71.1)	309.5 (77.1)	1,097 (74.2)
Canada	30 (7.6)	266 (8.3)	598.9 (6.5)	85 (22.9)	243.6 (18.9)	76.6 (19.1)	241 (16.3)
Mexico	96 (24.2)	223.5 (7.0)	393.2 (4.3)	29.3 (7.9)	128.7 (10.0)	15.2 (3.8)	140.7 (9.5)
Mercosur	202	356.9	1,238 (11 percent of all)	39.9	111	34	148.9
Brazil	166 (73.8)	234.9 (65.8)	778.3 (62.9)	23.5 (59.0)	57.8 (52.0)	20.5 (60.4)	78.6 (52.8)
Argentina	36	77	344.4	9.2	28.2	6.5	37.5
Paraguay	5	4.6	8.6	0.4	1	0.7	3
Uruguay	3	10.1	20.2	1.3	4.3	1.2	4.7
Andean Community	109	138	289.3 (2.7 percent of all)	26	46.5	21.4	62
Venezuela	23 (21.2)	69.4 (50.3)	105.8 (36.6)	15 (57.7)	18.5 (39.7)	9.0 (42.2)	20.8 (33.6)
Colombia	41	33.4	91.1	3.8	14.9	6.2	20
Peru	25	20.6	64.1	3.7	7	3.4	12.2
Ecuador	12	11.7	19.8	2.6	4.8	2	6.6
Bolivia	8	2.8	8.6	0.8	1.3	0.8	2.4

Caricom[a]	14.1	4.1	9.4	1.4	2.9	2.3	4.8
Haiti	8	1.5	2.8	0.2	0.1	0.4	0.6
Jamaica	3	2.6	6.6	1.2	2.8	1.9	4.2
CACM	32	21	48.4	4.4	12.8	5.6	19.1
Guatemala	11 (34.3)	7.9 (34.3)	19.3 (39.9)	1.2 (27.2)	3.1 (24.1)	1.4 (24.4)	5.2 (27.5)
El Salvador	6	3.6	12.1	0.9	1.5	1.1	3.5
Costa Rica	4	4.8	10.2	1.1	5.6	1.2	5.8
Honduras	6	2.6	4.7	0.8	1.9	1	2.8
Nicaragua	5	2.1	2	0.5	0.7	0.9	1.8
The Americas[b]	790	3,726.1	10,803.9	444.4	1,464.3	467.6	1,721.1

CACM = Central American Common Market.
Caricom = Caribbean Common Market.

a. CARICOM export and import data were only available for Haiti and Jamaica.
b. Chile, Dominican Republic, and Panama are included in the numbers for the Americas, but Cuba as well as some members of CARICOM are not because World Bank statistics did not include them.

Note: Numbers in parentheses are percent of the total.

Sources: For GDP, exports and imports: World Bank, *World Development Report 1999/2000: Entering the 21st Century*, 252-3, 268-9. For population: World Bank, *World Development Indicators 2000*, table 1.1, 13.

Table 8.2 US Exports to North America, South America, the European Union, Japan, and China, 1980-99
(millions of dollars)

Year	North America[a]	South America and Caribbean Basin[b]	EC/EU	Japan and China
1980	55,476	23,600	58,855	24,545
1985	66,922	17,221	45,776	26,487
1990	111,953	25,129	86,424	50,391
1995[c]	173,518	49,949	123,671	76,097
1999[c]	253,509	55,156	151,814	70,577

EC/EU = European Community or European Union.

a. North America is defined as including Canada, Mexico, and the United States.
b. The Caribbean Basin is defined as the governments of the Caribbean and Central America.
c. Data include exports of manufactured goods, agricultural goods, and all services.

Sources: US International Trade Administration, *U.S. Foreign Trade Highlights* (1985, 1988, 1992); Bureau of the Census, *Statistical Abstract of the United States* (various issues); International Trade Administration, *U.S. Total Exports to Individual Countries*, 1991-1999, http://www.ita.doc.gov/PRFrameset.html.

accepted the euro. Despite frequent summit meetings, Europe's leaders insist on retaining a veto on key decisions. This has made it difficult to consider reducing the mountain of subsidies provided under the Common Agriculture Policy. It has postponed a decision to change the formula for the regional policy to allow for the European Union's next enlargement. Absent a decision, the Union would bankrupt its budget. The Treaty of Nice in 2000 made limited progress in these directions, but still the Irish public rejected it in a referendum on 8 June 2001. It is difficult to deepen an organization after it has been widened.

Canada, Mexico, and the United States would promote market efficiency if they widened NAFTA to the rest of the Americas and deepened North American integration. Widening means an enlargement of the market, permitting even greater economies of scale. Deepening involves the reduction of internal barriers or distortions. Deepening is a far more complicated and difficult process, because it goes to the heart of how each government regulates its economy and provides for its citizens' welfare. Moreover, each government has groups, policies, or national symbols that it feels a need to protect. The Canadians, for example, are attached to their comprehensive health care system, regardless of its cost and its delays. The Mexicans are averse to allowing foreigners control of their petroleum. And the US sugar industry has rebelled at any effort to remove its subsidies. In each of these areas, an efficient policy would quickly collide with a powerful interest or symbol, making harmonization or compromise difficult.

Beyond these controversial areas, governments would benefit from negotiating uniform standards—for example, on safety, product design, or labeling, or on eliminating subsidies to declining industries or farms. Still, none of these decisions would be easy, and that led Doran—one of the most perceptive students of the debate on widening versus deepening—to characterize widening as "seductive" and relatively easy and deepening as "painful" but more important.[8] He favors both deepening and widening, but he believes that "deepening ought to precede widening, because widening adds diversity, and diversity leads to conflict over priorities and goals."[9] Whenever a new country joins the community, it often slows the integration process or vetoes the next steps. But his argument is based on a broader point:

> A liberal area based on advanced liberalization of trade, investment, and other rules that impinge on the economy will be much more of a community, and will be much more market efficient, than a looser, more diverse trade grouping of larger size that is still groping for a common denominator of progressive liberalization and standardization. Optimally, therefore, deepening ought to precede widening.[10]

Doran's argument is, to a great extent, based on the EU experience, but does it apply to the Americas? Once the FTAA is completed, the dispute-settlement mechanism would provide a built-in cost to any government trying to retreat or defect. Moreover, the FTAA will provide an incentive to deepen, because the removal of policy distortions will lead to more effective global competition. The major difference between North America and the European Union is the dominance of the United States. That has obvious disadvantages, but an advantage is that many of the decisions to deepen could be done in a de facto manner. Those who trade will follow the US standards. This may be what occurs on dollarization. Businesses find it easier to use the dollar as a standard, and over time, governments may find the decision on currency made for them. So it is quite possible that the dichotomy between widening and deepening might not be as compelling in the Americas as in Europe.

Moreover, a single approach toward integration might not be needed in the Americas; some deepening and widening can be done at the same time. If the three governments of North America decide to deepen their

---

8. For a thoughtful analysis of these issues, see the following two essays by Charles F. Doran: "When Building North America, Deepen Before Widening," in *A New North America: Cooperation and Enhanced Interdependence*, ed. Charles F. Doran and Alvin Paul Drischler (Westport, CT: Praeger, 1996), 65-89; and "Whither North America?" in *Toward a North American Community*, ed. Donald Barry (Boulder, CO: Westview Press, 1995), 271-81.

9. Doran and Drischler, *New North America*, xv, 66.

10. *Ibid.*, 69.

relations and establish some common organizations, the rest of the Americas can choose to follow or remain outside.

With regard to the question of which trade strategy makes the most sense for the United States, it is worth recalling that the very nature of the US political system seems to work against strategic thinking on trade— or, for that matter, on almost any field. There are simply too many actors and too much pressure, and that great hydra-headed, multibranched monster called the US government often ambles on several tracks at the same time. Strategists are often frustrated by a style that seems to dissipate US energies rather than concentrate them, but they should relax in this case: The objective of integrating the hemisphere might be best achieved by a multipronged approach. The United States should move quickly on negotiating the FTAA, and it should consult with its NAFTA partners on ways to deepen their relations. It might very well discover that the more channels one pursues, the greater the chance of achieving them all—at least in trade policy. One more benefit of *multiple trade negotiations* is that Latin Americans might prefer that to an approach in which Washington is applying its full weight.

Having said that, it would still be desirable if the United States had a plan with some priorities. First, it should deepen the North American Community and build organizations that will ensure that the integration process is smooth and effective. Second, it should continue to provide a support system under the Caribbean Basin countries, which are small, vulnerable, and strategically important. And third, Brazil and the United States should cooperate to bring the FTAA to an expedited conclusion.

The FTAA's members should be encouraged to adopt and adapt the organizations that are designed for a North American Community. For example, the idea behind the North American Commission—that a multinational advisory group could formulate a North American agenda— could be adapted to a wider FTAA. The Americas will need a hemispheric agenda, and the plans generated by the NAC—for example, on transportation or energy—could be adapted to the broader Community.

The Western Hemisphere and the WTO

Distinguished economists like Jagdish Bhagwati and Milton Friedman feared that NAFTA and other regional agreements could be stumbling blocks, preventing the Uruguay Round of Global Trade Negotiations from reaching a conclusion.[11] In fact, the opposite occurred. Soon after Congress

---

11. Jagdish Bhagwati, "Jumpstarting GATT," *Foreign Policy* 83 (Summer 1991); and "Milton Friedman Criticizes Regional Trade Agreements," *El Financiero International* (Mexico City), 1 June 1992, 3. For a full discussion of this debate as to whether NAFTA would be a stumbling or a building block, see Robert A. Pastor, *Integration with Mexico: Options for U.S. Policy* (New York: Twentieth Century Fund Press, 1993), chap. 6.

approved NAFTA, Europe and Japan, evidently fearful that the United States might exercise its regional option, accelerated the global trade talks, and they were completed in months.

The reason is that within each of the three great trade areas, one global power exerts disproportionate influence. Economically, the United States is preeminent in NAFTA; Japan plays a similar role in East Asia; and Germany does so in the European Union. What unites these three trading powers is the recognition that their global power is rooted in a rules-based, worldwide system. Their economies would be harmed if their only market were a regional one. All three have compelling interests in maintaining a world trading system. To the extent that the United States can deepen and widen its relationships in the western hemisphere, the world will also be better off, and Latin America will have options that it did not have in the past. The regional agreements also aim to create more efficient units for global trade and production by harmonizing or eliminating those barriers to trade and investment that have resisted global efforts. In brief, such "open" regional trade agreements are building, not stumbling, blocks.

There is another reason why proliferating regional integration agreements stimulate rather than impede serious global negotiations. In June 1999, the heads of state of the Mercosur countries and the European Union met in Rio de Janeiro to launch negotiations for "reciprocal trade liberalization, without excluding any sector and in accordance with WTO rules." Within a year, Mexico completed a free trade agreement with the European Union as well. Why? The Mercosur-European Union (MEU) talks were, in the view of Robert Devlin, an economist at the Inter-American Development Bank, "the EU's strategic response to the launch of the FTAA negotiations. As for Mercosur, the MEU process offered the promise of increased leverage for its FTAA negotiations."[12]

The *absence of negotiations* is the *worst disease* for free trade. The *best medicine* is *more agreements*, provided that they are nondiscriminatory and open, because they stimulate competition and encourage each group to catch up to its competitors.

Although the regional trade schemes define rules for businesses, the political dimension should not be overlooked. Democracy has not only increased the chances that regional trade agreements would be reached and maintained; these agreements have helped to maintain democracy among their members. The most obvious case in Latin America is Paraguay: Argentina and Brazil openly threatened the Paraguayan military that their country would be expelled from Mercosur if they dared overthrow their government.[13]

---

12. Robert Devlin, *The Free Trade Area of the Americas and MERCOSUR-European Union Free Trade Processes: Can They Learn Something from Each Other?* INTAL-ITD Occasional Paper 6 (Washington: Inter-American Development Bank, 2000), 7.

13. For an excellent case study, see Arturo Valenzuela, *The Collective Defense of Democracy: Lessons from the Paraguayan Crisis of 1996*, report to the Carnegie Commission on Preventing Deadly Conflict (New York: Carnegie Corporation, 1999).

From the beginning, the European Union encouraged democracy on its periphery by denying entry to Greece, Portugal, and Spain until each had free elections. Over time, the Union has become more insistent that its members and future members adhere to democratic principles, and the snub against Austria for electing a right-wing government was a recent public reminder of that. Since the Treaty of Amsterdam, the Union has insisted that entry by Eastern European governments would require adherence to very specific political criteria.

Democracy is valuable in the Americas precisely because its political history has been plagued by dictatorship. As the 21st century dawns, each country in the hemisphere, except Cuba, is committed to maintaining and deepening its democracy and helping its neighbors as well. But just as in economics, the political deepening of democracy is more problematic than its widening, partly because there is no consensus on what deepening means or how to do it. Some scholars equate deepening with consolidation, and define both as institutional and attitudinal respect for political systems of vertical and horizontal accountability.[14] Vertical accountability—between leaders and people—relies on free and fair election procedures that are judged as such by all the major political parties. Horizontal accountability means that each major institution of government respects other institutions' boundaries. The executive does not attempt to close the legislature or the courts; the courts obey the laws and the constitution, not the military, president, or prime minister; and the legislature is careful to respect the constitution if it finds just cause to impeach the president or members of the court. Many countries in Latin America have a fourth branch of government—an election commission and court—and the autonomy of those institutions is designed to safeguard both axes of accountability.

The principal risks to Latin America's democracies seem to stem from the weakness of their political parties, the hubris of their leaders, the paucity of well-crafted laws and regulations, and the arbitrariness of enforcement. Deepening democracy requires the careful development of political parties and the construction of legal restraints on the abuse or corruption of power. Almost all of the responsibility for preserving democracy rests with the people and institutions in each country, but the last line of defense is collective action. The FTAA, therefore, needs to incorporate a chapter on democracy that defines the rules for entry, punishment, and suspension of governments. In Quebec, the summit leaders announced their support for a "democracy clause" that would preclude unconstitutional regimes from being represented at summit meetings. But the leaders

---

14. See, e.g., Andreas Schedler, Larry Diamond, and Marc F. Plattner, eds., *The Self-Restraining State: Power and Accountability in New Democracies* (Boulder, CO: Lynne Rienner Publishers, 1999); and Larry Diamond, *Developing Democracy: Toward Consolidation* (Baltimore: Johns Hopkins University Press, 1999).

failed to define violations of democracy or the specific steps that the Community would take in response. An effort by the Peruvian government to develop a "Charter on Democracy" was set back at an OAS General Assembly in June 2001, but the OAS has continued to pursue negotiations to achieve consensus on such a Charter.

Entry into the FTAA should require acceptance of the rules and procedures of democracy. Elections need to be free and fair, and all major parties need to view them as such. The FTAA should associate with the Inter-American Court of Human Rights, based in Costa Rica, which should delegate to a distinguished committee the responsibility to observe and oversee any electoral disputes that cannot be settled by domestic institutions. All citizens of the Americas should have the right to petition before this body and seek redress both from their government and from the FTAA institutions. Serious violations of democracy should be judged like a trade dispute, in which a failure to comply with the court's decision would elicit sanctions of some sort—perhaps a withdrawal of trade privileges. A coup d'état would naturally evoke suspension from the FTAA, just as it would from the OAS, and the multilateral development banks would halt loans to the regime.

The Americas should accept nothing less. Indeed, the FTAA should go beyond the questions of membership or suspension and propose ways to nurture the roots of democracy, particularly in its weak neighbors. This democratic dimension would give real meaning to the concept of the Community of the Americas.

The Strategic Challenge of the 21st Century

Since the Second World War, the world has witnessed a remarkable expansion of free markets and trade. This has been both cause and consequence of the transfer of technology, the compression of distance and communications, the spread of universal values of human rights and democracy, and the strengthening of the rule of law within countries and among them. People, businesses, and societies have connected with each other in ways that have permitted the quality of life to improve demonstrably in all but the most isolated, poorest nations of the world. A global system has been created by private initiative and by decisions of nation-states.

This integration process has arrived at a critical moment. New forms of governance need to be established if the process is to continue, grow, and become more equitable. Global institutions—like the World Trade Organization—are not suited to negotiating the rules of deeper integration. There are too many members with too many diverse interests at too many levels of development. The noise of Seattle in November 1999 was just one sign of the WTO's incapacity to address this next challenge. The best arena is regional bodies, although even at this level there will be a clamor.

One of the most important challenges for the international community at the beginning of the 21st century is to define the space that will permit middle-income developing countries to graduate to the industrial world of trade and development. This is not to minimize the more serious problem of assisting the poorest people in the poorest countries, but other institutions—notably the World Bank and the regional development banks—are suited for that task.

NAFTA has been innovative in four ways and, as such, is a model for addressing this global, 21st century challenge. First, it has brought together countries on disparate levels of development whose histories are laden with deep-seated suspicion. Second, it has gone beyond eliminating tariffs and nontariff barriers, and has regulated and harmonized a range of policies in many sectors including foreign investment, services, and intellectual property rights. Third, it has recognized the importance of incorporating workers' and environmental rights, although it has done so only by insisting that each country enforce its own rules. Fourth, it has established a dispute-settlement mechanism to resolve trade and investment problems. These provisions have been implemented, some more effectively than others. But the problems that North America has encountered are not due to what NAFTA includes, but rather to what it omits.

The United States and its neighbors should proceed to establish a North American Community, but not at the price of a Free Trade Area of the Americas. Rather, both initiatives should be pursued simultaneously. The competition would be helpful. The deepening of NAFTA can preserve a special relationship among the three nations of North America, and its model might be of use to the FTAA in the future.

NAFTA's Premise and Promise

NAFTA's premise was that if the continent's three nations dismantled the barriers to trade and investment, the magic of a free market would better the lives of everyone. The free market is wonderfully designed to produce diverse and inexpensive goods, but it provides no answers to the collective problems that inevitably emerge from the market's failures, or even its successes. Without multinational organizations and uniform rules, the three governments cannot clean up pollution at their borders; they cannot reduce or stop illegal migration; they cannot manage or eliminate the hidden and illegal dimension of integration (drug trafficking, transnational crime, and money laundering); they cannot address the unevenness of taxes and welfare; and they cannot reassure those groups in each country that fear integration will endanger their livelihoods and values.

This book has developed a set of general principles and numerous specific proposals to allow the North American countries to redefine their relationship and thus to help them jump over the next hurdle of integration. First, the three countries should establish a North American Commission composed of distinguished individuals who are appointed *by* the three governments but are not *in* any of the governments. This Commission would set a continental agenda for the leaders of the three countries to forge new ways to facilitate integration. Second, the Commission should propose a North American Plan for Transportation and Infrastructure and should seek initial funding from the World Bank and the Inter-American Development Bank, with the understanding that the three governments would eventually provide the funds directly to build a North American network of roads, railroads, and shipping.

Third, the three governments need to devise collective mechanisms to handle the illegal flow of people, arms, goods, drugs, and so on across their borders. Numerous experiments are under way to find ways to untangle the dilemma between erasing trade barriers and impeding illegal trade, but even new devices—such as transponders—require a new kind of governance, because at the current time, there are too many jurisdictions within the three countries, let alone between them, to allow for a uniform standard. This challenge of devising practical systems of North American governance should be addressed by NAC and the three governments.

Fourth, I propose that the three governments create a development fund based on a regional policy that aims to lift the poorest regions of North America, much as the European Union has narrowed the disparities between its rich and poor member countries. Such a fund, which initially could be assisted and administered by the World Bank and Inter-American Development Bank, would invest most of its resources in infrastructure and education. The infrastructure should include new and modern roads from the border to the center and the south of Mexico, where it would link with the new Puebla-Panama Corridor. The fund also should establish community colleges in the poor states of Mexico, and also perhaps develop courses or research institutes on North American affairs in Canada and the United States. These colleges could also improve education in poor areas. The United States should work with its two neighbors to make sure that the Fund is well-financed so that it would do for North America what the European Union's Structural and Cohesion Funds have done for its four poorest members. It could lift both the economies and the spirits of the poor areas and begin to create a spirit of community that would have positive spillover effects on all the countries.

Such a proposal is quixotic if the governments remain bound to the old concept of sovereignty. The historic shield—the defense of sovereignty—stemmed from fear of the foreign, but modern democratic leaders have redefined sovereignty to permit them to reach across borders to deal with transnational problems. Public opinion surveys suggest that the people in all three countries are much less interested in abstract debates about sovereignty than about improving their lives and dealing with issues that their governments seem helpless to address. In this case, the lesson to be drawn from Europe's experience is eminently pertinent to North America. A French scholar defined that problem and the opportunity:

> Governments are naturally obsessed by issues of nationality. When emotion tends to color objective interests, disputes get more complex. Europe's citizens, however, are much more relaxed than their elected representatives about largely symbolic matters. They do not think in terms of sovereignty or nationality. They want to know who is in charge, who is responsible . . .[15]

People are far more pragmatic than their leaders give them credit for being. They are prepared to try radical ideas if they think doing so will improve the economy and their lives. Organizations count, however. Joining any international organization involves new obligations and constraints on a nation-state's behavior, but if one believes in a fair process and a uniform set of rules, then one wants to make sure the rules apply to everyone—and are enforced. In the end, such a system permits greater certainty, reliability, and trust and thus reduces transaction costs across the board. In that sense, *countries do not cede sovereignty, nor do they diminish their abilities by integration.* The *opposite* seems closer to the truth. Such agreements permit more efficient development, more effective autonomy, and greater ability to address transnational problems.

Why should we move toward a North American Community and from there to a Free Trade Area of the Americas? There are two simple answers to the question: It is the best way to avoid serious problems, and it is the best way to seize outstanding opportunities. In the middle of 2000, a Canadian trade negotiator wrote to other Canadians: "Should the current nine-year economic expansion in the United states weaken or end, Canadians may be reminded once again of how ugly US trade politics can become, how much Canada relies on good rules and procedures to keep US protectionism in check, and how the increasing sophistication and reliability of those rules and procedures have provided Canada with the capacity to resist US protectionist pressures."[16] The same argument applies in all three countries.

Unless the three governments develop policies to cover new problems, there is no certainty that existing rules will endure turbulent seas. If the United States fails to implement the agreement on sugar or trucks; or if

---

15. Dominique Moisi, "Caught between Enlargement and Globalization," *Financial Times*, 15 January 2001, 17. Moisi is the deputy director of the French Institute of International Relations.

16. Michael Hart, "The Role of Dispute Settlement in Managing Canada-U.S. Trade and Investment Relations," in *Canada Among Nations 2000: Vanishing Borders*, ed. Maureen Appel Molot and Fen Osler Hampson (New York: Oxford University Press, 2000), 94.

Mexico avoids its obligations on telecommunications; or if Canada refuses to modify or dismantle its agricultural marketing boards—then NAFTA could wither, and no country would escape the pain.

The United States has long understood that instability in Mexico could not be contained at the border. That is the national security rationale that underlies NAFTA. Migration pressures will not diminish in the short term, but a serious internal crisis could precipitate a massive outflow of refugees. A failure by Mexico to develop its natural gas and oil industry would not only hurt its development, it would not help California's. A union strike in Windsor, in Puebla, or in Detroit would quickly close down auto plants in the other cities. Unemployment would spread without regard to the border. Currency crises in Canada or Mexico or a recession in the United States would spread to the other parts of North America like the flu. *A problem in one part of North America can no longer be contained from affecting the other parts,* and that simple fact ought to concentrate our minds on the importance of transforming NAFTA into a Community.

Fear can motivate, but it can also paralyze. Hope and opportunity are better reasons to construct a model Community in North America. Already, North America's market is larger than that of the European Union, and industry is refashioning itself on a truly continental landscape. At the same time, trucks cannot cross the borders, and there is no organization to anticipate problems or plan for the continent's development.

The process of integration among disparate countries is not linear. Indeed, as trade and investment expands, it often triggers a reaction. Inefficient producers or worried unions seek protection, and politicians come to their defense. The other governments in the Free Trade Agreement then feel the same pressures from other businesses or unions, and the agreement risks unraveling. Similarly, as social integration through migration intensifies, subterranean anxieties are stoked, and nativist reactions, like "Proposition 187," are the result. This is the "Newtonian conundrum": every movement toward integration evokes an opposite, though not always equal, reaction. As the continent becomes more homogenous, it unleashes disintegrative pressures—from the Zapatistas in the south to the Bloc Quebecois in the north—that seek autonomy.

To sustain NAFTA, the three governments have to do more than just prevent defections. They need to deepen their collaboration and ensure that the benefits of freer trade are shared with those who pay the price of wider competition. A few voices can be heard calling for new North American institutions and policies to deepen NAFTA. In Canada, former Foreign Minister Lloyd Axworthy told a meeting at the North American Institute: "We all share the same concerns about wanting to deal with illicit drug trade, safeguard against terrorism and criminal activity. But we must develop a common, coordinated approach to these problems, not try to solve them by creating barriers for everybody that result in impossible lineups. We have not yet articulated what living together in a North American Community really means."[17]

From the south, President Fox of Mexico has proposed a common market: "We must be better friends, neighbors, and partners. By building up walls, by using arms, by dedicating billions of dollars like every [US] border state is doing to avoid migration—this is not the way to go. Instead of solving the problem, it has gotten worse."[18] His vision is the boldest. He wants to double foreign investment in Mexico to $20 billion annually and seeks a fund—similar to the one based on EU regional policy and the one proposed in this book—that would permit Mexico to grow by 7 percent a year and narrow its income gap with the United States. He recognizes that is the only way to stem migration northward.

US President Bush has a unique opportunity to structure a relationship that will have a profound effect not just on Canada and Mexico but also on the United States. It will require resources, new organizations, difficult negotiations, and most of all, a new perspective on the region. A commentator for the *Toronto Star* posed the issue concisely: "So the challenge is to create a North American Community whose vision goes far beyond trade and investment but without sacrificing cultural identity and core national institutions and values."[19]

The North American Community has much to learn from the European Union—about both what it should adapt and what it should avoid. But the New World does not want to replicate the bureaucracy of the Old or the many instruments the Union uses to reduce disparities between rich and poor countries. What distinguishes the North American approach from the European is the respect for the market. This market orientation has permitted North American efficiencies and the economies of scale that have helped fuel the region's restructuring and development. And indeed, the European Union is trying to replicate the US market's policies on labor flexibility and uniform standards.[20]

What Canada, Mexico, and the United States need is a North American perspective and a few lean organizations that can help coordinate the three

---

17. "Notes for Remarks by the Minister of Foreign Affairs to a Meeting of the North American Institute," Santa Fe, NM, 21 August 1998.

18. Cited in Kevin Sullivan and Mary Jordan, "Fox Seeks New Cooperative Era for North America," *Washington Post*, 14 August 2000, A1.

19. David Crane, "NAFTA Lacks a Sense of Community," *Toronto Star*, 23 August 1998.

20. See, e.g., Frits Bolkestein and Anna Diamantopoulou, "Workers without Frontiers; Governments Should Promote a Genuinely Free Market for Labour across Europe," *Financial Times*, 29 January 2001, 17. The authors are European commissioners for the internal market and for employment and social affairs, respectively. The article makes the case for facilitating the mobility of workers across countries and firms, much as the United States already does.

countries' multiple levels of governance and can accelerate integration without harming laggard regions. One option is to wait and let the market do its work, as the US South did for nearly 100 years. Or one can hasten the process by making targeted investments in infrastructure and education. What North America could learn most of all from the European Union is commitment. From its 1999 budget of $120 billion, the Union used about a third—$40 billion—for Structural and Cohesion Funds to reduce the disparities between rich and poor countries. Europe's gross product is smaller than North America's, and yet the Union spends about six times more on aid for its poor members as the United States spends on assisting its poor states. And the Union has programmed that annual aid to grow to about $70 billion by 2006.

If Canada and the United States contributed just 10 percent of what the European Union spends on aid, and if Mexico invested it wisely in infrastructure and education, Mexico could start to grow at a rate twice that of its northern neighbors. The psychology of North America would change quickly, and the problems of immigration, corruption, and drugs would look different. North America would have found the magic formula to lift developing countries to the industrial world, and that would be the 21st-century equivalent of the shot heard round the world.

Index

assimilation issue, 165
Association of South East Asian Nations
    (ASEAN)
    comparative focus, 14
    described, 25, 30-31
    expansion, 31
asymmetry of power, 16
    as defining characteristic in North
        America, 63
    high priority US, 150
    less in EU, 63
    NAFTA, 34
automotive sector, 72
    Mercosur, 174

bailout package, 4
balance of payments, 68
Benelux Union, 50
Berlin Wall, 25
Beutel Model, 57
bicultural society, in U.S., 165
bilateralism, 2
    differences between Canada and
        Mexico, 150
    dual, 103
    reasons for, 99, 147
    retreat to, 13
bilingualism (US), 165
Binational Association of Western
    Governors and Premiers, 103
binational commission meetings, 103
Bolivia, 174
    Mercosur, 14
border areas, 2
    customs, enforcement, and
        immigration, 120-22
    development approaches, 139
    northern Mexican economy, 137
    pollution, 137
    role of, 139
    traffic congestion, 92
    transport investment, 106
Border Environment Cooperation
    Commission (BECC), 76
border issues
    environmental projects, 76-78
    governors and premiers meeting, 103
    Mexican trucking, 84-85
    overview, 77
    pollution, 75, 76
    trade corridors report, 102
    transaction costs, 104
brain drain, 18
    Mexico, 82, 125

Brazil
    economic weight, relative, 176-77, 178t
    two-way trade with U.S., 177
Bretton Woods, 19-20
bureaucracy
    benefits and pitfalls, 62
    complaints to EU, 43
    loans to Mexico, 139
    NAFTA, 73-78
    State Department (US), 151, 152
    sunset provision, 100
Bureau of Western Hemisphere, State
    Department, 151
Bush administration, Mexican trucking,
    85
Bush, George H.W., immigration, 133
Bush, George W.
    common market, 2-3
    Guanajuato Proposal, 3
    immigration and energy, 133
    tax cut for wealthy, 37

cabinet meetings, 103
cabotage restrictions, 107
Canada
    attitudes to US, 157
    basic indicators, 7t
    culture of deference, 156
    customs union impeded by Mexico,
        143
    dispute settlement mechanisms, 74
    energy and sovereignty, 135
    exports, 9t
    FDI abroad, 72
    fears of US corporations, 71
    foreign policy, 87
    free trade background, 65-66
    GDP disparities among provinces, 37,
        38t
    health care system, 180
    imports, 9t
    independence, 64
    lumber products, 17
    NAFTA impact, 70, 80
    nationalism under Trudeau, 65
    North American trade, 10t
    Office of Canadian Affairs, 151
    population growth, 6
    rail merger, 93
    recession after FTA, 88
    responsibility to Mexico, 150
    role in Latin America, 140
    social cohesion concept, 13
    sovereignty issues, 135, 152

trade dependence on US market, 90
trade with US (growth), 13
US views of, 156-57
views of NAFTA, 160-61
wheat, 17
Canada-US, trade, NAFTA effects, 69
Canada-US Free Trade Agreement,
Mexican view, 66
Canada-US relations, 147-48
as community, 154
Canadian Trucking Alliance, 105
Canadian-US Partnership on border
trade and travel, 122
capital movements, 6
CAP. *See* Common Agricultural Policy
Cárdenas, Cuauhtémoc, 78
Cardoso, Fernando Henrique, 176
Caribbean Basin
immigration pressures, 128
US-Caribbean Basin Trade Partnership
Act, 173, 176
vulnerability, 172
Caribbean Basin Initiative, 24
Caribbean Community (Caricom), 172,
173, 178*t*
Caricom. *See* Caribbean Community
Castañeda, Jorge G., 3, 65
on immigration, 123
CEMEX, 73
Centers of North American Research and
Studies proposal, 101
Central America, 87
basic indicators, 179*t*
illegal migration to the United States,
124
Puebla-Panama Corridor proposal,
137-38
Central American Common Market
(CACM), 172, 173
Central Bank of North America
proposed, 114
Central and Eastern European
governments (CEEs), 48-49
Centre for European Policy Studies
report, 58
Chicago Council on Foreign Relations,
156
Chile, 174
Mercosur, 14
US trade talks, 14
Chrétien, Jean
common market, 3
tax cuts, 91

Chrétien, Raymond, 147
Chrysler, 72
Churchill, Winston, 19, 168
civic culture, 156
civil servants, EU, 43
Civil War (US), 64
Clinton, Bill
defense of NAFTA, 67
heading off peso crisis, 4-5
labor and environmental issues, 75
peso crash effects, 4
coalescing pressures, 84, 91-92
Cohesion countries, 50-51
education, 140-41
GDP growth, 53*t*
growth rates, 52
volatility tendencies, 61
Cohesion Funds, 45
distribution by country, 45, 47, 47*t*
Eastern Europe, 49, 50
Spanish membership, 47
spending, 45, 46*t*
Cohesion Report (1996), 50-51
Cold War, 25-26, 87
Colombia, 172-73, 178*t*
Commercial Vehicle Processing Center,
122
Commission for Environmental
Cooperation (CEC), 75
Commission for Labor Cooperation
(CLC), 75
Committee of the Regions, 45
Common Agriculture Policy (CAP), 43,
44
Eastern Europe, 49
rich-country subsidies, 61
veto powers, 180
common currency, 17
views of, 162-63, 163*n*
common external tariff (CET), Latin
America, 173
common market, 9
Andean Community, 173
Central American Common Market
(CACM), 172, 173
common market proposal, 132
Fox on, 13-14
labor mobility, 143
common policies for NAFTA, lacking, 83,
87-88
community
Canada/US relationship, 154
defined, 154

community colleges, 140-41
  Mexico, 142
  Portugal and Spain, 141
  proposal overview, 187
community of diversity, 18
competition policies, 108
conditionality, EU goals, 60
Confederation of Industrial Chambers of
    Commerce (CONCAMIN), 89
Congress (US), incentives at local level,
    149
consulates, Mexican, 132
contradictions, inherent in free trade, 16-
    17
convergence theories, 50
  EU goals, 60
  Leonardi, 57-58
convergence of values, 155-56
cooperative policies, idea of, 95-96
Coordinated Border Infrastructure
    Program, 106
Costa Rica, 185
Council of Ministers, 1
  described, 29
countervailing duties, 74, 85
  Canada lumber, 109
countervailing duties and antidumping
    (CVD/AD), 110
court, permanent, proposal, 103
coyotes (smugglers), 120, 121, 124, 133
crisis of 1994, 3-5
Cuba, 173
  approaches to, 17
  Canada and Mexico, 87
  common three-country approach, 111
  US sanctions, 87
Cuban Liberty and Democratic Solidarity
    Act ("Helms-Burton"), 87
cultural gap, narrowing, 150
cultural identity, 15
  union versus threat to, 144
  views of political union, 162, 163
currency
  Canadian depreciation, 113
  Canadian dollar rate, 110
  single currency issue, 17, 177, 180
customs union, 9
  proposal, 108
    Fox, 143

debt crisis of mid-1980s
  IMF conditions on Mexico, 66
  sovereignty issue, 39
Declaration on Workers' Rights, 174

deficit spending, 60
Delors I 5-year plan (1989-93), 44-45
Delors II 6-year plan (1994-99), 45
Delors, Jacques, 41, 44
democracy
  accountability issue, 184
  clause in FTAA, 184
  entry into FTAA, 185
  EU, 174
  Latin America, 174
    principal risks, 174
  as membership criterion, 60
  OAS charter on, 185
  political deepening debated, 184
  regional trade agreements, 173
"democratic deficit," 43
Democratic Revolutionary Party (PRD),
    78
Denmark, 29
Department of Regional Industrial
    Expansion (DRIE), 37
Deutsch, Karl, 153-54
development banks, 25
disintegrative pressures, 84, 88-91
disparities, among three countries, 18
disparity reduction issue
  ERDF (EU), 44
  European Community (EC), 41, 136
  EU goals, 60
  Mexico, 137
  See also regional disparities
dispute-settlement mechanisms, 30, 80
  NAFTA, 73, 74-75
    Chapter 11, 74-75
    Chapter 19, 74, 86
    Chapter 20, 74
  proposal for permanent court, 103
  rules-based desirable, 99
  softwood lumber issue, 109-10
divergence theories, 50
dollarization, 111-17, 111n
  Argentina, 111n, 112, 113n
  benefits argued, 113
  Canadian position, 111-12
  common currency, 114-15
  criticisms of, 113-14
  Ecuador, 111n, 112
  sovereignty issues, 112
  US economic dominance, 181
  US position, 112
Dominican Republic, 173
drayage system, 84, 105
Drug Enforcement Administration (DEA)
    of United States, 151

drug issue
Mexico
certification issue, 87, 148
seriousness, 148
unilateral US approach, 151
US blaming approach, 16
drug trafficking, 5, 6
free trade advantages, 17

East Asia
institutional dearth, 31, 32
intraregional exports, 20, 21f, 22t
Japan's role, 183
"new Asian challenge," 33
parameters of three regional trade
areas, 28t
regional vision lacking, 32
security community lacking, 32
structure of trade groups, 25
See also APEC (Asia-Pacific Economic
Cooperation)
Eastern Europe, 41
EU entry, 48-49
economic boom in US, 27
economic cohesion, definition, 44
economic competition, 26
nature of, 27
economic development
ideologies as surrogate weapons, 27
programs, 11
economic-gravity model, 20
economic growth
compared, 6, 7t
Greece, 55
Portugal, 55
Spain, 55
economic indicators
Canada post NAFTA, 80
Latin America, 178t-79t
Mexico, post NAFTA, 79
United States post NAFTA, 80
economic and monetary union, 9
economic motives, 23
economic shocks, 173
Economic and Social Research Institute
(Dublin), 54
Ecuador, 172-73, 178t
dollarization, 111n, 112
education
compared, 6, 7t
EU lessons, 190-91
funding, development banks, 138, 139
Mexico, compared to Portugal and
Spain, 141, 142t

plan proposed, 140-42
elections, 1
Mexico, 78-79
international observers, 153
Electoral Court, 78
emerging markets, Mexico as, 111
emigration
compared, 6, 7t
reducing disparities, 60
employer sanctions law, 128
employment, 68
adverse effects of NAFTA, 69-70
job loss from Mexican imports, 69-70
Mexico unemployment, 16
See also unemployment
end of the Cold War, economic themes,
27
energy plan proposal, 133-35
environmental issues
NAFTA dispute settlement, 74-75
northern Mexico, 137
pollution haven, 76
views of political union, 162, 163
environmental side agreements, 30
innocuous commissions, 75-76
escape valve, Mexico, 126
euro, 114
Europe
multiple identities, 154-55
postwar nation-state transcended, 41
Salinas overtures, 66
security issues, 23
sovereignty issue, 152-53
European Agriculture Fund, 43-44
European Coal and Steel Community, 28
security motives, 23
European Commission, 11
described, 29
North American Commission
compared, 101
sophistication, 43
European Community (EC), 8n
disparity reduction issue, 41
early regional policy, 29
first enlargement, 29
goals, 41
movement of labor, 143
widening vs. deepening, 177, 180
European Court
at Maastricht Treaty, 43
described, 29
European Economic Community (EEC),
8n

US-Canadian Free Trade Agreement, 72
foreign policy
  common approaches, 17
  NAFTA implications, 87-88
  third-country issues in NAFTA, 87-88
forests issue, 109-10
Fox Quesada, Vicente
  common market idea, 13-14
    customs union proposal, 143
    foreign investment doubling, proposal, 189-90
  election, 78
  EU studied, 2-3
  immigration
    energy tied to, 133
    immigrants as heroes, 120
    new US sensitivity, 131
    proposal, 123
    surrogate for other goals, 144-45
  Mexicans in the United States, 127
  NADBank, 78
  Puebla-Panama Corridor proposal, 137-38
  trilateral future issues, 98
France
  CAP, 49
  postwar trade, 19-20
free trade
  absence of negotiations, 183
  contradictions, 16-17
  disparities and equal opportunity, 98
  failures and problems of success, 186
  market orientation in North America, 190
free trade agreements, Canada/US, history, 64
Free Trade Area of the Americas (FTAA)
  democracy chapter needed, 184-85
  implications, 15-16
  negotiating style, 31
  organizational structure, 31
  road to, 175-77
  similarities to APEC, 31
  three governments on, 110-11
  timetable, 24-25
  unfulfilled, 4
    reasons for lack of progress, 175-76
  widening of NAFTA, 171

Galbraith, John Kenneth, 163-64
GDP
  Cohesion countries, 51
  compared, 6, 7t

Europe and North America compared, 33, 34t
Ireland, 52-53
per capita ratios compared, 63, 64t
General Agreement on Tariffs and Trade (GATT), origins, 20
General Motors, 72
geographical motives, 23
German Empire, 26
Germany
  CAP, 49
  in EU, 33
  power in trade bloc, 183
globalization, Latin America, 174-75
global system, 185
goals of NAFTA, 30
goods and Service Tax (GST) value-added tax, 88
governance
  new institutions needed, 185
  style, 30
government procurement, 108
governments
  attitudes toward, 155
  reorganization proposal, 150-52
government spending, comparative, 89
Gramm, Phil, 129, 144
Greece, 29
  economic growth, 55
  EU transfers, 56
  lack of progress, 57
growth rates
  Cohesion countries, 52
  Ireland, 52-54, 53t
Grupo Beta force of border agents, 121, 124
Grupo Industrial Bimbo, 73
Guanajuato Proposal, 3
gun control laws, 92

Haiti, 173, 178t
Hart, Michael, 99
health care debate, 91-92
health and sanitation, border regions, 76-77
hegemonic US corporate power, 12
Helms-Burton Act, 87
Helms, Jesse, 152
Hermin Model, 57
higher-level education, 60
high-speed rail corridors, 107
highway investment, 106
Hispanic population in United States, 132

mercantilism, 31
Mercosur, 14, 172
  basic indicators, 178t
  economic problems among members, 174
  Paraguayan coup attempt, 183
  trade agreement described, 173-74
Mercosur-European Union (EU)(MEU), 183
Meredith, Val, 102, 106-07, 108
Mexico
  attitudes to U.S., 157
  austerity measures, 89
  authoritarian political culture, 156
  automotive sector, 72
  basic indicators, 7t
  Central America, 87
  cheap labor, 70
  constitution on energy resources, 133
  Cuba, 87
  dependence on trade, 79
  energy issues, 134-35, 180
  exports, 9t
  FDI abroad, 73
  foreign policy, 87
  GDP disparities among states, 37-38, 38t
  history of distrust of US, 64-65
  imports, 9t
  manufacturing and employment, 88
  nationalism, 66, 153
  North American trade, 10t
  political development, 78-79
  as "pollution haven," 76
  real wages, 88
  regional policies, 12
  reversal on free trade, 66
  sovereignty issue, 39, 152
  trade (total), 9t
  trade with US, 68, 69
  trade with US (growth), 13
  US relations, 148
  US views of, 157
  views of NAFTA, 160-61
Miami Summit, 4
middle-income countries, 18, 60
  challenge of, 186
  Latin America, 177
migratory species, 76
mining, investments in Canada, 71
Ministry of International Trade and Industry (Japan), 27
monetary union proposal, 114-15

money laundering, 5, 86, 122
  sting operation, 151
Monnet, Jean
  sovereignty issue, 152-53
  unification, 168, 169
Morocco, 52
Mulroney, Brian, 65-66
multinational corporations (MNCs), 12
  Mexican, 73
  as North American companies, 73
multinational state proposal, 167-68
multiple trade negotiations, 182

NAFTA (North American Free Trade Agreement)
  asymmetry within North America, 33
  bureaucracy, 73-78
  Chapter 11, 103
  commercial tone, 96-97
  compared to EU functions, 29-30
  debates over, 67-73
  description, 66-67
  detailed comparison with EU, 33-38
  deteriorating US conditions, 67
  early initiatives, 65
  evaluation, 67-73
  focus of Canada and Mexico, 30
  innovative in four ways, 186
  modest benefits for US, 67
  parameters of three regional trade areas, 28t
  premise of, 186-88
  promise of, 188-91
  public relations campaign, 158
  US opposition, 30
  views of, 158-61
  widen or deepen?, 177, 180-82
NAFTA Free Trade Commission, 73, 74
NAFTA Land Transport Standards Subcommittee, 104
National Action Party (PAN), 78-79
National Council of La Raza, 77
nationalism
  Mexican, 66, 153
  Canadian, 65
national security rationale, 189
National Wildlife Foundation, 77
NATO (North Atlantic Treaty Organization), 32
natural gas, 134-35
neofunctional approach to integration, 168
neoliberalism
  NAFTA as product, 12

three regional groups, 27
Nexus generation, 158
nongovernmental organizations (NGOs), 132
    criticisms of, 75-76
nontariff barriers, former focus, 22
norteamericano, use of term, 155
North America
    basic indicators, 178*t*
    intraregional exports, 20, 22*t*
North American Commission (NAC), 11, 187
    framework of cooperation, 144
    for FTAA, 182
    proposal, 100-102
        European Commission compared, 101
        loans to Mexico, 139
        trade policy, 108-11
North American Community, 13
    diversity, 98
    EU lessons, 95
    proposals, 166-69
    spine and limbs, 96
North American confederation of nation-states proposal, 168
North American Customs and Immigration Force proposal, 121-22
North American Development Bank (NADBank), 76-77
    criticisms of, 77-78
    loans to Mexico, 139
North American Development Fund
    proposal, 135-40
    overview, 145, 187
North American Empire, 26
North American Framework Agreement (NAFA), 116
North American Institute (NAMI), 142
North American Monetary Union
    proposed, 114
North American Parliamentary Group (NAPG), 102-03
North American Plan for Infrastructure and Transportation (proposal), 104-08, 187
North American Planning Office
    proposal, 100
nuclear weapons, 26-27

OAS. *See* Organization of American States
Office of Canadian Affairs, 151

Office of North American Statistics
    proposal, 100
oil
    investments in Canada, 71
    Mexico exports, 68
open borders, effects, 125-26
Organization of American States (OAS), 31
    Canada entry, 157
    democracy charter, 185
organization of the book, 3, 14-16
Organization for Economic Cooperation and Development (OECD), single market program study, 58

Pacific Rim, 32
Paraguay, 183
partial-equilibrium model, 69
passports, "NAFTA" proposed, 123, 132-33
Pemex oil company, 134
Pereira Model, 57
Permanent North American Court on Trade and Investment, 103
Peru, 172, 178*t*
peso crisis, 3-5
    causes, 4
    dependence on foreign capital, 79
    effects, after NAFTA signing, 88
    long-term effects, 113
    as metaphor for NAFTA, 5
    NAFA too small, 116
    NAFTA effect, 67
    regional disparities, 89
    US bailout, 116
    views of NAFTA, 158
pluralistic security community, 154
political cultures, 156
political dimension, regional trade agreements, 183
political union
    underlying fears, 164-66
    views of, 161-64
politicians
    EU oversight and local involvement, 62
    North American Commission, 102
pollution, 76
population
    convergence in growth, 6, 7*t*
    Europe and North America compared, 33, 35*t*
    Hispanic in United States, 132
Portugal, 29

safety conditions, 104
safety net, 8
  cutting holes in, 27
  peso crisis, 88
  poor states, 51
safety standards, for trucks, 85
Salinas de Gortari, Carlos, 66
  energy, 133
  sovereignty, 153
Schuman, Robert, 168
Seattle WTO talks, 110
  what protests indicate, 185
Second World War, 19
secretariats, NAFTA, 74
security community, 32
security issues, 22
  Cold War, 25-26
  East Asia militarily lacking, 32
  instability in Mexico, 189
  NATO, 32
  nature of conflicts, 26
  pluralistic security community, 154
  postwar, 23
  regional models, 26
  rivalry between China, Japan and US,
    32
side agreements, 30, 75
single currency issue, 177, 180
Single European Act of 1986 (SEA),
    28-29, 44
Single European Market, 43
  convergence theories, 58
  study of effects, 58
smuggling
  coyotes, 120, 121, 124, 133
  free trade advantages, 17
  proposal overview, 187
  US reaction, 86
social charter, 13
social cohesion
  concept in Canada, 13
  defined, 44
  Delors introducing concept, 44
  premises of, 44
softwood lumber, 85, 109
South American Free Trade Area
    (SAFTA), 14
sovereignty issues, 15
  alternative approaches, 152-54
  Canadian energy policy, 135
  dollarization, 112
  historic shield, 187
  Latin America, 171

Mexican warnings, 171
Mexico, 39
  as obstacle, 39
  overview, 187-88
Spaak, Paul-Henry, 24
Spain, 29
  Cohesion Funds, 47
  economic growth, 55
  EU transfers, 55
  regional funds, 49
  rural colleges, 141, 142t
  unemployment in Andalusia, 51-52
special interests, 83, 84-86
Spinelli, Altiero, 168
State Department (US), 151
steel exports, 85
sting operations, 151
Structural Funds, 45
  convergence theories, 58
  cross-border cooperation, 50
  distribution by country, 45, 47, 47t
  Eastern Europe, 49, 50
  Ireland, 54
  spending, 45, 46t
  study of effects, 58
  targets, 45
stumpage fee price, 110
subregional trade agreements, Latin
    America, 172-74
"subsidiarity" principle, 43
subsidies
  Canada, 109
  Mexico, 109
  US, 108-09, 180
sugar industry, 79-80, 180
Summit of the Americas
  agenda, 171
  widening of NAFTA, 171
  See also names of individual summits
Suriname, 173, 178t
swap arrangements, 93
  for crisis situations, 115-16
  NAFTA, 116

tariffs
  former focus, 22
  Latin America, 172
  NAFTA effects, 68
tax policy
  Canada, 91
  comparative inequalities, 36-37
Teamsters, 84-85
technical advisers, 54
temporary-worker programs, 128-29

governmental reorganization proposal, 151-52
imports, 9t
independence, 64
Japan and China, 177, 180t
Latin America and Caribbean, 177, 180t
NAFTA impact, 80
North American trade, 10t
population growth, 6
power in trade bloc, 183
sovereignty issues, 152
sugar industry, 79-80, 180
trade (total), 9t
unskilled jobs, 127
urban/rural differences, 59
Uruguay Round, 24
regional agreements blocking, 182
US-Canada relations, as community, 154
US-Canadian border, 2
US-Canadian Free Trade Agreement (FTA), 13
foreign direct investment, 72
recession after, 88
significance, 24
US-Canadian Inter-Parliamentary Group, 102
US-Caribbean Basin Trade Partnership Act, 173, 176
US Exchange Stabilization Fund, 4
US General Accounting Office, 77
US-Mexican border. *See* border areas
US-Mexican Inter-Parliamentary Conference, 102
US Surface Transportation Board, 93

Venezuela, 172-73, 178t
vertical accountability, 184
views of NAFTA, 158-61
Canada, 160-61
Mexico, 160-61
US, 158, 160, 161
visas
for Mexicans, 130

"NAFTA" program proposed, 123, 132-33
volatility
currency, Canadian, 90
weaker countries, 91

wage differentials, Mexico-U.S., 126, 126n
War of 1812, 64
wastewater treatment, 78
water pollution, 78
weapons, 5, 26-27, 86, 87, 92
Western Hemisphere, World Trade Organization (WTO), 182-84
White House Office of the Special Trade Representative (STR), 24
withdrawal clause, 30
workers. *See* labor; labor mobility; labor side agreements; labor unions
World Bank
lending to Mexico, 138, 139
loans to Mexico, 140
on trading schemes, 14-15
World Trade Organization (WTO)
CVD/AD issue, 110
not suited for deeper integration, 185
origins, 20
regional integration agreements, 21
Seattle protests, 185
Seattle talks, 110
three governments on, 110-11
Western Hemisphere, 182-84
world trading system, postwar, 23-24
World Values Survey, 155-63

young people
Nexus generation, 158
North American identity, 158
political union views, 163

Zacatecas, Mexico, 125
Zedillo, Ernesto, 3
austerity measures, 136
heading off peso crisis, 4-5
Zoellick, Robert, 176

Other Publications from the Institute for International Economics

BOOKS

IMF Conditionality* John Williamson, editor
1983 ISBN 0-88132-006-4
Trade Policy in the 1980s* William R. Cline, editor
*1983*ISBN 0-88132-031-5
Subsidies in International Trade*
Gary Clyde Hufbauer and Joanna Shelton Erb
*1984*ISBN 0-88132-004-8
International Debt: Systemic Risk and Policy
Response* William R. Cline
*1984*ISBN 0-88132-015-3
Trade Protection in the United States: 31 Case
Studies* Gary Clyde Hufbauer, Diane E. Berliner,
and Kimberly Ann Elliott
*1986*ISBN 0-88132-040-4
Toward Renewed Economic Growth in Latin
America* Bela Balassa, Gerardo M. Bueno, Pedro-
Pablo Kuczynski, and Mario Henrique Simonsen
*1986*ISBN 0-88132-045-5
Capital Flight and Third World Debt*
Donald R. Lessard and John Williamson, editors
*1987*ISBN 0-88132-053-6
The Canada-United States Free Trade Agreement:
The Global Impact*
Jeffrey J. Schott and Murray G. Smith, editors
*1988*ISBN 0-88132-073-0
World Agricultural Trade: Building a Consensus*
William M. Miner and Dale E. Hathaway, editors
1988 ISBN 0-88132-071-3
Japan in the World Economy*
Bela Balassa and Marcus Noland
*1988*ISBN 0-88132-041-2
America in the World Economy: A Strategy for
the 1990s* C. Fred Bergsten
1988 ISBN 0-88132-089-7
Managing the Dollar: From the Plaza to the
Louvre* Yoichi Funabashi
1988, 2d ed. 1989 ISBN 0-88132-097-8
United States External Adjustment and the World
Economy* William R. Cline
May 1989 ISBN 0-88132-048-X
Free Trade Areas and U.S. Trade Policy*
Jeffrey J. Schott, editor
May 1989 ISBN 0-88132-094-3
Dollar Politics: Exchange Rate Policymaking in
the United States*
I.M. Destler and C. Randall Henning
September 1989 ISBN 0-88132-079-X
Latin American Adjustment: How Much Has
Happened?* John Williamson, editor
April 1990 ISBN 0-88132-125-7
The Future of World Trade in Textiles and
Apparel* William R. Cline
1987, 2d ed. June 1990 ISBN 0-88132-110-9

Completing the Uruguay Round: A Results-
Oriented Approach to the GATT Trade
Negotiations* Jeffrey J. Schott, editor
September 1990 ISBN 0-88132-130-3
Economic Sanctions Reconsidered (2 volumes)
Economic Sanctions Reconsidered: Supplemental
Case Histories
Gary Clyde Hufbauer, Jeffrey J. Schott, and
Kimberly Ann Elliott
1985, 2d ed. Dec. 1990 ISBN cloth 0-88132-115-X
ISBN paper 0-88132-105-2
Economic Sanctions Reconsidered: History and
Current Policy
Gary Clyde Hufbauer, Jeffrey J. Schott, and
Kimberly Ann Elliott
December 1990 ISBN cloth 0-88132-140-0
ISBN paper 0-88132-136-2
Pacific Basin Developing Countries: Prospects for
the Future* Marcus Noland
January 1991 ISBN cloth 0-88132-141-9
ISBN 0-88132-081-1
Currency Convertibility in Eastern Europe*
John Williamson, editor
October 1991 ISBN 0-88132-128-1
International Adjustment and Financing: The
Lessons of 1985-1991* C. Fred Bergsten, editor
January 1992 ISBN 0-88132-112-5
North American Free Trade: Issues and
Recommendations*
Gary Clyde Hufbauer and Jeffrey J. Schott
April 1992 ISBN 0-88132-120-6
Narrowing the U.S. Current Account Deficit*
Allen J. Lenz
June 1992 ISBN 0-88132-103-6
The Economics of Global Warming
William R. Cline/*June 1992* ISBN 0-88132-132-X
U.S. Taxation of International Income: Blueprint
for Reform* Gary Clyde Hufbauer, assisted by
Joanna M. van Rooij
October 1992 ISBN 0-88132-134-6
Who's Bashing Whom? Trade Conflict in High-
Technology Industries Laura D'Andrea Tyson
November 1992 ISBN 0-88132-106-0
Korea in the World Economy* Il SaKong
January 1993 ISBN 0-88132-183-4
Pacific Dynamism and the International Economic
System*
C. Fred Bergsten and Marcus Noland, editors
May 1993 ISBN 0-88132-196-6
Economic Consequences of Soviet Disintegration*
John Williamson, editor
May 1993 ISBN 0-88132-190-7
Reconcilable Differences? United States-Japan
Economic Conflict*
C. Fred Bergsten and Marcus Noland
June 1993 ISBN 0-88132-129-X

Corruption and the Global Economy
Kimberly Ann Elliott
June 1997   ISBN 0-88132-233-4
Regional Trading Blocs in the World Economic
System   Jeffrey A. Frankel
October 1997   ISBN 0-88132-202-4
Sustaining the Asia Pacific Miracle:
Environmental Protection and Economic
Integration   André Dua and Daniel C. Esty
October 1997   ISBN 0-88132-250-4
Trade and Income Distribution   William R. Cline
November 1997   ISBN 0-88132-216-4
Global Competition Policy
Edward M. Graham and J. David Richardson
December 1997   ISBN 0-88132-166-4
Unfinished Business: Telecommunications after
the Uruguay Round
Gary Clyde Hufbauer and Erika Wada
December 1997   ISBN 0-88132-257-1
Financial Services Liberalization in the WTO
Wendy Dobson and Pierre Jacquet
June 1998   ISBN 0-88132-254-7
Restoring Japan's Economic Growth
Adam S. Posen
September 1998   ISBN 0-88132-262-8
Measuring the Costs of Protection in China
Zhang Shuguang, Zhang Yansheng, and Wan
Zhongxin
November 1998   ISBN 0-88132-247-4
Foreign Direct Investment and Development: The
New Policy Agenda for Developing Countries and
Economies in Transition
Theodore H. Moran
December 1998   ISBN 0-88132-258-X
Behind the Open Door: Foreign Enterprises in the
Chinese Marketplace   Daniel H. Rosen
January 1999   ISBN 0-88132-263-6
Toward A New International Financial
Architecture: A Practical Post-Asia Agenda
Barry Eichengreen
February 1999   ISBN 0-88132-270-9
Is the U.S. Trade Deficit Sustainable?
Catherine L. Mann/*September 1999*
ISBN 0-88132-265-2
Safeguarding Prosperity in a Global Financial
System: The Future International Financial
Architecture, Independent Task Force Report
Sponsored by the Council on Foreign Relations
Morris Goldstein, Project Director
October 1999   ISBN 0-88132-287-3
Avoiding the Apocalypse: The Future of the Two
Koreas   Marcus Noland
June 2000   ISBN 0-88132-278-4
Assessing Financial Vulnerability: An Early
Warning System for Emerging Markets
Morris Goldstein, Graciela Kaminsky, and Carmen
Reinhart
June 2000   ISBN 0-88132-237-7

Global Electronic Commerce: A Policy Primer
Catherine L. Mann, Sue E. Eckert, and Sarah
Cleeland Knight
July 2000   ISBN 0-88132-274-1
The WTO after Seattle
Jeffrey J. Schott, editor
July 2000   ISBN 0-88132-290-3
Intellectual Property Rights in the Global
Economy   Keith E. Maskus
August 2000   ISBN 0-88132-282-2
The Political Economy of the Asian Financial
Crisis   Stephan Haggard
August 2000   ISBN 0-88132-283-0
Transforming Foreign Aid: United States
Assistance in the 21st Century   Carol Lancaster
August 2000   ISBN 0-88132-291-1
Fighting the Wrong Enemy: Antiglobal Activists
and Multinational Enterprises
Edward M. Graham
September 2000   ISBN 0-88132-272-5
Globalization and the Perceptions of American
Workers
Kenneth F. Scheve and Matthew J. Slaughter
March 2001   ISBN 0-88132-295-4
World Capital Markets: Challenge to the G-10
Wendy Dobson and Gary C. Hufbauer,
assisted by Hyun Koo Cho
May 2001   ISBN 0-88132-301-2
Prospects for Free Trade in the Americas
Jeffrey J. Schott
August 2001   ISBN 0-88132-275-X
Measuring the Costs of Protection in Europe:
The European Commercial Policy in the 2000s
Patrick A. Messerlin
August 2001   ISBN 0-88132-273-3
Lessons from the Old World for the New:
Constructing a North American Community
Robert A. Pastor
August 2001   ISBN 0-88132-328-4

SPECIAL REPORTS

1   Promoting World Recovery: A Statement on
    Global Economic Strategy*
    by Twenty-six Economists from Fourteen
    Countries
    December 1982   ISBN 0-88132-013-7
2   Prospects for Adjustment in Argentina,
    Brazil, and Mexico: Responding to the Debt
    Crisis*   John Williamson, editor
    June 1983   ISBN 0-88132-016-1
3   Inflation and Indexation: Argentina, Brazil,
    and Israel*   John Williamson, editor
    March 1985   ISBN 0-88132-037-4
4   Global Economic Imbalances*
    C. Fred Bergsten, editor
    March 1986   ISBN 0-88132-042-0

5 **African Debt and Financing***
Carol Lancaster and John Williamson, editors
May 1986   ISBN 0-88132-044-7

6 **Resolving the Global Economic Crisis: After Wall Street***
Thirty-three Economists from Thirteen Countries
December 1987   ISBN 0-88132-070-6

7 **World Economic Problems***
Kimberly Ann Elliott and John Williamson, editors
April 1988   ISBN 0-88132-055-2
Reforming World Agricultural Trade*
Twenty-nine Professionals from Seventeen Countries
1988   ISBN 0-88132-088-9

8 **Economic Relations Between the United States and Korea: Conflict or Cooperation?***
Thomas O. Bayard and Soo-Gil Young, editors
January 1989   ISBN 0-88132-068-4

9 **Whither APEC? The Progress to Date and Agenda for the Future***
C. Fred Bergsten, editor
October 1997   ISBN 0-88132-248-2

10 **Economic Integration of the Korean Peninsula**
Marcus Noland, editor
January 1998   ISBN 0-88132-255-5

11 **Restarting Fast Track*** Jeffrey J. Schott, editor
April 1998   ISBN 0-88132-259-8

12 **Launching New Global Trade Talks: An Action Agenda**   Jeffrey J. Schott, editor
September 1998   ISBN 0-88132-266-0

13 **Japan's Financial Crisis and Its Parallels to US Experience**
Ryoichi Mikitani and Adam S. Posen, eds.
September 2000   ISBN 0-88132-289-X

14 **The Ex-Im Bank in the 21st Century: A New Approach?**   Gary Clyde Hufbauer and Rita M. Rodriguez, eds.
January 2001   ISBN 0-88132-300-4

WORKS IN PROGRESS

The Impact of Increased Trade on Organized Labor in the United States
Robert E. Baldwin
Trade Flows and Productivity
Martin Baily
New Regional Arrangements and the World Economy
C. Fred Bergsten
The Globalization Backlash in Europe and the United States
C. Fred Bergsten, Pierre Jacquet, and Karl Kaiser
The U.S.-Japan Economic Relationship
C. Fred Bergsten, Takatoshi Ito, and Marc Noland
China's Entry to the World Economy
Richard N. Cooper
The ILO in the World Economy
Kimberly Ann Elliott
Can Labor Standards Improve Under Globalization?
Kimberly Ann Elliott and Richard B. Freeman
Reforming Economic Sanctions
Kimberly Ann Elliott, Gary C. Hufbauer, and Jeffrey J. Schott
Free Trade in Labor Agency Services
Kimberly Ann Elliott and J. David Richardson
IMF and the World Bank
Michael Fabricius
The *Chaebol* and Structural Problems in Korea
Edward M. Graham
The Benefits of Price Convergence
Gary Clyde Hufbauer, Erika Wada, and Tony Warren
Leadership Selection in the Major Multilaterals
Miles Kahler
The International Financial Architecture: What's New? What's Missing?
Peter Kenen
Imports, Exports, and American Industrial Workers since 1979
Lori G. Kletzer and Robert Lawrence
Job Loss from Imports: Measuring the Costs
Lori G. Kletzer
Globalization and Creative Destruction in the US Textile and Apparel Industry
James Levinsohn
APEC and the New Economy
Catherine Mann and Daniel Rosen
Dollarization, Currency Blocs, and US Policy
Adams S. Posen
Germany in the World Economy after the EMU
Adam S. Posen
Sizing Up Globalization: The Globalization Balance Sheet Capstone Volume
J. David Richardson
Why Global Commitment Really Matters!
J. David Richardson and Howard Lewis
India in the World Economy
T. N. Srinivasan and Suresh D. Tendulkar
Inflation Targeting
Edwin Truman
Curbing the Boom-Bust Cycle: The Role of Wall Street
John Williamson
Debt Relief: Where Does It Stand?
John Williamson and Nancy Birdsall

DISTRIBUTORS OUTSIDE THE UNITED STATES

**Australia, New Zealand, and
Papua New Guinea**
D.A. Information Services
648 Whitehorse Road
Mitcham, Victoria 3132, Australia
tel: 61-3-9210-7777
fax: 61-3-9210-7788
e-mail: service@dadirect.com.au
http://www.dadirect.com.au

United Kingdom and Europe
(including Russia and Turkey)
The Eurospan Group
3 Henrietta Street, Covent Garden
London WC2E 8LU England
tel: 44-20-7240-0856
fax: 44-20-7379-0609
http://www.eurospan.co.uk

Japan and the Republic of Korea
United Publishers Services, Ltd.
Kenkyu-Sha Bldg.
9, Kanda Surugadai 2-Chome
Chiyoda-Ku, Tokyo 101
Japan
tel: 81-3-3291-4541
fax: 81-3-3292-8610
e-mail: saito@ups.co.jp
**For trade accounts only.
Individuals will find IIE books in
leading Tokyo bookstores.**

Thailand
Asia Books
5 Sukhumvit Rd. Soi 61
Bangkok 10110 Thailand
tel: 662-714-0740-2 Ext: 221, 222, 223
fax: 662-391-2277
e-mail: purchase@asiabooks.co.th
http://www/asiabooksonline.com

Canada
Renouf Bookstore
5369 Canotek Road, Unit 1
Ottawa, Ontario K1J 9J3, Canada
tel: 613-745-2665
fax: 613-745-7660
http://www.renoufbooks.com

India, Bangladesh, Nepal, and Sri Lanka
Viva Books Pvt.
Mr. Vinod Vasishtha
4325/3, Ansari Rd.
Daryaganj, New Delhi-110002
India
tel: 91-11-327-9280
fax: 91-11-326-7224
e-mail: vinod.viva@gndel.globalnet.
ems.vsnl.net.in

Southeast Asia (Brunei, Cambodia,
China, Malaysia, Hong Kong, Indonesia,
Laos, Myanmar, the Philippines, Singapore,
Taiwan, and Vietnam)
Hemisphere Publication Services
1 Kallang Pudding Rd. #04-03
Golden Wheel Building
Singapore 349316
tel: 65-741-5166
fax: 65-742-9356

**Visit our Web site at:
http://www.iie.com
E-mail orders to:
orders@iie.com**